THE STORY OF SOY

THE STORY OF SOY

Christine M. Du Bois

REAKTION BOOKS

For the service they have rendered to humanity:
In loving memory of Sidney W. Mintz, and in honour
of soy scholars William Shurtleff, Akiko Aoyagi
and Theodore Hymowitz.
And, as always, in appreciation of Laurence U. Buxbaum

Published by Reaktion Books Ltd
Unit 32, Waterside
44–48 Wharf Road
London N1 7UX, UK
www.reaktionbooks.co.uk

First published 2018
Copyright © Christine M. Du Bois 2018

Printed and bound in Great Britain
by TJ International, Padstow, Cornwall

A catalogue record for this book is available from the British Library

ISBN 978 1 78023 925 5

CONTENTS

INTRODUCTION: HIDDEN GOLD

In 1904 two grand imperial powers locked into unspeakably violent combat over control of a single small, steep hill. At stake was power over a strategic land rich in timber, coal, wheat – and soy. Soldiers atop '203 Meter Hill' had a crucial vantage point for domination of lucrative Port Arthur. They rained machine-gun, rifle and artillery fire down on their enemies, who in response shot lethal mortar fire upwards. The attacking army doggedly persisted, sending thousands of men struggling upwards to kill and themselves rapidly be slain – 'human bullets' they were called. The losses on both sides were great; in little more than two months, some 20,000 soldiers perished. In the end, the attacking Japanese triumphed over their Russian adversaries, wresting control of 203 Meter Hill, Port Arthur and, ultimately, prized Manchuria in northeast China, with its copious harvests of soybeans.[1]

Soy provided an incentive for conflict as well as food for the Japanese army, fodder for Russian horses and oil to make soap for both armies. The Russo-Japanese war of 1904–5 also saw many new technologies in combat, including barbed wire, the self-powered machine gun and mines. Massive steel warships battled spectacularly at sea, making critical use of early radio communications. The two armies' clash at the inland city of Mukden in 1905, for which more than half a million men were mobilized, was perhaps the largest battle of modern times to that point – the Battle of Leipzig in 1813 in the Napoleonic era being the only other contender for that bloody distinction.[2]

Its scale and modernity have led some historians to consider the Russo-Japanese War a 'dress rehearsal' for the First World War.

Because of the conflict's impact on balances of power, some have even referred to this struggle for economic control of Manchuria as 'World War Zero'.[3] Its after-effects proved far-reaching and varied. In Japan, cheap soy protein became more available to the population, while Japanese traders in Manchuria became rich from commerce in soy. Japanese dependence on soy in their diets would, over time, spur them to purchase it on a massive scale from the United States and Brazil. In the immediate aftermath of the war, Japan grew more imperialistic. Meanwhile in Russia, domestic disgust with the czarist government's war performance catalysed the Revolution of 1905, which in turn fomented conditions for the 1917 Communist Revolution. Simultaneously, seeing Russia's weakness, Germany was militarily emboldened. Elsewhere, activists in colonies around the world took inspiration from a non-Western people's defeat of a major European power.

This war, over strategic territorial control, over trade in raw materials, and specifically over soy, is often neglected. In this way, the war is like the bean itself: shaping our world in multiple ways, while largely hidden or ignored. Yet, as this book will show, soy's importance to human diets and the world economy has only increased since the Russo-Japanese War.[4]

Soy is a significant source of oil for manufacturing and food. Subjected either to mechanical pressing or chemical extraction, soybeans yield 15–20 per cent oil.[5] Soon after the Russo-Japanese War, commercial interest in that oil grew substantially. Manchurian farmers had increased production of soybeans during the war in response to demand from both armies; once the soldiers were gone, they sought to continue selling their expanded harvests. At the same time, Japanese traders in Manchuria realized that in Europe the prices of plant oils for soap, paints and other industrial goods had recently risen. These enterprising middlemen therefore priced Manchurian soybeans competitively and managed to sell a shipment to oilseed crushers in England. Pleased with the results, the crushers ordered more, sparking years of highly profitable Asian trade to northern Europe.

From the 1930s on, soy oil became less of a component in industrial products and more of an ingredient in human diets. Its presence as food, first in shortening and margarines, and then for cooking and frying, eventually predominated. As demand for edible

Soy for success: a woodcut from the Russo-Japanese War shows soybeans thrown to revellers disguised as ogres, a Japanese tradition. The woman tosses beans to bring luck to hungry soldiers.

plant oils increased in the twentieth century, soy oil production soared. Today soybeans are second only to palm trees as the largest source of vegetable oil worldwide; in 2016–17 companies around the globe processed over 57 billion litres (12½ billion gallons) of soy oil – enough to fill about 23,000 Olympic swimming pools.[6]

Soy is far from useful merely because of its oil, however. During the war with Russia, the Japanese fighters survived in part on the protein in fermented soy and on dried frozen tofu, which is lightweight for long marches and also made from soy. These foodstuffs strengthened soldiers for their arduous tasks. Soybeans are, in fact, about 35 per cent protein and unusually nutritious among plant sources as an alternative to meat.[7]

This felicitous circumstance derives from biochemistry. Proteins are built of amino acids, nine of which are crucial to the human diet. Eating a variety of plant proteins can provide all nine essential amino acids, but if a diet lacks variety, consuming a higher quality protein provides a short-cut alternative. High-quality proteins are easily absorbed in the digestive tract and contain, already assembled, an appropriate balance of the essential amino acids; typical examples of such proteins are eggs and meat. Yet once soy has been heated sufficiently, it also provides just such a protein, becoming a less expensive source of essential amino acids than animal proteins. Chickens, pigs, cattle and even farmed fish are all fed soy protein in order to augment their growth; when humans eat soy directly, they are cutting out these 'middleman' animals in the delivery of vital amino acids to their own bodies.

Yet despite the inefficiency of producing livestock for meat, domestic animals are raised on soy on a vast scale. Processed soybeans are the largest global source of protein in animal feed, and each year animals consume well over 90 per cent of all soy protein on the planet.[8] During the last seventy years, thanks to the assiduous efforts of the American Soybean Association (ASA) and private companies, the model of feeding animals soy and fortified grains to mass-produce meat has spread globally, a phenomenon accelerating as emerging middle classes demand a meatier diet. Defatted soybeans have become so dominant in animal feeds that other protein sources are measured in a unit called 'SME', for 'Soybean Meal Equivalent'.

Earth's 21 billion chickens and turkeys eat the most soy, consuming nearly half the supply of high-protein meal that remains after the oil has been extracted from the beans.[9] Wryly remarking on this feed regimen, Brazilians have referred to chickens as 'soybeans with wings'. Thus, although colloquially 'chicken feed' means 'a small amount of money', the soy meal that composes around 40 per cent of poultry feed brings big profits at the powerful Chicago Board of Trade (CBOT) and other commodity markets.[10] Soy meal's total futures market was valued at roughly $11 billion in 2012.[11] Yellow soybeans earmarked to grow chicken wings are the agricultural equivalent of Harry Potter's famously desirable Golden Snitch.

Producing soybeans for animal feed has mixed impacts on human diets; sometimes it makes better nutrition available to the poor in the form of cheaper meats, but sometimes it actually makes access to protein more difficult, rather than less. Large landowners at times replace traditional protein crops, such as other kinds of beans grown for human consumption, with soy destined for export. In local marketplaces, the poor therefore find their traditional protein sources less available and priced higher than before – sometimes priced quite out of reach.

The use of soy-plus-grain as feed has also promoted the massive 'factory farming' of animals that, on the one hand, lowers the prices of meats through economies of scale, and on the other, subjects animals to cruelty and environments to dangerous agglomerations of waste. The issues are complex, and in each situation there are always winners and losers, positive impacts and negative ones. Thus the increased affordability of meat has contributed to the world-wide doubling of pork consumption and a spectacular quadrupling of chicken consumption since 1960.[12] Lower prices for meat have pushed down the cost of other proteins as well. This lowering of costs has helped the percentage of the earth's population that is malnourished to decrease steadily. Increased access to protein has meant stronger immune systems in developing countries, and fewer children's intellectual abilities permanently damaged.

Improved affordability of meat has come at the expense of animal welfare, however. Recently in the U.S., the pioneering country for the 'factory farming' of animals, each year over 5 million sows spent most of their lives in pregnancy stalls so tiny that their flesh pushed up against the bars.[13] Sows in such conditions cannot turn around or sleep on their sides as pigs prefer; they become weak from lack of exercise; they have high rates of urinary tract infections; and they exhibit odd behaviours associated with boredom and frustration, such as head weaving, tongue rolling and bar biting.

Affordability of meat also creates environmental hazards – strikingly, an oxygen-deprived zone in the Gulf of Mexico, an area that in 2016 was larger than the U.S. state of Connecticut or the British province of Northern Ireland.[14] This 'dead sea' is filled with algae feeding on the fertilizer run-off from Midwestern crops grown to fatten up pigs, chickens and cattle. The algal decay drains the ocean of oxygen, making this massive area essentially devoid of life other than algae and bacteria.

In Maryland's Chesapeake Bay, about one-fourth of the chemicals encouraging algal blooms come from the water's pollution with livestock manure and poultry litter (a combination of poultry bedding, uneaten feed, loose feathers and excrement). In 2008 researchers estimated that about 75,000 metric tons of the bay's clams and worms had failed to grow or were killed off yearly because of poor water quality in the bay's dead zones.[15] Such organisms serve as food for the bay's beloved, tasty blue crab, whose numbers had been declining. Fortunately, recent programmes to protect the bay have improved its ecological balance.

Both the benefits and problems associated with soy as animal feed are amplified by the scale on which soy is used. Whole soybeans and the two products separated by crushing the beans – the meal and the oil – together constitute one of the most traded crops worldwide, at over 211 million metric tons in 2015.[16] Unsurprisingly, in recent years the world's top-earning crop exported to a single nation has been whole soybeans sold to China.[17]

Soy production and trade have sometimes increased so fast that financial markets, storage systems and transportation networks have struggled to accommodate them. In the 1960s and early 1970s, American analysts referred to soy with awe as 'The Cinderella Crop' because of its dizzying rise over forty years from lowly forage to profit powerhouse. But this Cinderella has sometimes ascended too quickly, as the bottlenecks at Brazilian ports in 2013 demonstrated. The combination of a bumper crop that year, along with Brazil's inadequate transportation infrastructure and the long distances between growing areas and the ports, led to chaos: 24–32-km (15–20-mile) lines of trucks waiting to unload at the port of Santos, and over two hundred ships queued up at ports, some waiting two months before being filled and heading to China.[18] Exasperated, the Chinese cancelled some of their orders, even as Brazilians frantically scrambled to haul soy to less crowded ports in the north of the country.

The immense trade in soy puts the bean at the centre of tough trade negotiations and disputes. The 2013 quarrel between Brazil and China was not their first over soy. In 2004 the Chinese had rejected multiple shipments of Brazilian soy, arguing that it was contaminated with pesticide-infused seeds not approved for human consumption in China. Immediately Brazil inspected its exports more closely – while also protesting that the rejections were really motivated by reduced Chinese demand for soy chicken feed in the wake of that year's bird flu outbreak. Brazil threatened to lodge a complaint with the World Trade Organization (WTO), but as soy commerce between the two nations picked up again, Brazil backed away from litigation.

As the genetically engineered (GE) crop with the largest global area,[19] soy has figured in a different, protracted WTO dispute. In the 1990s, the European Union (EU) curtailed its cultivation of GE plants and sale of foods with GE ingredients. In 2003, disappointed with commercial diplomacy on these issues, the governments of the U.S., Canada and Argentina filed WTO grievances against the EU.

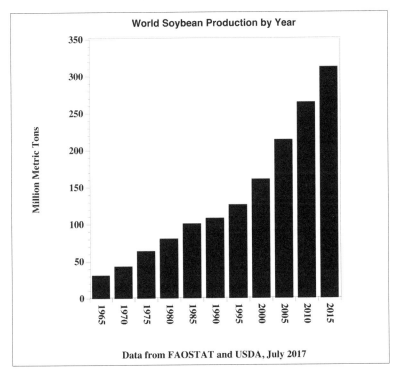

Fifty years of world soybean production.

Three years and many expert testimonies later, the WTO deemed the EU's behaviour inconsistent with its obligations as a WTO member. Nevertheless, the culture clash over what constitutes appropriate agricultural technology, and how a society decides what is safe for humans and ecosystems, did not fade. It was not until 2009 that the EU and Canada settled their GE dispute (Canada's principal concern was about GE canola, or rapeseed), and not until the following year did the EU and Argentina similarly work out their differences (principally over GE soybeans).[20] In November 2017 the disagreement between the U.S. and the EU was still not fully resolved.

The U.S. has much at stake, since it is by far the world's largest producer of GE crops: some 40 per cent grow on U.S. soil.[21] Because over 90 per cent of America's annual soy harvest is genetically modified,[22] soy is the most common of its GE crops. The U.S. is, moreover, the largest producer of soy in the world and the second-largest exporter of whole soybeans after Brazil.[23] Soy and soy products – again, mostly genetically modified – constitute the pre-eminent U.S. agricultural export, bringing in over $20 billion in 2016.[24] The U.S. government and agribusiness community take seriously anything threatening GE soy in world markets.

Soy is not only valuable to U.S. farmers for income, but also to alternate in fields with maize (in American English, 'corn'). Cultivating soy enhances the soil precisely in the way maize needs: maize is always hungry for nitrogen and tends to deplete it quickly in fields. Soy, by contrast, belongs to the legume category of plants, which pull nitrogen right out of the air. Soy uses that nitrogen for its own metabolism. It accomplishes its air-to-plant nitrogen feat through a startlingly tight symbiosis with the bacterium *Bradyrhizobium japonicum*.

Nitrogen, our atmosphere's most common element, is required by all life forms for production of proteins. In the air, however, nitrogen exists in a state that plants cannot use; it is everywhere, yet inaccessible. The nitrogen has to be 'fixed' into a molecular structure suitable for plants. Hence a soy seedling engages bacteria in a multi-step process of fixing, in which plant and bacteria take turns influencing each other.

First, soy sends chemicals into the soil that attract *Bradyrhizobia* and encourage their reproduction. The bacteria attach themselves to soy root hairs. Secreting their own special chemicals, the attached

Nitrogen-fixing nodules on soy roots.

bacteria induce the root hairs to curl and form tiny tubes within them. These coiling tubes are 'infection threads'. Next, the bacteria proliferate within an expanding network of such threads. Eventually the threads burst, sending multitudes of bacteria straight into the host seedling's cells. The infected cells form small nodules all over the roots.

These nodules absorb air from tiny spaces in the soil. Bacteria and plant together now produce an enzyme, nitrogenase, which fixes the nitrogen in the absorbed air into a desirable structure. But the 'fixing' reaction requires very specific conditions, and here the extraordinary symbiosis continues, like a complex dance between partners who have adapted to each other's every move. One condition is that most of the oxygen pulled with the rest of the air into the nodules must be kept isolated from the nitrogen-fixing reaction – so together bacteria and seedling create a special protein called leghaemoglobin. This protein is similar to the haemoglobin in human red blood cells, and like haemoglobin, it closely controls the amount of oxygen available to its environment.

The nitrogen-fixing reaction requires a great deal of energy. The plant, whose leaves create biologically useable energy through photosynthesis, sends energy down to the bacteria. Impressively, when nitrogen fixation happens within a legume nodule – instead of in a factory producing artificial nitrogen fertilizer – plants' capacity to harness sunlight for energy can replace our burning of fossil fuels in fertilizer manufacture.

Thus the bacteria gain food energy from a soy plant's photosynthesis, and the soy gains nitrogen from the activity of the bacteria. Then when the soy roots eventually decay, they leave behind some of their nitrogen – now in a plant-useable form – in the soil. All life on earth benefits from this process, as legumes' ability to fix nitrogen helps maintain the planet's chemical balance, providing soil nitrogen for the many non-nitrogen-fixing plants at the beginning of vast food chains.

Because of this symbiosis between legumes and bacteria, when farmers rotate soy and maize/corn through their fields, as they do in huge swathes of the American Midwest, the need for manufactured nitrogen fertilizers – the source of much pollution – is reduced. Less need to burn fossil fuels in manufacturing fertilizers leads to less greenhouse gas pollution. Moreover, farmers save on fertilizer costs, helping to keep food prices lower. Soy provides a winning double play.

Unfortunately, soy cannot supply all the nitrogen that maize needs, and even some soy itself requires artificial nitrogen fertilizer. Hence combining soy with maize in animal feed means that soy facilitates a regimen that does stress the environment – and yet, because of soy's symbiosis with *Bradyrhizobia*, the environment is less polluted than when animal feeds contain proteins from sources that cannot fix nitrogen. Soy in animal feeds, compared to other proteins, helps reduce the planet's nitrogen-fertilizer problems.

Soy is also quite useful to food companies, primarily for its oil but also in small quantities for its protein and lecithin. All over America, soy is the source of 'vegetable oil' used in commercial frying and baking; Brazilians also cook with soy oil a great deal. Lecithin, found in eggs, soy and other organic substances, is used worldwide for its colloidal properties, which help integrate one ingredient microscopically within another. In feeds, it helps distribute fat in tiny particles, enhancing fat absorption in animal guts and so plumping up livestock with more calories.

In countless processed foods, lecithin emulsifies, smoothly joining liquids that otherwise would not mix. In margarine it prevents 'bleeding', or separation of water from the fats, and it reduces splattering of margarine during frying. Lecithin is an antioxidant as well; in fortified margarines it helps protect vitamin A from oxidative destruction. It is added to manufactured breads and cakes, where it improves tenderness and delays staling. In chocolate, it decreases the time needed to grind the beans and mix ingredients, and it permits more even coatings on confectionery or candy bars. Lecithin makes peanut butter creamier and more uniform. It improves the dispensability and wettability of instant powders such as dry milk, cocoa mix and cake mixes. Such food applications require only small amounts of lecithin, often just 0.1–2 per cent of a product's contents.[25]

Like lecithin, soy protein appears in processed foods – again, in small quantities. In meats, sausages, breads and cakes it functions to bind moisture into the food. In soups and gravies it binds water to solids, thereby thickening the liquid. In meats and cheeses it can have a gelatinous effect, 'setting' the food into a defined shape. In doughnuts it binds loose fat, leading to a product that tastes richer without seeming greasy. In bakery items soy protein locks in flavours. In whipped toppings, mousses and angel food cakes, it traps gas to create a foamy texture. In breads it boosts bleaching for a consistent bright colour.

As a primary ingredient, soy protein appears in ready-to-eat bars for breakfast, snacks for athletes and meal substitutes. It figures in protein shakes aimed at consumers craving thick sweet drinks but preferring something healthier than an ice-cream shake. In meat substitutes for vegetarians, soy protein simulates the texture of animal muscle. For vegans in particular, it appears in soy 'cheese' and 'yoghurt' and in frozen desserts. And, of course, soy protein is a major component of traditional Asian soy foods: tofu, soy milk, the young soybeans known in Japanese as edamame, miso, soy sauce and Indonesian tempeh.

Beyond its roles in feed, food and soil renewal, in South America soy is a vital yet problematic engine of rural development and export earnings. Oddly enough, its dynamism there was first spurred by the fates of Peruvian anchovies. In 1973–4, a band of warm water in the Pacific, El Niño, reduced the normal circulation of cold currents from the deep ocean. Anchovies living near the surface depend on the upwelling of nutrient-rich water. Without it, the anchovies were in distress. Peruvian fishermen did not adjust their catches to protect them; instead they nearly depleted the waters of the remaining healthy specimens. Ravaged by weather and workers, the fishery collapsed, unable for a decade to regain its original numbers.

The anchovies of Peru had generated profits from the 1960s until 1973 because the catch was ground up and sold as animal feed. The sudden disappearance of fishmeal from international markets provoked anxiety in the administration of u.s. President Nixon. Officials reasoned that demand for soy meal to replace the anchovies would surely swell. Although a surge in soy prices would benefit American farmers, it would hurt meat producers. The meat industry would see reduced profits, and surely would also pass some of their increased costs to consumers by raising prices on chicken, pork and beef – perhaps substantially. Inflation was already bouncing upward; the rise in meat prices would surely exacerbate it – or so the thinking went.

The solution, the administration thought, was temporarily to prohibit u.s. farmers from exporting soy. The total ban lasted just days, replaced by a system that reduced but did not completely cut off u.s. soy exports. That system, in turn, only lasted a few months before normal trade resumed. But it was long enough to send soy prices outside the u.s. skyrocketing, and utterly shock a nation that until then had been profoundly dependent on u.s. soy, both for animal feed and human food: Japan.

The Japanese wasted little time in finding another country whose infant soy agriculture they could nurture. Determined never to be bound to a single supplier again, they diligently helped Brazilian farmers expand soy cultivation from their temperate southeast into their vast, near-equatorial Centre-West region. For 21 years, Japan financed research into pest management and the development of soy varieties adapted to the Centre-West's soils and daylight length. The Japanese also helped qualified farmers to enlarge their operations. Their investments, along with those of Brazil's government and citizens, paid off: within forty years, Brazil had increased production fifteen-fold,[26] shifting from a minor player in soy markets to vying with the U.S. for primacy in exporting whole soybeans.

Other South Americans jumped on the bandwagon. In the 1970s, rapid growth in EU soybean consumption for animal feed, as well as the 1973 jump in soy prices, motivated Argentines to invest in soybeans. The central government, wanting to strengthen the nation's industrial capabilities, offered strong financial incentives for Argentines to crush soy prior to export. Consequently, in just two decades Argentina catapulted to global leadership in trading soy oil, and by 1997 was also the top exporter of soy meal.[27] Observing these success stories, farmers in Paraguay and Bolivia followed suit. For these cultivators, the road towards a brighter future is paved with soy. Unfortunately, in all South American countries serious environmental problems accompany soy production – especially habitat loss for indigenous species.

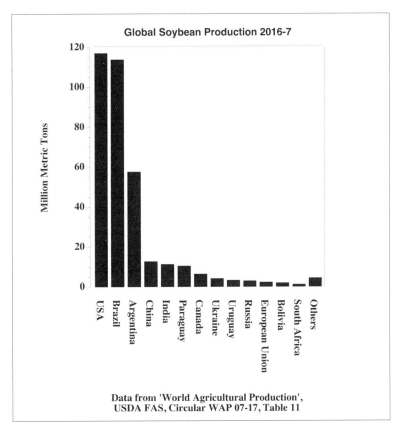

Soybean-producing nations.

One way or another, in the twenty-first century soy will figure in the destinies of much of the world's population. Soy will play a significant role in producing meat, and maybe also in replacing meat as an inexpensive source of protein. If grown under four conditions – by small farmers, sustainably, for local human consumption, and in developing countries – soy could effectively reduce the chronic malnutrition afflicting 815 million people.[28] Making full use of soy's potential to aid the undernourished will not be simple. But safeguarding populations from protein malnutrition is morally imperative; experimenting with soy towards this end is worthy.

Soy will also have many industrial uses in this century. Already U.S. packaging and newspapers often tout their soy ink, made from the bean's oil. Invented in the U.S. in the 1980s, soy ink is now gaining popularity elsewhere, notably in Korea, Japan and Taiwan. Soy oil is also found worldwide in caulking compounds, disinfectants, dust control agents, electrical insulation, epoxies, pesticides, linoleum backing, anti-corrosive and anti-static agents, paints, plasticizers, protective coatings, putty, soaps, shampoos, detergents, vinyl, waterproof cement and wallboards. It is even employed during metal casting.

Soy lecithin serves as an anti-sludge additive in motor lubricants, an anti-gumming agent in gasoline and a particle disperser in many products where soy oil also appears. Lecithin emulsifies both cosmetics and oil-drilling fluids. It softens leather. It is an anti-foaming agent in the manufacture of paper, alcohol and yeast.

Soy protein has myriad industrial uses as well, in creating adhesives, antibiotics, waterproof emulsions for roofs and septic tanks, leather substitutes, paints, particle board and plywood, plastics, polyesters and other textiles. It can be formed into a biodegradable plastic for disposable food containers, reducing the burden of landfills. It can decrease the energy expended to make disposables, since it requires less energy than other plastics for its manufacture.

Engineers keep adding to the bean's remarkable applications. Recent innovations include soy-oil hydraulic fluid for elevators – more environmentally friendly than other hydraulic products – and foam cushions from soy oil for Ford vehicles. Research is progressing on soy-fibre nappies. A scientific team in Britain is developing soy-based wound dressings.

In many wares, soy replaces a petroleum product. Soy oil used directly as fuel is particularly intriguing. Such biodiesel is currently pricier than ordinary diesel, but it burns more cleanly, releasing less of the particulate matter that harms lungs and hearts. Since it derives from agriculture, biodiesel is also renewable. When it burns, it smells better than conventional diesel. Although soy biodiesel could never provide a large portion of the fuel powering modern lifestyles, it is nevertheless growing in importance as the world gravitates towards cleaner energy.

Soy is thus filled with possibilities. This chapter's sketch of soy's little-remarked importance only scratches the surface. Later chapters explore its rise on several continents, its uses during the Second World War and the 'factory farming' of livestock, its ecological and nutritional impacts, its genetic modification, its role in world trade and its transformations into fuel.

WITHIN THOSE CHAPTERS, religious movements, strongman military conquest, bold entrepreneurship, passionate scientific enquiry, colourful and eccentric personalities, fiercely criticized companies and contracts and startlingly creative uses for soy all combine to make these small beans the focus of a compelling tale. Their story begins with the first great innovators – the anonymous peasants of China's Yellow River valley and Manchuria, to whom we now turn.

Myriad consumer and industrial products feature soy.

ONE

ASIAN ROOTS

For thousands upon thousands of years, people in northern China gathered the wild ancestors of modern soybeans. The individual who first thought to plant those beans – to choose where they would grow, and to tend them for a better harvest – was illiterate, as was his or her whole society. Thus soy's domesticators left no written record of their momentous actions. But based on extensive archaeological evidence, we can imagine a reasonable scenario for that first spark of an idea, that notion to put beans into the ground and care for them.

Our imagined scenario begins with a young girl named Dawei, and on that pivotal day she was bored. Sunshine alternated with shade in flecks over the black waters – today the swamp was like a giant glittering tortoise shell. Perhaps she plucked a flower from a floating lotus, adding the blossom to her basket. 'I have so many flowers now,' she whined to her older sister, 'Isn't that enough?'

'You have to help out like everybody else,' Chongde snapped. 'This is a big festival.'

'But I want to go home and watch Uncle Li make a new flute.'

'All right,' Chongde relented. 'Go back – but take the path along the rice paddy. About halfway down I saw some wild beans; pick them on your way home.'

'Thanks!'

Dawei extricated herself from the muck and skipped along the path. Three flowers tumbled from her basket; she stooped to retrieve them. As she did, she noticed a clump of beans her sister hadn't mentioned. Each of their hairy pods bulged with one or two more seeds tucked inside than usual. 'Mama will be interested in these,' Dawei mused.

At a bend in the trail, Dawei found the beans that Chongde wanted her to gather. Dawei placed bean pods under the flowers in her basket until her fingers were irritated from the pods' rough surfaces. She would help cook most of the beans later, she knew. But the seeds from the slightly fuller pods – maybe Mama would plant them. Mama didn't usually plant beans, but Dawei knew that sometimes her mother separated out the biggest millet seeds and then put them in the ground. So maybe Mama would do the same with these beans, and soon they would grow near the house.

Dawei headed home. She did not know it, but her selection of more fertile pods was historic: the beginning of the domestication of soy.

SOY BELONGS TO THE PLANT GENUS *Glycine*. At the turn of the twentieth century, when the Western world was only just starting avidly to grasp the utility of soy, the people of northeast Asia already had millennia of experience with the remarkable versatility of plants in this genus. And so we can plausibly imagine this scene 9,000 years ago near the village of Jiahu in northern China, in which a young girl discovers a superior strain of wild soy and chooses to bring it to her farmer mother. The evidence for soy at Jiahu at that time is very strong, although it is not clear that the abundant beans found there were cultivated, rather than simply gathered from unfarmed spaces where they grew on their own. But it is conceivable that Jiahu in its oldest period was indeed the place of soy's first domestication.[1]

Significantly larger soybeans than those at Jiahu have been found in other archaeological sites in China and Japan from a mere 5,000 years ago.[2] Larger beans are associated with domestication: farmers tend to select the biggest beans for planting, since they wish to reproduce a crop of large beans in the next season. Smaller beans are eaten and therefore do not have offspring. Over time, repeated farmer selection of the largest beans leads to bigger and bigger ones. Perhaps, then, it was at one of these other locations, and not Jiahu, that wild beans were first transformed into a cultivated crop. Most likely, soy was independently domesticated several times and in several different locations in northeast Asia.[3]

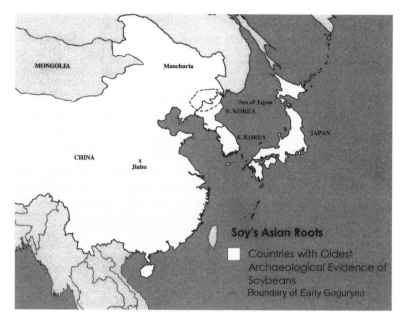

Geography of soy's Asian roots.

One might wonder if knowing exactly where and when soy was first domesticated matters. Aside from knowledge for its own sake – adding details to humanity's story – deducing how soy was domesticated could shed light on the human choices that shaped soy genetics. Such insight could kindle new ideas among current soy breeders and geneticists. And yet, surprisingly, the most impassioned interest in this Neolithic mystery is neither academic nor agricultural. Instead it is, of all things, geopolitical.

China and South Korea have long contested the right to boast of first taming wild soy.[4] The argument centres around who may claim the heritage of an area that is now in Manchuria and North Korea – were the ancient people in that region Koreans, or were they Chinese? The tussle over bragging rights has escalated since 2002, when the 'Northeast Project' of the Chinese Academy of Social Science declared that the ancient kingdom in that region, called Goguryeo, had not been an independent Korean state but rather a regional government within China's empire. In 2004 the Chinese Foreign Ministry deleted Goguryeo from their web page about Korea. Then South Koreans discovered that certain Chinese scholars (supported by the central government) were 'appropriating' various historical figures, events and artefacts treasured by

Korean nationalists. The Chinese scholars claimed that these Korean national emblems were more truly Chinese. South Koreans erupted in indignation – and contentious claims of their own. Mutual outrage included arguments over who could justly claim soy as their gift to the world. Chinese Internet posts accused Koreans of arguing that soy milk is a Korean invention. Unfortunately, such unsubstantiated allegations inflamed anti-Korean sentiment among the Chinese, even in Taiwan.

Meanwhile, South Koreans searched for hidden Chinese motives for what they experienced as a serious cultural affront. Were the Chinese creating a conceptual framework for eventually claiming North Korea, should the Pyongyang government collapse? Reciprocally, the Chinese worried that South Korea might wish one day to annex other lands that the Chinese saw as theirs. High officials from China and South Korea engaged in discussions to ease tensions. North Korea's government made a statement criticizing the Chinese scholars but mostly stayed out of the controversy.

Ironically, the ancient people of Goguryeo would not have considered themselves either Korean or Chinese. The Goguryeans had their own identities, and the peoples in what are now South Korea and China would have seemed quite foreign to them. The glory for what ancient East Asians did with soybeans belongs to the ancients themselves, rather than to any modern national identities. But humans like to take history – even the history of soybeans – and through creative imagination bend it to serve new purposes.

Imagination reveals how important soybeans have been in Asian societies, for people rarely mythologize or reinterpret phenomena unless they are central to their lives. Thus a Japanese tale from 712 CE depicts a divine origin for soy. The Shinto sun goddess, hearing of a distant food goddess, sent the moon god to contact her. When the moon god arrived, the food goddess produced rice, fish and meat from her mouth, set them on tables and presented them to him. Repulsed by this offering from her body, the moon god refused to eat and instead killed his hostess. When the sun goddess learned of this deed, she sent a messenger to examine the murdered goddess's corpse. What the messenger found was glorious: from the goddess's head sprang cattle and horses, from her forehead millet, on her eyebrows silk worms, in her belly rice and in her life-giving genitals, wheat, soybeans and red beans.[5]

Modern geopolitics and evocative myths aside, from assorted evidence one can reconstruct much of soy's long history in Asia. Chemical profiles of soybeans from archaeological sites, written histories, diaries, religious texts, folk songs and sayings, poetry, legends and recorded contracts for labour, trade and weddings – even murals – all proffer insights.

In China, for centuries soy was appreciated as a reliable crop and useful fodder for animals – but as a food, it was deemed too coarse for anyone but those toughing out a hard life. Soy shared its lowly status with wheat, since refinements in processing these plants were undeveloped, and both were rather difficult to prepare and digest. Although soy is an excellent source of protein when thoroughly heated, when undercooked it actually interferes with protein digestion. Under-processed soy can also cause flatulence. It was a problematic crop; whenever possible, the Chinese ate millet and rice instead.

In approximately the third century BCE, a method of preparing soy was devised to yield a prized, more expensive food than ordinary boiled and steamed soybeans. The new technique produced *shi*, a salty, chunky, fermented soy relish. By 173 BCE, all but the poor considered shi essential, as evidenced by a famous history scroll. It detailed the exiling of Prince Liu An for fomenting a revolt against his cousin, the emperor. Compassionately, the emperor allowed Liu An to leave with a retinue of servants and necessities: firewood, rice and the beloved condiment, shi.[6]

By the first century BCE, shi had become affordable for Chinese commoners. In that century, a master imposed on his rebellious servant an 'agreement' delineating the house boy's duties and specifying that he could consume only water and simple cooked soybeans. The youth wept when he heard of this and other privations in the arrangement. A diet of endless, plain cooked soybeans was no longer acceptable even to the servant class. The chastised servant knew well that other foods were available, and that shi was a better kind of soy. Fortunately, the master recorded his galling 'agreement' and the servant's reaction to it in a clever rhyme, motivating posterity to save it for millennia.[7]

Soybeans were also in Korea at this time, and eventually they were transported back and forth between Korea and Japan. A chemically analysed 'family tree' of the proteins in Asian soybeans

In this 18th-century woodcut, a Japanese family throws and eats soybeans in order to expel demons.

indicates that since at least the third century CE, and perhaps earlier, soy was being moved across the Sea of Japan.[8] An increasingly diverse soy culinary culture began emerging in these countries.

Back in China, by the early centuries CE not only was shi available, but also *jiang*, a smoother, more refined soy condiment that included wheat flour. Versions of jiang also existed in Korea. In Japan it was probably adopted sometime after 500 CE when immigrant Koreans taught the Japanese how to make it. There it came to be so highly prized that for a time Japanese high officials were paid with jiang as salary.

An alternative explanation for how jiang came to Japan posits Buddhism as central. Buddhist doctrine arriving from China and Korea discouraged meat eating; monks especially were vegetarians. Monasteries became centres of experimentation with plant-based alternatives to meat, and monks travelling for study or missionary work spread soy-processing techniques throughout Asia. The tale of Ganjin, a venerated Chinese monk who sojourned to Japan in 753 is therefore credible: it is said he brought dried fermented soybeans, used to make early Japanese jiang.[9]

A Korean woman crushes boiled soybeans to make a fermented paste in the early 20th century.

No matter how jiang reached Japan's shores – perhaps both the learning-from-Korean-immigrants and the brought-by-a-Chinese-holy-man stories are true – clearly the Japanese gradually adapted jiang to create *miso*, a soy paste often including rice or barley. As fermented soy products became cornerstones of their national cuisines, the modifications that jiang underwent in Korea and Japan profoundly shaped the culinary preferences of their populations. Especially notable in Korea was the addition of hot peppers hardly a century after discovery of the New World introduced peppers to world trade; the resulting fiery soy paste is called *koch'ujang*.

Another major soy product was also being invented, improved upon, carried around by Buddhist travellers and commercialized during the early centuries CE, and perhaps even before. As milling equipment improved, the Chinese experimented with grinding a wider variety of crops. One outcome was wheat flour, and from that, many types of breads and noodles. But soybeans are less cooperative. When ground, their substantial oil content yields lumpy flaking, rather than a smooth powder. What to do with such flakes?

Because China's peasants never tolerated any waste of food, they must have searched for a way to use the unwieldy soy mash. An obvious choice was to cook it in water the way they cooked whole beans. A soy gruel was born. Then at some point, someone drained excess cooking water from the gruel and used the fluid separately, and eventually even ground the beans with water from the start to obtain a thicker version of this new liquid. This novelty was soy milk. Although soy milk did not become popular in China until the eighteenth or nineteenth century CE, before then it played a crucial role as a precursor ingredient for tofu.[10]

Exactly when and how someone first curdled soy milk, and then pressed the curds to make a semi-solid block of tofu, is a mystery made all the more intriguing by myth and academic guesswork. Medieval Chinese legend states that tofu was invented by Liu An, the same prince who was exiled for his supposed plot to overthrow the emperor. Liu An was a great scholar at whose gatherings brilliant men exchanged ideas. Did the method for making tofu evolve out of these gatherings? Did Liu An learn to make tofu from the alchemists whose works he studied? Or was the legend of his inventing tofu itself an invention of later Buddhists – a way of promoting tofu consumption by associating it with a hero from the past? The mythical aspect of Liu An's relationship to tofu is well illustrated by one writer from the fourteenth century CE, who proclaimed that Liu An 'ate tofu, grew younger, eventually sprouted wings, and ascended to heaven'.[11]

Then there is the perplexing tomb art from China's Henan Province, discovered in 1959. In a tomb from the Later Han period (25–220 CE), a mural depicts something that might be the making of tofu. Although no beans are shown, steps used in preparing tofu – soaking, grinding, filtering, stirring in coagulant for curdling and pressing – are all visible. But a crucial step – heating – is missing. Some scholars argue that the mural must therefore be about wine production, not tofu. Others contend that the mural's intent was to show specialized equipment, and since heating required no special instruments, that step was omitted even though it was, in fact, being performed. If this latter interpretation is correct, then tofu existed at the beginning of the Common Era, and perhaps even before. 'Not so fast,' the first set of scholars protests, posing a vexing question: if tofu existed so long ago, then why was there not even a hint about it in Chinese writings until centuries later?[12]

Dating the origin of tofu is thus problematic. What of the technique – how did it develop? Possibly the first soy curds formed as a mishap when a cook added unrefined sea salt to soy gruel. Sea salt contains magnesium chloride, which curdles the proteins out of crushed soy in liquid. A cook may have noticed such curds and creatively worked them into a cheese-like semi-solid. By around 950 CE, a Chinese text mentioned tofu as common in markets, so this accidental discovery would have occurred well before then.[13]

The analogy to cheese brings up two other theories about tofu's origins. The ancient Chinese did not extract milk from animals for human consumption; they found this practice among other peoples disgusting. They may have been intrigued, however, by the cheese and yoghurt production of the peoples along their borders. Nomadic tribes migrating south to China from about the third century CE used milk from cows, camels, yaks, goats, sheep and horses in fermented products. Although the Chinese considered these tribes barbarians, they eventually enjoyed some of their dairy foods. Appreciation perhaps led to imitation, as the Chinese observed chemicals coagulating mammalian milk; they may have tried sprinkling such substances into soy milk to see what would happen. It is even possible that the word 'tofu' derives from a Mongolian word for soft cheese, *rufu*.

Possibly inspiration for curdling soy milk came instead from the south. This theory centres on a legendary Buddhist monk named Bodhidharma, depicted in art as an irascible man with a thick moustache and shaggy beard, and said to have perfected meditation by staring at a wall. He was perhaps from Persia or South India – both dairying cultures. In the sixth century CE he apparently introduced to China the enigmatic form of Buddhism known as Zen – and possibly also the straightforward art of curdling liquids, which the Chinese then applied to soy milk. Support for this theory is weaker than evidence for the northern nomads' influence.[14] In any case, tofu and its value as an animal-protein substitute were clearly known in China by the time of the Tang Dynasty (618–907 CE), when the people called it 'small mutton'.

From Tang China, tofu spread as Buddhists took it with them on their travels. Folklore suggests, for example, that tofu had a Buddhist origin in Vietnam. A very old Vietnamese folk song proclaims, 'If you want to enjoy tofu with traditional soy sauce, sharpen your knife and scissors, shave your head, and become a monk.'[15] Several other lands adopted tofu – notably Japan, where it became a ubiquitous, everyday yet deeply appreciated food. Traditionally, tofu shops were as common in Japan as corner bakeries in France, and just as the French will debate at length which baker makes a better baguette, so also the Japanese are acutely aware of subtle differences in tofu from different shops.[16] Tofu thus moved beyond its role as a meat substitute for Buddhists. Indeed, the earliest known written reference to tofu in Japanese appears in the diary not of a Buddhist monk, but of a Shinto priest, who in 1183 CE mentioned it as a shrine offering.[17]

Legend posits a different sort of introduction for tofu in Indonesia: military conquest. Currently the Javanese town of Kediri specializes in tofu production, which tradition dates to an invasion in 1293 CE. Historical records indicate that China's Mongol emperor, Kublai Khan, repeatedly demanded tribute from the Javanese king Kertanegara – but the latter defied him and even had one of the Khan's messengers cut deeply in the face. Retaliating, Kublai sent 1,000 square-sailed warrior ships, which in their galleys presumably carried tofu and tofu-making equipment.

Meanwhile, trickery lurked. A rival Javanese king assailed Kertanegara's lands; some of the invaders went undetected until it was too late. Kertanegara was killed, and his rival became king. Kertanegara's vengeful son-in-law then directed the Mongols, just arriving, to assault his father-in-law's usurpers. Deceived into thinking they would punish the king who had humiliated their Khan, the Mongols followed the son-in-law's directions to Kediri. There

Japanese miso soup with cubed tofu makes use of soybeans in two different ways.

they killed the new king and routed his army. But, abruptly, their Javanese allies turned on the Mongols, assaulting them ferociously. The Mongols realized they had been used, like a giant weapon, in an internal Javanese conflict – and now that several months had passed since their first landfall, the season's monsoon winds were winding down. If the Mongols waited much longer, they would be trapped without useful winds for six more months in very hostile territory. They fled. But, according to the people of Kediri, they left behind their tofu-making techniques, for which the town folk are forever grateful.[18]

The most iconic Indonesian soy food is *tempeh*. The word, unlike the names of so many other soy products throughout Asia, does not have a Chinese origin; tempeh seems to have developed in central Java. A Javanese saga – written in 1815 but set in the 1600s – twice mentions tempeh, so if the tale has historical accuracy for details of everyday life, then tempeh was first created some 500 years ago.[19] It is made by soaking, dehulling and partly cooking soybeans. A mild acid such as vinegar, and then a fermentation starter including spores of a particular mould, are mixed with the beans. The mould flourishes in the slightly acidic environment. In Indonesia, this mould, *Rhizopus oligosporus*, naturally occurs on the leaves of 'sea hibiscus' trees; the

Indonesian tempeh is made by fermenting whole soybeans and is a good source of vitamin B12.

tempeh-making technique was possibly discovered when someone was interrupted halfway through cooking some soybeans and left them in contact with hibiscus. Within a day or so the soybeans were firmly connected by the mould's white branching threads. The end product was high in protein and had a nutty flavour that the Javanese appreciated, so they refined methods for producing it.

Today tempeh is still valued for its hearty contribution to meals and snacks. When produced using both mould and certain bacteria, tempeh provides vitamin B12, which is essential to human metabolism, blood and the nervous system. Most people obtain vitamin B12 through eating animal products, but vegans, and vegetarians in societies with limited dairy consumption, require a bacterial source such as tempeh.

The 1815 references to tempeh appear in the *Serat Centhini*, a collection of Javanese tales. In one passage, a group travels through a haunted forest. They hear hunters pursuing game animals, yet see no other people. Suddenly a woman in their group screams and faints. Revived, she tells of her frightening vision – a fierce man attacking her. With great relief, then, the group reaches a friendly village, where a prominent family kindly serves them a feast. Their hosts' tempeh and other dishes offer comforting contrast to the terrors of the forest. The tale suggests that by the time it was penned, tempeh was well established in Java.[20]

Asians have found myriad ways to ferment soy, which efficiently breaks down the beans' anti-nutritive and flatulence-causing chemicals and preserves them for long periods. *Oncom* is a fermented Indonesian product typically made with peanuts, but sometimes instead with dregs from the first stages of tofu production. The soy pulp is fermented with a *Neurospora* mould that gives oncom a bright orange hue. Oncom is often critiqued as tasting stale – yet for those accustomed to it, when fried with spices it is an enjoyable snack.

Tamari, from Japan, is a thick liquid by-product of fermenting miso; it is used as a seasoning. *Natto* also comes from Japan. Made from soybeans briefly fermented with *Bacillus subtilis*, it accompanies other dishes such as miso soup, rice or salad. Although its musty flavour, whiff of ammonia and slimy consistency make natto unappealing to many, even among the Japanese, vegetarians have long recognized the value of its protein, vitamins and minerals. An amusing Japanese story from the feudal period pays homage to natto.

Interpretable as a parody of the struggle between twelfth-century clans, personified vegetarian and animal-based foods vie with one another for superior rank. Lord Natto is the leader of a vegetarian food army that triumphs over forces led by Lord Salmon.[21]

The fermented soy food that most astonishes the uninitiated is 'stinky tofu', a Chinese concoction with a variable recipe. Producers proudly guard the details of which precise ingredients and method they use. This dish exudes an odour noticeable even from a distance; one rarely prepares it at home, lest the neighbours take offence. Generally, making stinky tofu begins with the fermenting of soy milk; various flavouring ingredients are added – potentially bamboo shoots, melon, herbs, salted shrimp, animal organs or eggs. Fermentation occurs when ambient bacteria, or added bacterial starter from a previous batch of stinky tofu, cause ammonia to form; the resulting change in pH encourages other species of bacteria to invade, adding their own metabolic activities to the chemical brew. The 'brine' now smells like rotting, unwashed athletic socks – or manure. It is ready for the tofu, which is steeped in the liquid for up to one week. Having taken on the brine's aroma, as tofu easily does with liquids, the newly stinky tofu is either simmered in a stew, stir-fried or deep fried as a snack with chilli sauce and pickles. Its flavour is pungent but mercifully milder than its smell. Stinky tofu is a startling food that, like a particularly ripe, reeking and formidable Roquefort cheese, the local connoisseurs love, and many (often even those who make it) cannot help but despise.[22]

But the ultimate fermented soy food, in terms of its conquest of cuisines worldwide, is soy sauce. Sauces made from the liquid remaining after soy fermentation seem to have existed in China before the Common Era, and in Korea and Japan by the seventh or eighth centuries CE. Fermented from a base of salted soy, such sauces possibly included a bit of wheat flour, mushrooms, shrimp eggs or other flavourings. Unfortunately, a paucity of records about them in earlier centuries makes it difficult to trace their development.

Legend asserts that in southcentral Japan in the 1200s, a prominent Buddhist monk was the first miso producer to collect tamari liquid, a predecessor of true soy sauce. He taught the technique to the local populace.[23] In the mid-1500s it seems that someone there added roasted, cracked wheat to the fermenting mash and then employed specialized equipment to squeeze liquid (and maximal flavour) out of the mixture. The resulting thin, delectable sauce was costlier than tamari and hence a luxury for at least another hundred years, exported by sea to nobles in distant areas of Japan, and even to China. Eventually, as soy sauce was produced on a larger scale, its price declined enough for the regular population to enjoy it. Its importance to ordinary Japanese is shown by the fate of two 1871 taxes levied on soy-sauce production. By 1875 pressure to remove the taxes had grown sufficiently that the government repealed them, noting (perhaps ruefully) that soy sauce should be sheltered from excess taxation because it was, after all, a necessity.[24]

Along with other foods, fermented soy tickles human taste buds with the pleasure of *umami*. Like the tastes of sweet, sour, salty and bitter, umami is perceived by the tongue through specialized flavour receptors. With umami, receptors detect the amino acid glutamate. In Japanese, the word 'umami' means 'flavour of deliciousness'. Combined with soy sauce's versatility for cooking – and the assiduous marketing efforts of the world's largest soy sauce company, Kikkoman – this deliciousness has made soy sauce the most popular soy food on the planet. A working-class teen in the Dominican Republic adds a dash of soy sauce and vinegar to her scrambled egg batter; an Afrikaaner dad grills meats marinated with soy sauce; a Portuguese housewife makes *trinchado* stewed beef with peppers, garlic, red wine, herbs – and soy sauce; food websites suggest adding soy sauce to vanilla ice cream to conjure up a butterscotch flavour (really!).

This extended look at Asia's prowess in fermenting soy is not to neglect that continent's *unfermented* soy foods. Asians have been wonderfully inventive with soy. From tofu they have made many other foods: deep-fried tofu puffs; thinly sliced, flavoured and baked tofu chips; frozen tofu; pickled tofu; smoked dried tofu; freeze-dried tofu (a staple with a long shelf life found in most Japanese kitchens – just soak in hot water before using in stews); tofu fried and stuffed with other ingredients such as minced fish and hot peppers; tofu in myriad types of stir-fry dishes; tofu in soups; and sweet tofu puddings.

There are still more. Unfermented soy foods include:

- edamame – chewy young soybeans straight from the pod, steamed and served with a little salt;

- *yuba* or 'beancurd robes', the yellowish 'skin' that forms on the top of cooling soy milk. This skin is scooped up and dried, or semi-dried, in sheets. It can be used to wrap dim sum, or else carefully folded onto itself to imitate the texture of chicken breast or other meats;

- tender new shoots from just-sprouted soybeans, today added to stir fries and salads, and eaten in the early centuries CE in China for their supposed medicinal effects on numb joints and muscles;

- watery soy drinks with sweet flavourings – but never with so much extraneous flavour as to mask their prized, slightly beany taste;

- soybeans roasted and ground into flour, appreciated in confections for its nutty flavour; and

- unfermented soy pulp, used to provide texture for various recipes – especially in Japan, where it is seen as very healthy and is known as *okara*. Recently in Japan, okara has also been used to make yarn and biodegradable cat litter. Okara serves as livestock feed throughout East Asia.

Among other non-food uses, for generations in Asia the soy plant has served as green forage for domestic animals; it is high in protein and low in fibre compared to grasses. Soy meal has been used as organic fertilizer for other crops; by about 1905 the Japanese employed more soy meal 'cake' than traditional fish cake to enrich their soils.[25] At that time much of Japan's soy fertilizer came from Manchuria, and after 1910, from annexed Korea as well, providing further motivation, beyond the Japanese taste for soy foods, for them to covet economic and political control over their neighbours.

Soy has been grown and consumed in farther-flung locations across Asia. In Kazakhstan, soybeans were planted around 1870 by a Chinese Muslim minority, the Hui, many of whom descend from ancient Silk Road travellers.[26] Although soy became established in Kazakhstan among this ethnic group, other Kazakhs did not plant soy until the twentieth century, and then only in modest quantities.

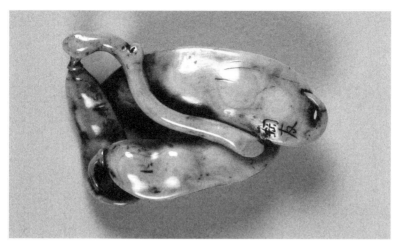

In the early 19th century, edamame boiled on the stem inspired artist Yamaguchi Okatomo to create this small ivory sculpture.

Meanwhile, soy continued to generate interest in other Asian regions. At Asia's border with Europe, in what is now the Republic of Georgia, by 1910 one company sold soybean 'coffee'.[27] The first known commercial soy product in the Transcaucasus, soy coffee had originally developed in areas that are now in Italy and Croatia. Soy coffee was thus a Western recipe for an Eastern crop, fittingly marketed in Georgia at the crossroads of continents.

WESTERN INGENUITY with soybeans stretched back to the seventeenth century. European and American experiments with soybeans prior to 1900 were a prelude to the twentieth century's passion for the crop in the New World. Risk, genius, zeal, collapse, triumph, anxiety: we shall see that, as in Asia, the burgeoning story of soy in the West runs the gamut of human experience.

TWO

EUROPE EXPLORES AND EXPERIMENTS

A century after Columbus discovered the New World, a young Italian named Francesco Carletti spent eight years travelling overwhelming distances – the first non-sailor to circumnavigate the globe without government sponsorship. Returning home, he reported to the Florentine court all he had seen. In the account, we see through European eyes the opportunities, curiosities and miseries of the Age of Exploration.[1]

Carletti did not live in gentle times. He and his merchant father set out to purchase Africans in the Cape Verde islands. Despite the younger Carletti's troubled conscience, the two men acquired 75 enslaved individuals, packed them into a ship and crossed the Atlantic. En route several died, their corpses thrown overboard. The merchant pair sold the survivors in South America.

Father and son decided to expand their trip in search of tradable goods. In Peru, Carletti met Spaniards becoming fabulously wealthy from the back-breaking labour of indigenous silver-mine workers; in the Philippines he watched gamblers bet on cocks armed with miniature scimitars with which to disembowel one another. Upon arrival in Japan, Carletti witnessed the crucifixion of Christian missionaries and converts; in the woeful aftermath of a Japanese invasion of Korea he observed the marketing of vast numbers of Korean slaves. Then in Macau father and son were imprisoned as possible smugglers; later the father fell ill and died.

On Carletti's way home, Dutch sailors attacked his ship, stealing all the treasures he had so painstakingly obtained. When he finally reached Florence, Carletti had nothing to sell – but he fascinated the court with strategic information. He had a thousand cross-cultural details to impart, of political, military and economic importance. One of these details especially concerns us, as Carletti was the first European to describe a food made from soybeans (something Marco Polo, centuries earlier, had neglected). In Nagasaki, Carletti had noticed not only the Japanese versions of the harshness of the age, but also their inventions, including a ubiquitous seasoning he spelled *misol*.

Carletti understood that miso was made from

> a sort of bean that abounds in various localities, and which – cooked and mashed and mixed with a little of that rice from which they make the wine already mentioned, and then left to stand as packed into a tub – turns sour and all but decays, taking on a very sharp, piquant flavour. Using this a little at a time, they give flavour to their foods . . .[2]

In the decades that followed, other European travellers described tofu and soy sauce but seemed not to know that they came from beans. Only in 1712, when the German explorer Engelbert Kaempfer published a 900-page description of Japan, did Europeans gain more understanding of soybeans.

Kaempfer was brilliant, and employers of various nationalities sought him out. In the 1680s he ended up in Japan, where he was engaged as a physician for the Dutch traders on Dejima island, and also charged with preparing a scholarly description of Japan.

Studying that isolationist nation proved challenging. By then employees of the Dutch East India Company were the only Europeans allowed in Japan, and with rare exceptions they were never permitted to leave Dejima, on pain of death. Dejima is tiny, barely big enough for a few warehouses and twenty homes. The Europeans were provided with a retinue of Japanese translators, servants and guards, but the Japanese were prohibited from teaching their language to them.

Kaempfer overcame this stifling atmosphere through kindness and competence. He began learning Japanese on his own, and towards his handlers he was generous with medicines and liquor. He won the friendship of his Japanese personal servant, and through him discreetly obtained Japanese books. Kaempfer also travelled twice to and from the capital to provide medical advice to the wealthy, which allowed him to make myriad observations to discuss with his servant.

The resulting scholarship began filling a gap in which Europeans had had no concept of growing soy themselves, or of preparing their own soy foods. In his 1712 oeuvre, Kaempfer detailed both the plant and methods for making soy products. Then, in a posthumous history, he described soy as one of Japan's principal 'fruits of the field':

> Daidsu, that is, Daidbeans, is a certain sort of Beans, about the bigness of Turkish Pease . . . next to the Rice in use and esteem. Of the meal of these beans is made what they call Midsu [miso], a mealy Pap, which they dress their Victuals withal, as we do with Butter. What they call Soeju [soy sauce] is also made of it . . . which they eat at meals to get a good Stomach. This Soeju is imported by the Dutch and brought even into Holland.[3]

During Kaempfer's stay in Dejima, the Dutch seemed unaware of the ingredients in the Soeju they traded. Yet it was a commercial success, and it has even been speculated that King Louis XIV of France, the mighty 'Sun King' who filled his court with every luxury, procured it in the late 1600s as a mysterious, exotic seasoning for his banquets.[4]

More historically certain is the availability of soy sauce in London in the 1670s, as described by the philosopher John Locke.[5] Soy sauce would become a base for many different sauces in British cooking. By 1818 Lord Byron's humorous poem 'Beppo: A Venetian Story', which is partly about English visitors to Italy at the time of Lent, would highlight the ubiquity – even necessity – of soy in the cuisine of the English upper classes:

> And thus they bid farewell to Carnal dishes,
> And solid meats, and highly spiced ragouts,
> To live for forty days on ill-dress'd fishes,
> Because they have no sauces to their stews –
> A thing which causes many 'poohs' and 'pishes',
> And several oaths (which would not suit the Muse)
> From travellers accustom'd from a boy

To eat their Salmon, at the least, with Soy;
And therefore humbly I would recommend
'The Curious in Fish-Sauce', before they cross
The Sea, to bid their Cook, or wife, or friend,
Walk or ride to the Strand, and buy in gross
(Or if set out beforehand these may send
By any means least liable to loss)
Ketchup, Soy, Chili-Vinegar, and Harvey
    [a brand of sauce that included soy],
Or, by the Lord! a Lent will well nigh starve ye . . .[6]

By bringing Europeans beyond merely upper-class appreciation of soy to a detailed understanding of the plant, Kaempfer was the forerunner of numerous European soy scientists. Not all of them became its champions; indeed, an Italian agriculture professor in the 1850s declared soy 'disgusting and absolutely no use as a bean [to eat], nor is it of any worth as an oilseed'.[7] But in nineteenth-century France there was a receptive group, the Zoological Society for Acclimatization, whose mission was to introduce new animals and plants to the French. The Society's members were the first Europeans to promote soy cultivation actively in a Western country.

France was a promising region for inquisitiveness about soy. In that country especially, nobles who engaged in 'lowly' occupations of mechanical labour, crafts or retail commerce risked having their high-born privileges revoked. They therefore invested in land, and many passed leisure time in horticultural experimentation – an appropriate pastime for a gentleman. Meanwhile, France's missionaries and colonizers in Asian countries sent back soy recipes and seeds. It was from the French consul in China that the Acclimatization group received its first soy seeds in 1854. France's passion for wine and cheese also inspired people to try their hand at making tofu, seen as a bean cheese. In 1869 a French scholar compared tofu to soft cow's milk cheese, proclaiming that this 'pea cheese, fried in fat like potatoes, is truly a delicacy'.[8] But the French were especially interested in 'ripening' soy to make fermented tofu, soy sauce and miso. The Society for Horticulture in Marseilles even created red- and white-wine fermented tofus and reported that the local population enjoyed them.[9]

The French used soy oil, too. In 1855 a Frenchman praised soy oil as lacking the 'bitterness or sharpness from rapeseed . . . oil, [and] with the addition of a little lard . . . [it] becomes similar in flavour to second grade olive oil'.[10] Then in 1868 Hippolyte Mège-Mouriès invented margarine, and within a few decades French scientists devised the process of hydrogenating vegetable oils. Hydrogenation gives oils a more solid consistency and longer shelf-life – convenient for margarine. Over time margarines came to contain large quantities of soy oil, made possible when the English developed a solvent method for removing oil from the beans. This method was cheaper than the older system of screw-pressing the beans to squeeze the oil out.

German speakers also forged ahead with soy research. Germans would eventually engineer the most advanced solvent extraction systems in the world and sell their equipment in foreign markets. Austrians made contributions as well, beginning in Vienna with the Universal Exposition of 1873.

The Exposition was a world's fair, and the Viennese went to great lengths to 'wow' visitors. Nearly 26,000 exhibitors presented cultural artefacts, live entertainment, new technologies and horticultural arts from many lands to the public. Over six months, 7 million people attended. Among the displays were soybeans grown in China, Japan, Mongolia, Transcaucasia and even Tunisia. Opportunely, the chancellor of Austria's Royal School of Agriculture, Friedrich Haberlandt, stopped by and obtained the seeds of nineteen varieties of soy. For the next five years – which would be, unfortunately, his last – Haberlandt distributed seed extensively to colleagues and farmers, thereby initiating hundreds of experiments with soy cultivation in central Europe. Based on the data collected, on his historical research and on his own testing of soy-processing techniques, in 1878 Haberlandt published *Die Sojabohne*, the first book devoted to soy in any Western language.

Haberlandt died before he could see all that his work inspired: fifty years of soy research in Vienna and greater interest in soy throughout Europe. French work had emphasized soy's food uses, and Haberlandt too was interested in soy foods – soy 'chocolate', 'coffee', grits for a version of polenta and flour in breads. He proposed replacing garden peas with soybeans in the Austrian army's pea sausage. But, crucially, Haberlandt also envisaged feeding soy to livestock.

From a present-day perspective, eminent soy historians William Shurtleff and Akiko Aoyagi deem Haberlandt's impact seminal. Haberlandt's promotion of soybeans for animal feed was prescient, leading, as Shurtleff and Aoyagi explain, 'to a major reevaluation of the soybean's potential in Europe'.[11] Within a few decades of Haberlandt's visit to the Universal Expo, agricultural scientists had devised preliminary methods for processing soy into feed. The enthusiastic response of farmers would eventually create a global stampede to convert soy protein into animal flesh.

Haberlandt also saw soy's potential as cheap nourishment for the underprivileged. He argued that if properly prepared, soy would 'someday play a major role in the diets of the poor . . . With its fat . . . it will replace lard, and with its protein it will supply strength.'[12] His influence was so great that for a time in Austria, in Germany and even among some in France, soy was called 'the Haberlandt bean'.

Haberlandt's book immediately stimulated a French researcher, Nicolas-Auguste Paillieux, to compile years of the Acclimatization group's findings into a French tome.[13] Paillieux would become the first to recommend soy for diabetics; chemical analyses had revealed that the bean is low in starch. The French would produce baked soy goods for diabetics until the early twentieth century, benefiting that population but unfortunately lending an aura of 'therapeutic necessity' to the bean. In France, where delectable eating is nearly a right of citizenship, touting a food as medically useful does not broaden its appeal.

In this culinary environment, a gifted Chinese biochemist educated in France, Li Yuying, laboured to adapt traditional Asian soy foods to French tastes. He opened Europe's first modern soy food factory near Paris in the early 1900s. There he and his employees made soy milk, soy 'yoghurt', Roquefort and Camembert-flavoured tofus, soy sauce, soy sprouts and roasted soy flour for bakery products. Li hired Chinese students to help finance their stays in France; he was an early employer in French work–study programmes that would in due course include a teen named Deng Xiaoping, the future premier of China.

In May 1911 France's Acclimatization group engaged Li to prepare their annual breakfast showcasing little-known foods. Li served bread, jam, cheeses and 'ham' – all made from soybeans. Around

Enthusiasts and entrepreneurs in Europe experimented with making soy yoghurt.

that time, he also held the world's first soy foods press conference, serving an eleven-course soy meal to hundreds of top journalists and officials. He next translated his Chinese book on soy foods into French. The opus was published in 1912 and was widely discussed among French agronomists.[14]

But Li was too far ahead of his time, and his factory closed after a few years; he returned to China. To the average Frenchman, the slightly beany taste of soy simply did not belong in cheeses and baked goods. True, as agronomist Léon Rouest noted in 1921, soy cheese was feared by the cheese industry in France.[15] Cheese makers worried: what if the French came to love this food that was cheaper and easier to produce than dairy cheeses? But dairymen need not have fretted. Today, a century and a half after the dissemination of soy seeds in France began, and a century after Li opened his factory, the French rarely include soy protein in their diets. Instead, they feed it to animals, just as Haberlandt long ago suggested.

Even the Frenchman Paillieux argued that emphasizing soy for food was the French pioneers' mistake. He noted that in Austria–Hungary, where soy as human food was secondary to its applications in animal husbandry, there had been increasing demand for wide swathes of soy cultivation, while in France 'we were still cultivating [soy] . . . between the rows in the kitchen garden for use as food.'[16]

Ultimately, the exigencies of war propelled serious interest in soy within France and Europe as a whole. The Russo-Japanese conflict of 1904–5 provided Europe with a case study in soy's utility for armies. Brutal though that war was, it was sufficiently old-fashioned and geographically delineated for military officers from several nations to observe the action safely from nearby hills, and even to feel comfortable travelling between the sides to study how each was housed and provisioned. The Japanese used soy as human food more extensively than the Russians, but even the Russians consumed some soy – the first time a large group of Europeans had ever done so. One conclusion the Europeans drew was that soy could be an

The Chinese tradition of fermenting tofu did not seem strange to the French, who have their own long tradition of fermenting strong cheeses.

important military supply. Another, more tragic, conclusion was that to win a war, one should send great volumes of well-nourished men directly into the fight, and when they are mowed down, send more until the enemy is worn out – a strategy leading to the deadlocked, blood-soaked trenches of the First World War and the deaths of at least 8.5 million men.[17]

In 1907 the English began the first large-scale imports of soy-beans to Europe, bringing them from Manchuria to crush, primarily for industrial oil. Other European nations soon followed suit. Mean-while, the military build-up that would eventually trigger the First World War loomed, with colonial rivalries exacerbating tensions. Each European power wanted an empire more potent than the others'. Agricultural prowess was an important avenue to success; the possibilities for extracting raw materials from subjugated lands dazzled Europe. Experiments with soy agriculture in tropical climes were part of those efforts.

The Dutch and the French had an advantage, because for a long time their Indonesian and Indochinese possessions were the only fully fledged European colonies in East Asia. These places happened to be ideal for investigating soy. Thus Dutch researchers studied alternating soybeans with rice in Indonesian fields, and they part-nered with a bakery in Amsterdam that made bread for diabetics from Indonesian soybeans. A French military pharmacist, Armand-Aron Bloch, also applauded soy, recommending that his nation's troops in Indochina consume tofu for its nutritional value, low cost and pre-servability when dried in thin sheets.[18] But other European countries made attempts, too: the Belgians, for instance, introduced soy to the Congo in 1908. Catholic missionaries there trained schoolchildren to ask for a soy beverage as 'Monseigneur's milk'.[19]

The Germans took a different tack. For decades Brazil had had a monopoly on rubber, a critical industrial and military resource. The English then subverted the Brazilians: in 1876 explorer Henry Wickham sneaked tens of thousands of rubber seeds out of the Amazon to England, from whence they were profitably grown in Ceylon and British Malaya. The Germans had no such plantations. They recognized that having their own supply of rubber – or a good substitute – would reduce their vulnerability during war. So they invested in research, and in 1909 two Germans patented a rubber substitute made from soy oil.[20] But these efforts were ultimately disappointing. Soy-based rubber had some uses during the 1930s and the Second World War around the world, but cheaper synthetic rubber made from petroleum soon overtook the market.

Just before the First World War, Germany imported and crushed more soybeans than previously – partly because the price of other industrial oils had risen above that of soy oil, but partly also because in 1906–7 German soy scholar Emanuel Senft had published a positive appraisal of the Japanese army's soy food rations.[21] During the First World War itself, Germans used soy flour for protein in civilian and army diets, and soy oil both as food and in industry. They even extracted glutamic acid from soybeans to enhance the flavour of a beef-tea drink served in German hospitals. Similarly, Austria sought to improve its soldiers' and population's protein intakes with soy products.

In France in 1914, after the army requisitioned traditional dry legumes, soy appeared in civilian markets as a substitute. By 1917 the French were making soybean soups and baked products using soy flour. The army ate soy breads and crackers, and army cooks often replaced the meat powder in rations with soy. One could even find plain soybeans in a can for soldiers.

But the Great War also had negative effects on European soy food development. In England, a small company had been making soy margarine, cakes, breads, 'cocoa' and 'chocolates' before the war, but when German submarine warfare caused soybean imports to dry up, the owners emigrated to America. Germans gradually also had to forego soy products, as the Allied blockades of the North and Adriatic Seas prevented them from replenishing their supply of beans. They had stockpiled soy before 1914, but the war dragged on far longer than anyone expected. The lack of soy oil was particularly problematic. Germany would not forget this lesson, as we shall see later.

In the immediate aftermath of the First World War, however, the keenest interest in soy came from the new Soviet Union. Japan's earlier defeat of Russia had acutely impressed soy's usefulness upon Russian leaders. After the Russo-Japanese War, private Russian businessmen had continued trading Manchurian soybeans, exporting them to the motherland and especially to Western Europe through the Siberian port of Vladivostok. Russia used soy for their growing margarine industry, and the Soviets continued this trend.

In 1924–5 disaster struck the Volga German Autonomous Soviet Socialist Republic, a region originally colonized by eighteenth-century German settlers in Russia. Writing to an American benefactor, one citizen explained:

> Over the last three months it has still not rained one time . . . our fields and gardens and forests are really parched . . . Provisions, whether for man nor beast, are quickly disappearing . . . Our government seeks to console our discouraged farmers not to lose heart . . . Now, already many are without Bread, worn down, half naked, and grasping, again condemned to wander and beg and in this way seek to eke out a living, but that will also not be possible for very long.[22]

Such misery, on the heels of the 1921–2 Russian famine, motivated authorities in Moscow to invest in soybeans. They engaged a prominent Hungarian researcher, Laszlo Berczeller, to help them with modern soy processing. Berczeller travelled to and from the USSR for several years, met with Stalin to discuss soybeans and in 1930 was named Honorary General of the Red Army. His work dovetailed with other Soviet efforts, their newsprint proclaiming, 'Plant soybeans and you plant meat, milk, egg omelets!'[23] A British official elaborated:

> In the Five Years' Plan Russia has set aside vast tracts . . . for the cultivation of the soya bean. There is a soya bean Research Institute at Moscow. An exhibition of soya bean foods was held where 300 varieties of soya bean dishes were . . . served to the representatives of trade-unions, factories, engineers, Soviet Press, and the Red Army. The food was unanimously pronounced to be excellent . . . rickets and consumption are treated by Soyolk [Berczeller's soy flour] . . .[24]

Also in the Soviet repertoire were soy toffee, soy pies and soy *kumis* – kumis being a slightly alcoholic Central Asian beverage traditionally made from fermented mare's milk.

In Western Europe, recovery from the Great War spurred renewed uses for soy. Events in Denmark were particularly striking. Danish farmers made their livelihoods exporting wheat. But the

American plains were awash with excess wheat; between 1919 and 1921 its price dropped more than 50 per cent. Farming wheat in Denmark had become a money-losing exercise as cheap American imports flooded European markets. The enterprising Danes came up with a solution: import soybeans from Manchuria, feed them to livestock and develop a new economic base exporting butter and bacon. This plan worked very well, as the typical mid-size Danish farm was not as efficient for the production of wheat as larger American farms – but it was ideal for the intensive care of animals. Soy thus helped rescue the Danish economy.[25]

In Germany, researchers continued to work with soy in the 1920s and '30s. Among them was a spirited soy breeder named Lene Mueller, whose investigations took her on travels worldwide. In 1927 she was shipwrecked in Asia and had to be rescued from the sea near Java. Yet her passion for enquiry refused to quit, and she kept travelling, planting and experimenting. She eventually married another soy researcher, and they named their daughter Soja.[26]

Meanwhile in the Netherlands and Britain soy oil was foundational to a prominent business merger: in 1929 the Dutch margarine company Margarine Unie joined with the British soap maker Lever Brothers. In the following decades, the new 'Unilever' company became a giant with over 400 brands, including Dove soap, Hellmann's mayonnaise and margarines Flora, Promise, 'I Can't Believe It's Not Butter' and Country Crock. In revenue terms, it was the third-largest consumer goods company in the world in 2009,[27] and still dealing in large quantities of soy: this company alone purchases about 1 per cent of the world's soy output.[28]

Unilever was formed the same year that Laszlo Berczeller visited Italy at the request of dictator Benito Mussolini, who was considering whether to mandate the manufacture of soy polenta and breads. Eventually Mussolini established an institute to research soy utilization, and he ordered the fortification of military breads with soy flour. But in Catholic Italy the connotations of soy bread were not merely military. Following Berczeller's lead, one Italian journalist referred to soy bread as 'manna', invoking the heavenly sustenance for God's chosen people.[29]

Of course, the year 1929 also saw colossal stock market crashes and the onset of the Great Depression. Germany, already struggling and resentful of the reparations it paid to the Allies following the

First World War, suffered deeply from the depression. Hardship allowed Adolf Hitler's seductive jingoism to flourish, and he resolved to protect the German economy while preparing for war. His regime tried to wean itself from Manchurian soybeans, promoting soy cultivation – but since Germany's latitudes are not ideal for growing soy, the Germans instead swayed farmers in southeast Europe to plant it and trade it exclusively to them. A 1938 British article explained that

> The great German chemical concern, I. G. Farben, has succeeded in concluding an agreement by which a considerable part of Rumanian land has been put under cultivation of soya beans, of which it holds a monopoly of purchase. Rumania is forced in exchange to take corresponding quantities of German industrial products . . . [30]

The reporter outlined how the financial system underlying this arrangement enabled 'Germany to exercise powerful economic influence on Rumania'. During this period, German demand similarly stimulated soy production in Bulgaria and Hungary.

The I. G. Farben company had also, in 1933, acquired the German patent for Berczeller's superior-quality soy flour. In 1938 the German army's High Command published a 71-page cookbook of soy recipes, mostly with that flour as an ingredient. Soy was clearly part of Germany's war plan. Ironically, Berczeller, who dedicated his life to making good soy flour available to the masses, and who took great interest in how soy could alleviate human suffering, found his product integral to the most violent conflict the world has ever known. As Shurtleff and Aoyagi explain, his flour supported the very regime that would also cause him great personal anguish:

> In 1934, as anti-Semitism was increasing in Germany, Berczeller was divorced by his German wife, who turned pro-Aryan/Nazi. This was a great blow . . . As a Jew, Berczeller was forced to flee Germany during the war. He hid in France but emerged malnourished, and died poor and unknown in 1955.[31]

Soybeans bolstered all sides during the Second World War, although in the conflict's final years, soy agriculture, trade routes and stockpiles all faltered in Europe and Asia. Soy instead took a trajectory that was oddly parallel to that of one of its champions, Dr Artemy Horvath.

Horvath was born in 1886 in Russia to an aristocratic father who prepared soy 'coffee' for the south Russia market. The younger Horvath was studious, becoming an expert in the chemistry of fats and oils. Because he and his wife had aristocratic backgrounds, they were forced to flee the Russian heartland during the Revolution. Their first child was born in Russia's soybean-port of Vladivostok. Before long, they were safe in China, and by 1923 Horvath was in charge of research into soybean nutrition in Beijing, funded by America's Rockefeller Foundation. Horvath read widely about soybeans, including the works of Li Yuying and Laszlo Berczeller, and in 1927, in China, he published a review of human knowledge about soy.

Also in that year, he accepted a position in New Jersey with the Rockefeller Institute for Medical Research. By 1932 he had co-founded a U.S. soy foods company, and from 1933 to 1939 he experimented with soy at the University of Delaware. Beginning in 1940, he devoted himself fully to the union of free enterprise and science, spending the next two decades researching, patenting, publishing, founding a second company and flourishing in America – always with soy.[32]

Like Horvath, soy itself began a great shift in the 1930s. For millennia, soy's centre of cultivation had been Manchuria, but in the 1930s U.S. production rose and rose, until by 1942 U.S. soy harvests outstripped Manchuria's.[33] For decades, the centre of soy research had been Europe, but in the 1930s the U.S. also surged ahead in that domain. In America, a combination of university research and private enterprise spurred early growth in soy cultivation and processing. Horvath, with his Chinese and European soy experiences, university professorship and immigrant business success story in America, shared much with his beloved beans.

Horvath was certainly not the first European to promote soybeans in America; indeed, the first soy foods factory in what is now the U.S. had exported soy noodles and sauce to Britain as far back as 1765. Benjamin Franklin had also taken an interest in soybeans, having learned of them, while serving as the U.S. ambassador to France, from the director of Paris's Jardin des Plantes. But Horvath's soy story serves as a particularly apt microcosm of the story of the bean itself.

THE EARLY EFFORTS with soy in America foreshadowed today's vast plantings of soy in the New World. The choices that a variety of individuals and institutions made during those preliminary years in America created the twists and turns of the next chapter in soy's ascendance.

THREE

THE YOUNG COUNTRY AND THE ANCIENT BEAN

Thomas Jefferson had two serious, intertwined problems. First, he was deeply ambivalent about owning slaves. On the one hand, he held racist and paternalistic views of African Americans; on the other, he believed that slavery was a 'moral depravity' and 'hideous blot' flouting the laws of nature. He also believed that slavery presented a grave danger to the new United States. But he could not divine how to maintain the southern economy, and his role in it, without the ultra-low cost of coerced labour. His best guess was that enslaved people should gradually be emancipated – voluntarily on the part of their owners, as he thought befitted the owners' rights in a democracy – and then the former slaves be expatriated so that their resentments could not boil over into violence.

Yet Jefferson emancipated very few of his own slaves – because of his second problem. Like many Virginia planters, he grew tobacco, a profitable but labour-intensive and soil-exhausting crop. Tobacco depletes soil of its nutrients, notably nitrogen, much more quickly than many other crops. In consequence, before the advent of synthetic fertilizers, tobacco farmers regularly had to acquire and clear virgin land, at considerable expense. This difficulty pushed Jefferson into sizeable debt, as did his penchant for expensive goods. Upon his death, as he knew they would, Jefferson's creditors demanded that nearly all his slaves be sold to pay his financial obligations. Jefferson had declined to emancipate his slaves, in order to protect his legal heirs from burdensome debts. The plantation's enslaved community was cruelly split up and scattered.

What if Jefferson had planted soybeans instead of tobacco? In Georgia an English sailor, Samuel Bowen, had already demonstrated that in the New World soybeans could be gainfully grown, processed and exported as soy noodles and sauce.[1] Soy is very sensitive to the length of the day, which is determined by latitude – but Virginia's latitude is just fine. In fact, the region of Virginia where Jefferson lived is at the 38th parallel, which also cuts through the middle of the Korean Peninsula, a venerable region of soy agriculture. Soy could have been grown in eighteenth-century Virginia; indeed, generations later in the twenty-first century, soybeans were not only cultivated in Virginia, they were the state's most profitable crop.[2]

Although Jefferson believed in soil renewal through crop rotation, the particular nitrogen-fixing crops he sowed were not lucrative. Because he did not plant soy, he could not produce and export that luxurious seasoning, soy sauce, to Europe (soy sauce was much more expensive in that era than today). Jefferson remained caught in the debt cycle spurred by tobacco's tendency to ruin the soil; and he freed less than 2 per cent of the hundreds of slaves he owned over his lifetime.[3] These aspects of his personal economic history were linked. Could soy have helped this brilliant, ambivalent man outgrow his own hypocrisy? Perhaps. Jefferson believed that a farming society was most conducive to genuine democracy and that introducing new crops benefited the nation. But his views on agricultural and social arrangements did not push him to any pioneering work with soy, or any transformation of the agricultural economy. Those tasks were each left for later eras.

Major soy cultivation in the New World had to wait until the twentieth century. Before then, however, Asian immigrants brought soy foods to Hawaii and America's West Coast. Tens of thousands of Chinese men joined California's scramble for gold from 1848 to 1855, and by 1880, about 9 per cent of the state's population was Chinese.[4] Sidelined by discrimination, they stuck together. Their customs were thus preserved, and by 1899 the U.S. Department of Agriculture (USDA) reported that vendors in San Francisco's Chinatown sold imported yellow and black dried soybeans, tofu and soy sauce.[5]

In the same period, Japanese immigrants also arrived in the U.S. In 1879 Mr Saheiji Mogi of the Kikkoman Company formally registered his brand in California, six years before it obtained legal protection in Japan.[6] He began exporting soy sauce from Japan to Japanese immigrants in the western U.S. Around 1900 some of those immigrants opened soy sauce factories of their own in Hawaii and San

José, California, as well as tofu shops and small miso manufacturers in California's cities. America's introduction to soy foods was on its way.

In the early 1900s an extraordinary Chinese woman, Yamei Kin, also boosted American awareness of soy foods. Orphaned in China at the age of two, she was raised by American missionaries. Through opportunities afforded by the family's tutelage and travels, Kin became fluent in Chinese, English, Japanese and French. As a young woman she obtained a medical degree in the U.S. and then worked in Asia spreading Western medical knowledge, setting up and heading clinics. Like her foster parents, she became a kind of missionary, lecturing, organizing and writing – for American medicine among Asians, and for Asian soybeans among Americans. As she explained to the *New York Times Magazine* in 1917,

> The world is in need of tissue-building foods . . . and cannot very well afford to wait to grow animals in order to obtain the necessary percentage of protein. Waiting for an animal to become big enough to eat is a long proposition. First you feed grain to a cow, and, finally, you get a return in protein from milk and meat. A terribly high percentage of the energy is lost in transit from grain to cow to a human being . . . in China we take a short cut by eating the soy bean, which is protein, meat, and milk in itself . . . human nature is about the same everywhere, and the Chinese don't care for a monotonous bean diet any more than other people. So they have taken this soy bean and managed to invent a great many . . . products.[7]

Dr Kin's work included helping the USDA and U.S. army during the First World War adapt soybeans to American palates. Later, in Beijing, she educated a visiting soy researcher, Palemon Dorsett, about the numerous Asian soy pastes used in dipping sauces, condiments and flavourings.

Mr Dorsett, along with Charles Piper and William Morse, was an investigator for the USDA – a trio with an enduring impact on America's soy agriculture. In 1905 Piper became head of the USDA's forage crop division; he soon hired Morse to grow and test soybeans near Washington, DC. The two recognized that the limited number of soy varieties available to American farmers was hampering the crop's success. Seed choice is essential for prosperous farming, as distinct varieties respond better or worse to differences in climate, soil conditions, latitude, pest populations and market demands. Piper and Morse discovered that only eight cultivars – varieties bred for desired characteristics – had been grown in the u.s. before 1898.[8] They set about rectifying this situation.

Over three decades, the two worked with Dorsett and USDA explorer Frank Meyer to bring 3,000 soy samples to the u.s. from China, Japan, Korea and India. Then, in 1929, the USDA sent Dorsett and Morse on a two-year tour through Asia. Dorsett focused on northeast China, with which he was familiar from a previous expedition; combined, the two trips enabled him to add about 1,000 soy seeds to the USDA collection.[9]

Meanwhile, Morse not only collected soy but studied soy-processing techniques. Both men brought family members on this splendid adventure. They also found companionship among other soybean advocates and plant scientists they encountered in Asia – Dr Kin in Beijing; in Seoul, the famous Soviet botanist Nikolai Vavilov (who later angered Stalin and starved to death in prison); and by chance on a train in Manchuria, the German soy breeder Lene Mueller. In that period, the community of soybean researchers was small, and the paths of all the top investigators eventually led to that corner of the world. Their shared passion for the bean was great. Thus despite Dorsett's having suffered for months in China from double pneumonia, upon returning to the u.s. he summed up the trip by nostalgically exclaiming, 'Oh! The romance of it all!'[10]

Commemorating the expedition's fiftieth anniversary, soy geneticist Theodore Hymowitz wrote admiringly that in Asia, Dorsett and Morse collected seeds and other sources of plant DNA from

> fruit and vegetable markets, food and flower shows, experiment stations, botanical gardens, seed companies, farms, factories making soybean and other food products, processing plants, and from the wild . . . The explorers returned with 3,350 black-and-white still pictures . . . 210 publications, 341 different soybean food products.[11]

In addition, they obtained 2,774 m (9,100 ft) of motion-picture negatives. About their extensive collection of soy vines, one colleague joked, 'we have enough soy varieties now to tangle up the feet of everybody from one end of the country to the other.'[12] Forty-one of the collected soybean varieties became u.s. cultivars. They were given colourful names such as 'Agate', 'Emperor', 'Fuji' and 'Wolverine'. Agronomists crossbred other samples to create cultivars adapted to particular u.s. conditions. Most of the expedition's varieties were bred for human consumption as edamame, rather than animal feed; currently, therefore, they make up only a small percentage of American soy.[13] Yet those Asian varieties have proved a valuable source of alternative DNA for soy breeding, enabling researchers to grow new strains to resist escalating pest problems.

After the expedition, Dorsett retired from the USDA. Morse, by contrast, continued researching soybeans and promoting their agriculture in a long and fruitful career with the USDA. Hymowitz has rightly called Morse 'the father of soybean production in North America'.[14] He played a central role in preparing the u.s. to become a soybean powerhouse after the Second World War – and he lived long enough to see that momentous transformation.

USDA researchers were not the only ones exploring soy in early twentieth-century America: Seventh Day Adventists (SDAs) devoted much energy to devising new soy foods. The religion arose in the 1840s in New York State from a movement of believers expecting Jesus's imminent return. Adventists share many doctrines with older Protestant denominations but place a distinctive emphasis on healthy lifestyles (in consequence, on average they live ten years longer than other Americans). Many SDAs are vegetarians, in keeping with the teachings of their prophet, Ellen White. They take a keen interest in high-protein plants and have concocted many flavourful meat substitutes, often from soybeans.

One of their groundbreaking soy food developers was John Harvey Kellogg, who is most famous for inventing, with his brother W. K., the breakfast cereal known as cornflakes. (W. K. is best remembered for founding the Kellogg Company, which today sells food in over 180 countries.[15]) After obtaining a New York University medical degree, John served as chief physician at the Battle Creek Sanitarium, an SDA health resort in Michigan. Although the Adventist church eventually expelled Dr Kellogg for heresy, he was nevertheless a grand contributor to SDA lifestyles through his work on vegetarian foods. His teachings influenced hundreds of thousands, as well as powerfully inspiring other SDA soy pioneers.

Some of Kellogg's new soy foods had textures reminiscent of meat. These 'meat analogues' became prototypes for products marketed by Loma Linda Foods and other Adventist companies. Even today, U.S. supermarkets sell products that Kellogg helped formulate. The MorningStar Farms brand, for example, is a direct descendant of Kellogg's enterprises; some of its burgers are still made from textured soy protein.[16]

Soy protein was not, however, the most remunerative part of the plant in early twentieth-century America. Soy oil was far more valuable, for a variety of reasons. Boll weevil infestations of American cotton were limiting the amount of cotton oil available. Europe, with a growing population and little oilseed production, depended on foreign oilseeds and oil. The First World War cut trade in Manchurian soy; simultaneously Europe required yet more soy oil for the skyrocketing production of nitroglycerine for combat explosives. A major shortage developed.

U.S. observers saw these difficulties pushing the price of soy oil upwards. Accordingly, clever crop-processing entrepreneurs convinced both the farmers they wanted to buy from, and the manufacturers they wanted to sell to, to embrace soy.

A turning point came with Illinois corn processor Gene Staley's announcement that he would begin crushing soybeans in the autumn of 1922. He publicized this plan through newspapers, farm magazines, letters, pamphlets and company representatives who visited farming communities. Staley further promised farmers that he would buy all the soy they could grow. Many responded enthusiastically: the spring of 1922 saw a fivefold increase in Illinois's soy plantings. Metaphorically, the 'soy train' had left its station.

But Staley also arranged for a literal soy train! In the spring of 1927, the Soil and Soybean Special train carried exhibits about the exotic bean to rural communities:

> The six-car train contained exhibits . . . on soybean planting, cultivation, processing, and utilization . . . It also had two cars converted into motion picture theaters and a lecture car. Between March 28 and April 17, a total of 33,939 people passed through the train as it traveled 2,478 miles and made 105

scheduled stops. Prizes were awarded and Gene Staley even went aboard for some parts of the trip. When a reporter asked Staley if he had any hobbies, the latter replied, 'Soybeans – just soybeans'.[17]

At this time soy oil was mainly used in the manufacture of paints, soaps and varnish. But Americans were also trying the oil as human food. Manufacture of soy margarine expanded in the u.s., with continual improvements in its flavour. Threatened, the American butter industry successfully lobbied for anti-margarine laws. Margarine sales were subject to extra taxes, and in some states manufacturers could not add yellow colouring to make the product look like butter.

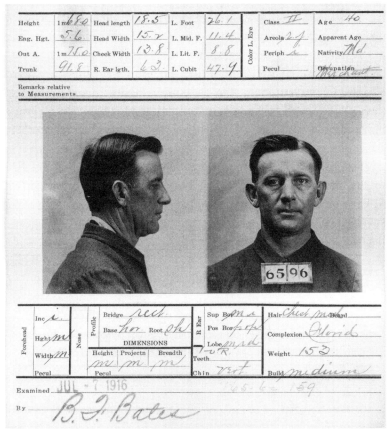

In 1916 John R. Seymour was sentenced to two years in u.s. federal prison for selling tax-free, contraband margarine. The rise of cheap soy-oil margarine was of great concern to the dairy industry, which had succeeded in obtaining laws taxing margarine and punishing anyone committing 'crimes against butter'.

In late nineteenth-century New Hampshire, margarine had even had to be coloured pink to make it look strikingly different from butter – a requirement overturned by the U.S. Supreme Court.[18] Eventually the margarine industry obtained repeal of all the anti-margarine laws – but it took several decades.

There were new developments in the use of soy protein as well. In 1909–10 Dr John Ruhräh performed the first studies on feeding a soy-enhanced suspension to infants suffering from diarrhoea. Diarrhoeal conditions, it must be remembered, can cause fatal dehydration, particularly in babies. This early soy-based infant formula contained full-fat soy flour, condensed cow's milk, barley flour and minerals. It included a bit of salt which, when combined with the natural sugar in the soy flour and cow's milk, helped to rebalance the babies' physiology. Ruhräh recommended his product both for diarrhoea and whenever sterile cow's milk for weaned babies was not available. For his dedication to childhood nutrition, a Baltimore school was named after him in 1930; no doubt over the years it has educated many students who were nourished with soy infant formula. Today such formula is recommended for babies with cow's milk allergies who are not breast-fed (though medical researchers still overwhelmingly recommend breast milk).

Seventh Day Adventists were also developing soy infant formulas, notably a medical missionary to China, Dr Harry Miller. Miller gained first-hand knowledge of soy food processing at an SDA medical college; Dr Kellogg mentored him. In 1903 Miller and his wife left for China, where they

> found great poverty and malnutrition. They both learned Chinese, dressed like the local people, and even adopted the hair style of a long queue and shaved pate. They also ate Chinese foods, and soon Miller was visiting local tofu shops, learning about and sampling tofu, yuba, curds, soymilk, and the like.[19]

Returning to America in 1911, Miller became a surgeon and medical superintendent at the SDA's Washington Sanitarium and Hospital. The hospital served vegetarian foods. It ran into difficulties during the First World War, when the U.S. government requisitioned all the foods that a local dairy had previously provided the hospital with.

Miller worked around this problem by creating soy-based alternatives to dairy products.

In 1925 Miller returned to China to spearhead a new network of SDA medical facilities. Troubled by China's high infant mortality, he again turned to soy. Friends teased him: shouldn't a distinguished surgeon find a more elegant hobby than beans? Unwavering, in his free time he tested production methods in a small factory behind the hospital. He sought to devise a soy milk that lacked 'beany' flavours – one that orphaned infants who were increasingly being dropped off at the hospital would readily accept.

His 'aha' moment came in the mid-1930s. In his kitchen experimenting with a suspension of finely ground soy particles in water, he suddenly 'heard a divine voice behind me that said "Why don't you cook it longer with live steam?"'[20] Miller was apparently unaware that steaming was a known technique. He tried it; staff and patients alike praised the improved soy milk.

In 1936–7 he expanded his tests, feeding hundreds of young children at his Shanghai clinic. The children received one of several preparations: soy milk formula, fresh cow's milk or various Western prepared baby foods. The analysed data pointed to the efficacy of soy formula as an infant food; Miller published them in the widely read *Chinese Medical Journal*.

He also opened a full-size soy milk factory, which soon employed men on three-wheeled cycles attached to home-delivery carts brimming daily with 3,000 quarts and 4,000 half-pints – over 6,600 litres. A mere eight months after the factory opened, however, bombs destroyed it during Japan's invasion of Shanghai. Miller and his family left Shanghai, and less than two years later, China itself. In the meantime, however, he had obtained a U.S. patent for his system of making soy milk.

Back in the U.S., Miller continued to develop and sell soy products. Only his infant formula, Soyalac, won much U.S. acceptance – except during the Second World War, when his other vegetarian products sold well because of the meat shortage. Yet even with Soyalac he had difficulties, as the dairy industry and USDA pressured him not to label the product 'milk'. Adding to his frustration, the American Medical Association refused to endorse Soyalac unless it was marketed only narrowly for infants allergic to cow's milk (around 2–5 per cent of babies in developed countries[21]). Fortunately for his business, Miller did manage to sell powdered soy milk and other soy products in the Philippines and China.

Miller's legacy has continued to be felt on two continents. Shurtleff and Aoyagi assert that 'most of the remarkable expansion of interest in and production of soy milk that has taken place throughout Asia during the last half of the twentieth century can trace its origins directly back to the work of Dr Miller' through people influenced by his efforts.[22] In 1956 the Taiwanese president Chiang Kai-shek awarded Miller the Blue Star of China for indefatigable service to the Chinese people.

In the u.s., Miller eventually sold his business to Adventists for a markedly low price. Shurtleff and Aoyagi elaborate:

> Dr Miller had always believed that [his] process for making soy milk was not something that he had originated; the key to it had been a gift to him from a higher power. Thus, he felt it was simply not his to sell. So he gave the process to the Adventist church but sold the rest of the business to Loma Linda Foods . . . and loaned them the money to buy it.[23]

Soyalac was marketed in the u.s. for decades. In 1989 a Dutch infant-formula company bought the brand from Loma Linda, but eventually discontinued it. Yet the name Soyalac lives on: a Mexican company revived it early in the twenty-first century for plain and flavoured soy milks marketed to children, the elderly and people with various medical conditions.

The u.s. successes of soy-based infant formulas, of other soy foods and of soy in industrial products depended in no small degree on government support. Under President Lincoln the federal government created the USDA, which eventually would pay for the research done by Piper, Morse and Dorsett. The government later gave federal lands to every state to sell for funds to create colleges. The newly created institutions were required to include programmes in practical domains such as engineering and agriculture. At these 'land-grant' institutions, agronomists studied pest management, soil health and crop breeding. Laws in 1887 and 1914 stipulated that the knowledge gained was to be shared not only with students, but directly with farmers. Plant varieties bred there had to be publicly accessible.

The importance of government support in soy's U.S. history must not be underestimated. As agronomists John Gardner and Thomas Payne assert, in the past 'the biological development of improved soy genetics, varieties and production was contributed mostly by the public sector, whereas the private sector [mostly] contributed soybean . . . processing and product development.'[24] In 1980, 70 per cent of U.S. soybean acreage was planted with public-sector seed.[25] Recent decades have witnessed a shift towards more privately bred, patented seed in the U.S., but the genetic precursors of those new seeds came from government-sponsored expeditions and breeding programmes.

During the Great Depression, the federal government took the further step of protecting American soybean agriculture against competition from cheap Asian imports. Various tariffs on soy imports were imposed from 1913 until 1936. Most stringent was the Smoot-Hawley Tariff of 1930, named after two senators who sponsored it. The ASA (American Soybean Association) successfully lobbied for it to include soy tariffs. Raising import duties on thousands of products, the legislation provoked retaliatory levies from America's trading partners. Global trade faltered. Like a pitiless bird of prey, the Great Depression fed on this weakness. Yet U.S. soy agriculture was not hobbled; it flourished.

Farmers of traditional crops saw their incomes plummet. There was simply too much food compared to the money Americans had to buy it. A solution would be to grow less, with relative scarcity then causing food prices to rise, and the amount each farmer was paid per unit of crop also rising. But each grower preferred that other farmers make the sacrifice of selling less. No one was willing to make the first move to change the quantity he or she cultivated. The federal government stepped in; it paid farmers to grow *less* corn, wheat and cotton. But soy was under no such restriction; because it benefited the soil, the government encouraged its expansion.

Much of the soy was destined for industry. The Glidden Company, for example, used soy in paints, cosmetics and plastics. A largely forgotten genius at the forefront of Glidden's soy work was Dr Percy Julian, an African American research chemist in an era when black Americans struggled greatly to receive any education beyond primary school.

Julian was born in 1899 to a family that intensely valued learning. The Julians were well acquainted with hardship – a slave owner

u.s. Department of Agriculture employee plants soybeans in Washington, DC, in 1931.

had cut off two of the grandfather's fingers because his 'property' had dared to become literate. Percy would encounter violence, too: in 1950, as a successful scientist, he moved to an all-white Chicago suburb. Racists soon bombed his property near the bedrooms of his sleeping children; fortunately they were unhurt. He was not always rejected, however, finding support among journalists, his colleagues at Glidden and some neighbours.

Julian had completed a doctorate in organic chemistry in Vienna and spoke fluent German, so he was ideally suited to help Glidden in two ways. First, he set up their newly imported German extraction equipment; second, he developed products from chemicals naturally within soybeans. His team purified soy protein to replace the more expensive milk casein that Glidden previously used to waterproof cartons and to fill the tiny pores in paper. Julian's soy protein isolate also became a key ingredient during the Second World War in Aer-O-Foam, used to extinguish fires. This product, affectionately nicknamed 'bean soup' by the u.s. navy, smothered oil and gasoline fires on ships, saving thousands of servicemen's lives.

Julian also devised the mass synthesis of testosterone and progesterone from a soybean chemical. Over time this would prove an important advance for developing birth control pills, for preventing premature births and for treating infertility, sexual dysfunction, menstrual and pregnancy disorders and hormonal imbalances. Prior to this breakthrough, the hormones were extremely expensive, as they were extracted in minute quantities from the spinal cords of huge quantities of animals.

From 1949 Dr Julian worked on inexpensively synthesizing a new wonder drug, cortisone. Cortisone began as a treatment for rheumatoid arthritis; today it and other corticosteroids are used extensively to combat inflammation, to regulate the immune system and to assist with breathing disorders, heart failure, certain cancers, adrenal insufficiency and septic shock. Julian began his research by synthesizing corticosteroids from soy, although eventually he extracted the needed chemical from a wild yam.[26]

Another African American who worked with soy, albeit less extensively than Julian, was the illustrious George Washington Carver. Within months of his 1896 appointment to Alabama's Tuskegee Institute, Carver conducted field trials with soy as a soil builder. He experimented with soy foods on numerous occasions,

Percy Lavon Julian was a soy chemist who pioneered industrial and medical uses for the bean. He was inducted into the National Inventors Hall of Fame in 1990. The u.s. Postal Service released this stamp in 1993.

trying his hand at soy Christmas confectionery (with pecans and dried sweet potatoes), a creamy soy powder for baking, a soy breakfast gruel (which he recommended with fruit purée for u.s. soldiers), soy sprout salad, soy-peanut soup and soy-cream-cheese wafers. Carver especially enjoyed sharing his concoctions with the man who, above all others, twentieth-century Americans associated with soybeans: Henry Ford.

Ford was a visionary, gifted, bigoted, complicated man, with much about him to criticize, and much to praise. Among his commendable attitudes was a deep interest in helping American farmers survive the Great Depression. His company prolifically innovated in the field of 'chemurgy', the study of chemical components in plants and their potential applications within a broad array of industries. Ford was also far ahead of his time in fashioning many new foods from crops. His business was mostly automobiles, but his mind and heart reached far beyond to utopia.

He was so utopian, in fact, that he commissioned an idealized town, Fordlândia, in Brazil's Amazon Basin, to obtain rubber for Ford vehicles. The town had strict social rules, free housing, a modern hospital, streets laid out in the style of a quaint American village – and, alas, much cross-cultural and worker–owner conflict. Tree diseases led to its demise, and the rubber production was moved to another Ford town, Belterra. The Ford company eventually sold Belterra's failing plantation to the Brazilian government. Today Fordlândia is a minor tourist attraction as a ghost town.[27] Belterra survives mostly because it lies along Brazil's grand 'soybean highway', where soy travels long distances through roads and rivers for export. Eight companies are currently investing in the region near Belterra, counting on further expansion of infrastructure for soy transport. This destiny for Belterra is tremendously fitting for a place with Ford connections, because although rubber did not work out for Ford, in many ways soybeans did.[28]

In the u.s., Ford and his chemists cooked up ingenious uses for soy in meat substitutes, textiles and plastics. By 1931 Ford had instructed his chemurgy staff to focus on soy to the exclusion of other crops. He eventually purchased some 24,000 hectares (60,000 acres) in Michigan for planting three hundred soy varieties.[29] Like Staley in Illinois, he assured local farmers that if they, too, cultivated soy, the Ford Motor Company would buy it.

George Washington Carver experimented with soybeans and shared ideas about soy with Henry Ford.

In 1934 the company showcased its soy inventions at the Chicago World's Fair, attracting over a million visitors and much media attention. Shurtleff and Aoyagi describe the scene:

Ford brought in an entire barn from his childhood home . . . planted a plot of soybeans around it, put up a sign 'The Industrialized American Barn' over the door, and set up inside it an elaborate display featuring one of his small farm-scale solvent extraction plants and a soyfoods kitchen. Soy protein was molded into plastic parts and soy oil, extracted on the spot, was used to fuel a diesel engine, which ran a generator that produced all the electricity for the display . . . Large seeded, vegetable-type soybeans were deep fried and served like salted peanuts to visitors, providing most with their first taste of soybeans. Moreover, a press luncheon, featuring fourteen soy-based dishes . . . was served to 30 wary reporters; it included 'Celery stuffed with soybean cheese' [tofu], and 'Cocoa with soymilk', and ended with ice cream made from soymilk; no meat was served.[30]

Ford's team researched improving the production of soy milk, as Ford considered cow's milk a disgusting repository of tuberculosis and other bacteria. Ford himself regularly drank soy milk sweetened with maple syrup. In 1942 the company built a laboratory named after Ford's fellow luminary and friend George Washington Carver, dedicating it to the production of soy milk and other soy protein products.

Ford's engineers also discovered how to extrude soy protein through spinnerets to make a durable fibre. They blended it with wool for the sidewall upholstery in autos. A top Ford official gushed about the feat:

> In order to give you an idea of what the comparative costs will be between wool and soybean fibre, it takes 2 acres of grazing land to support one sheep a year. The average wool yield from one sheep is 8 pounds. On the other hand 2 acres of land will produce 400 pounds of soybean protein.[31]

Soon, however, mass production of soy fibre lost out to a DuPont invention, a less expensive, petroleum-based textile – nylon. Yet the early twenty-first century has seen renewed interest in soy for vehicle seating. Today numerous Ford vehicles use soy-based foam as the padding inside seats. Soy carries the cachet of being more eco-friendly than petroleum-based foams.

Ford also consigned vast quantities of soy oil to the creation of enamel paints for his cars. By 1935 the paint, soy-plastic horn button, gearshift knob, window knobs, accelerator pedal and timing gears of each Ford auto together consumed a bushel of soybeans.[32] In 1936 *Time* magazine dubbed Ford 'A bean's best friend'. In 1940 newspapers across the u.s. published a photo of Ford taking an axe to an auto made with soy plastic. Ford, a master of public relations, wished to promote soy plastic as tough and durable, although the photo misled since the axe was not sharp and the car's frame did not actually contain much soy.[33] Nevertheless, soy was a major part of the car's non-structural parts, and 'the plastic car' captured America's attention as metal shortages developed early in the Second World War.

WHEN THE U.S. entered that war, however, Ford factories all converted to military manufacturing, dropping their work with soybeans. Ford sold his soy-processing equipment and formulas to others, who built on his successes with new enterprises. Although the war ended Ford's professional involvement with soybeans, as we shall see for the country as a whole, it marked a great beginning, a pivot towards pre-eminence as the earth's soybean superpower.

FOUR

SOY PATRIOTIC

The soybeans were fermenting in their incubator, and the submarine reeked of fusty soy natto – like mouldy clothes someone had tried to clean with ammonia. Japanese sailors were inured to the scent; 23-year-old Sub-Lieutenant Katsuhisa Ban barely noticed it anymore. He had other things pressing on his mind. He had been assigned to assault an American ship, USS *Chicago*, a cruiser that had survived the attack on Pearl Harbor. Now, in May 1942, the ship was moored in Sydney Harbour, Australia. Katsuhisa Ban had been chosen to climb from the mother submarine into a nimble, ferocious midget sub she carried and fire torpedoes at the American vessel. In preparation, he wrote to his mother, and surely with the other sailors he ate protein-rich natto for strength. He hoped to bring honour to his country and family: he did not expect to survive.

Two other midget subs failed to reach the *Chicago*, and their crews committed suicide rather than face the disgrace of capture. But Katsuhisa Ban got close enough to fire his weapons. Visual conditions were poor, and he missed, hitting a seawall next to a dormitory ferryboat for Australian sailors. The ferry sank; 21 sailors died. Meanwhile, Katsuhisa Ban's midget disappeared – to be discovered 64 years later by amateur scuba divers. It became clear then that Katsuhisa Ban had had enough strength – just not enough oxygen. He suffocated before managing to rendezvous with the mother submarine. In 2007, his family joined Australian and Japanese dignitaries in a ceremony honouring his bravery.[1]

Here, as with so many incidents, tracing the uses of soy provides a lens both on the colossal designs and on the individual human experiences of the Second World War. Studying soy illuminates

During the Second World War the Japanese military ate natto, a protein-rich fermented soy food, for strength.

facets of the war while, reciprocally, studying the war clarifies how and why the mid-twentieth century transformed soy cultivation and utilization. During the war soy was crucial to militaries, civilians and prisoners. Its availability was at times a matter of life and death and, like other nutrient-dense foods, it could be as critical to warfare as bombs, ships, planes and guns. In turn, the war catapulted it to enormous economic significance in the post-war period.

Beyond Japanese submarines, the war witnessed Canadian soldiers sprouting soybeans as fresh vegetables in the barren Arctic.

The u.s. military was intrigued by Japanese soldiers' consumption of *Inarizushi* like these.

The Canadian navy ate soy biscuits. The Nazis fed their army soy flour mixed into noodles, cabbage and potatoes. They gave them small biscuits fortified with soy flour, complementing a more sinister Nazi 'pep' supplement made from methamphetamine – a forerunner of today's global scourge of crystal meth addiction.

Other military uses of soy included a canned version of *Inarizushi*. This popular Japanese dish is named for the Shinto spirit Inari who, fittingly for imperialist Japan, promotes worldly success. Inarizushi is a pouch of fried tofu stuffed with rice; the name derives from Inari's alleged appetite for fried tofu. The u.s. Board of Economic Warfare, studying enemy provisioning of soldiers, considered Inarizushi a kind of sandwich.[2] Japanese infantrymen also consumed either miso powder or soy sauce daily, carried around in their rucksacks.

The u.s. had its own tactical uses of soy. American soldiers consumed it in soup powders and as a nutritious extender in pork sausage. In addition, as a 1943 American propaganda film effused, troops in mobile warfare need a [highly] compact ration, so the army has developed the now-famous K ration, the completely streamlined meal. Originally designed for para-troops, K proved ideal for tank busters, commandos, and all isolated units. Each package contains a balanced, vita-min-rich meal. A day's ration weighs about 2 pounds . . . [It is] adapted to all climactic conditions from the tropics to the frigid zones. Each item in K had to be super-nutritious, but also appetizing . . . we find ways to use such highly nourishing staples as the soy bean, which is easily produced in great plenty.[3]

Thus for both Axis and Allied military personnel, soy protein was a vital resource during the war. Soy oil was also more widely consumed as other edible fats became scarce; in the u.s., industrial uses of soy oil after 1939 dropped dramatically so that the oil could be used in margarine and cooking.[4]

The Nazis recognized soy's strategic importance even before the war began. They valued their commerce with China, yet recog-nized Japan's growing might: in 1931 Japan had wrested from China the region of Manchuria, at that time the centre of world soybean production. Seeking a major Asian ally and unsure which to court, Hitler and his aides dithered. Ultimately, they aligned with the power controlling Manchuria. They remembered Germany's terrible suf-fering during the First World War when it had run out of edible oils – dietary fat is essential for bodily functions, including the absorption of several vitamins. They deemed Japan a more reliable partner than China, both diplomatically and as a source of precious soy. Eventu-ally, the Nazis bartered cannons to Japan in exchange for soybeans, not only for food but also to make nitroglycerine for Germany's own cannons.[5]

The Nazis also negotiated with the Soviet Union for raw mater-ials, including soy traded from Manchuria through Russia. Since Hitler's planned invasion of Poland would be likely to provoke an Allied blockade of German sea trade, the Nazis needed alternate access to metal ores, petroleum, rubber, wheat and soybeans. They considered the Soviets a logical choice for an economic pact, despite profound differences between the two regimes. The Soviets, in turn, wanted German machines. In August 1939 the two countries signed an agreement that provided Germany with 167,000 metric tons of soybeans over two years.[6]

But Hitler did not want mere trade with the Soviets. He envisaged a German takeover of all central and eastern European territories to control their natural resources; the 60 million non-Germanic people living there were slated for extermination, expulsion or enslavement, including the planned murder of 50 per cent of Russians. The Nazis gave this extraordinarily depraved vision the banal name 'General Plan for the East'. In accord with the plan, Hitler attacked the Soviets in 1941 with the largest invasion force in history.

In the end, with conquest of the USSR unexpectedly difficult, the Germans found themselves with insufficient edible oil – the very predicament they had dreaded. After war broke out between these two empires, German consumption of soy oil dropped dramatically. The Germans still received soy from Romania, but it was not enough.

Worse, thousands of Allied bombs almost completely destroyed Germany's oilseed-processing factories. The immense Hansa oilseed mill in Hamburg, for example – a world-leading, ultra-modern facility handling over 1,000 metric tons of soybeans daily – saw intense warfare. On 24 July 1943, during the Allied 'Operation Gomorrah', British planes dropped 350,000 incendiary bombs on targets including the Hansa mill, which burned to the ground.[7] Hamburg soon suffered a tornado of fire 460 m (1,500 ft) high, caused by a whirling updraft. Some 40,000 people died during the campaign, vast areas of the city became wasteland and the oilseed industry was a shambles. Hitler avoided touring the ruined city, which represented the beginning of the end for the Nazis.[8]

The Japanese seemed better situated to avoid a soy shortage. After all, they grew soy, since it was fundamental to their cuisine: miso paste for protein in peasant diets, and various fermented soy foods as culinary essentials among all social strata. By the early twentieth century, however, Japan could not grow enough soy for her own needs; indeed, the value of Japanese soy imports had increased four-hundred-fold between 1882 and 1902.[9] The bulk of the soy came from Manchuria. Securing tighter control of that flow significantly motivated the 1931 conquest.

The imperial government then solidified dominion over Manchuria – while offering a safety valve for Japan's overpopulated, destitute countryside – by spurring Japanese peasants to migrate there. Government agents advertised Manchuria as an empty territory waiting to be tilled by poor Japanese farmers – a land that, like the American West, offered a new start, and riches, to hard workers. This propaganda failed to consider Manchuria's energetic resident population, which had productively cultivated soy and rice for generations. Japanese officials envisioned, instead, relocating 1 million Japanese households there. Food scholar Lizzie Collingham explains:

> The usual Japanese method for obtaining land for the settlers was simply to misclassify it as uncultivated, ignoring the Chinese and Korean peasants' farms. The farmers were evicted or coerced into 'selling' their land for artificially low prices. In 1941 many of them were still waiting for their payments.[10]

The arriving Japanese hired some of the evicted Chinese as farm labourers. But the Japanese found life in Manchuria far from idyllic; they were subject to raids by the resentful Chinese, the farming was difficult and they were lonely. Then in 1945, when the Soviet army seized Manchuria from Japan, the colonizers were abruptly abandoned; the Japanese army made no effort to evacuate them. Desperate, their men folk hastily assembled in doomed militia. Women and children hid in the mountains by day and fled for their lives at night, scrounging food from fields or from compassionate locals. Collingham summarizes their fates:

> Of the 220,000 farmer settlers, around 80,000 died. About 11,000 of them met a violent end at the hands of the avenging Chinese, some committed suicide, and about 67,000 starved to death. The remaining 140,000 traumatized survivors were eventually repatriated to Japan.[11]

But Japan's Manchurian conquest proved hollow even before the territory was lost. As the Second World War progressed, Japan was less and less able to benefit from its colonial control. Early in the war, imports of Manchurian soy had been crucial to feeding both the home population and Japan's far-flung military. This was particularly true after Allied blockades made rice imports from Southeast Asia difficult, and Japan's central government replaced rice with whatever else was available – especially sweet potatoes and soy – in city dwellers' rations. Food deprivation led to creative government suggestions for using soy to make strange foods palatable; one article, for instance, urged people to boil the larvae of bees, dobsonflies, dragonflies and long-horned beetles in soy sauce to season them.[12]

But eventually the soy ran out, too. From 1943 on, submarine warfare against Japanese merchant ships shrank the soy imports coming from Manchuria across the Sea of Japan; the Japanese navy revealed itself woefully unprepared for enemy submarines in home waters. Adding to the intense submarine harassment, in 1945 the u.s. air force's 'Operation Starvation' dropped 12,000 mines around Japan's coastline, further crippling trade routes. The assaults were brutally effective: from 1943 to July 1945, Japan lost hundreds of merchant ships. Few vessels remained to supply Japan either with food or war materiels.[13]

By 1945 huge heaps of Manchurian soy lay rotting on wharves in Korean ports while Japan's urban dwellers withered. People struggled to prepare government recipes listing dubious alternatives – used tea leaves, silkworm cocoons and sawdust.[14] There were reports of people fermenting salvaged waste to concoct a soy sauce substitute. The scarcity of soy not only affected diets directly, but made farming other crops more onerous. Before the war, Japan had depended on imported fishmeal, chemicals and soy meal as fertilizers; with imports drastically curtailed, cultivators expended much time and labour collecting excrement in order to boost the fertility of Japan's meagre soils.[15]

Meanwhile, in North America other Japanese also longed for soy. Yanked from productive lives and coerced into barebones u.s. and Canadian internment camps, they sought comfort in familiar dishes. For two years, the Japanese at Wyoming's Heart Mountain camp converted soybeans hauled into the community into some 900 kg (2,000 lb) of tofu daily, feeding 10,000 of their fellow interns.[16] Similarly, at the freezing-cold Tashme camp in British Columbia, Japanese at a small factory manufactured enough soy sauce and miso to supply all of Canada during the war. Japanese in the camps also sometimes received soy gifts. In January 1944 the newspaper at Idaho's Minidoka Internment Center excitedly proclaimed that a special shipment would soon arrive: 440 kegs of soy sauce and fifteen barrels of miso, courtesy of the International Committee of the Red Cross.[17]

Throughout the conflict, soy products also nourished prisoners of war. Tempeh was vital to prisoners in Indonesia, New Guinea, Singapore and Hong Kong. In Indonesia, the Japanese incarcerated a Dutch former Olympic-rower-turned-botanist named Pieter Roelofsen. Since the Japanese gave inmates' nutrition the lowest priority, Roelofsen drew on his scientific knowledge to prepare soy tempeh for his fellow prisoners.[18] After the war he published an article on the severe protein shortage they had suffered and on tempeh's role in reducing mortality.[19]

From 1942 until 1946 in Dutch Indonesia, microbiologist André Van Veen was also a captive of the Japanese. After his release, he wrote that due to fuel shortages in the camps, soybeans were often undercooked, making them indigestible for prisoners with dysentery. But fermenting these semi-raw beans as tempeh rendered the soy more assimilable, preventing many deaths from protein malnutrition. Van Veen had thrown himself into such efforts.[20] In appreciation, after the war the Dutch government knighted him into the Order of Orange-Nassau, an honour reserved for those making special contributions to society.

Via a complex trade route, tempeh also figured prominently in nourishing Indonesians and Europeans who were not prisoners but were stranded in New Guinea. Wars are fought to expand empires, and empires mobilize to support wars; the two processes endlessly intertwine, as the Japanese and Dutch connections to New Guinea and soy during the Second World War illustrates.

Japan attacked New Guinea in early 1942. The Allies responded forcefully, and the area quickly became engulfed in warfare, with the safety and food supplies of all civilians at risk. Dutch colonial administrators, European missionaries and European and Javanese scholars, traders and support staff on the western side of the island were abandoned by the war-wary shippers who normally brought them food from the Netherlands East Indies.

For all these immigrants to New Guinea, soybean tempeh was familiar, fairly easy to prepare and high in protein and vitamins. But they ran out of soy. For two years they did without, and their fungal cultures for tempeh fermentation died for lack of soybeans to keep them going. Then American ships came to the rescue, bringing soy out of their own plentiful stores. But without a way to ferment the American beans, the immigrants were forced to boil them into a mash, which they found quite unpalatable.

The tendrils of empire offered a solution. South America's Dutch colony of Suriname had a population of ethnic Javanese; their ancestors had come as indentured servants when liberated slaves of African descent had shunned working for their former masters. Suriname's Javanese had starter cultures for tempeh. Learning of the New Guinea problem, in early 1945 a Dutch official in New York wrote for help to a botanist in Suriname. Safe passage from the New World to New Guinea was by then possible, and within days, a plane had delivered the starter culture. Soon kitchens of the Dutch colonial government in New Guinea were making tempeh for the residents, much to their relief.[21]

In distant Russia, the siege of Leningrad impelled a more desperate clutching at soy foods. Soon after the Nazis attacked the Soviets, the German army closed a cordon around Leningrad, blocking all land routes from which its residents could access food. Thus began a siege that would last 872 days and prove the deadliest in history, taking between 700,000 and 800,000 lives through German bombardment, the ill fortune of an unusually cold first winter and, especially, through starvation.[22]

The first few months were the hardest; the Soviets had not yet found a safe way to get food across Lake Ladoga to the city's trapped citizens. Leningrad's residents had government-issued ration cards, but hardly anyone actually received what the cards promised. Adolescents found themselves particularly tormented: despite teens' high metabolic needs, beyond the age of eleven they no longer qualified for the extra food permitted to children. Teens had to find alternate sources of food to keep from starving; many failed. Some managed to obtain industry jobs, coveted because at factory canteens, workers could take their ration coupon worth only a pitiful handful of groats and trade it for, instead, three whole bowls of yeast soup and a bottle of soy milk.[23]

Soon Leningrad's new mothers found themselves too undernourished to produce breast milk. The city government officially provided babies with soy milk, but supplies were so low that each infant only had the right to 100 ml (4 fl. oz) daily – a right that was sometimes only theoretical. When there was not enough soy and other foodstuffs, women resorted to fierce creativity in order to feed their families. Historian Darra Goldstein explains:

> Tested by want, they searched their apartments for edibles in the form of tooth powder, Vaseline, glycerine, cologne, library paste, and wallpaper paste, which they scraped from the walls. They tore books apart and gave their children the glue off the bindings . . . The resourceful women of Leningrad painstakingly retrieved old flour dust from the cracks in the floorboards and licked decades of spattered grease from the kitchen walls, savoring it slowly.[24]

One woman, finding her breasts not merely dry but rather completely gone, and the soy milk ration far too small for her screaming daughter, pricked her arm and let her child suck mama's blood. If only there had been more soy, more grains, more sustenance of any kind!

Of course, not everyone in Leningrad was saintly. In the winter of 1941–2, after all the city's pets, rats and birds had been consumed and rumours of cannibalism circulated, a food supplier was arrested, along with his assistant, for illegally profiting from the sale of several thousand kilograms of soy and wheat flour.[25] They were neither the first nor last to prosper from others' misery – even though wartime food crimes could be punished with immediate execution.

In late 1942 the Battle of Stalingrad evolved into a mirror image of Leningrad's horror. Germany's 6th Army found itself encircled in a 'pocket' in Stalingrad (the Germans aptly called it a 'cauldron'). Unfortunately for the Nazis, they had many soldiers trapped there, and not enough aeroplanes to bring them the dried soy and other lightweight foods so useful in airlifts. By February 1943 the starving Germans had run out of ammunition and provisions and were forced to surrender, turning the tide of war in Europe. Once again, soy was coveted, soy saved lives and for far too many people, soy – or any type of nourishment – arrived too little, too late.

By comparison, wartime food woes in the United Kingdom seem tame. Britain had previously depended on overseas imports for 70 per cent of the population's calories.[26] But Nazi submarines attacked civilian vessels in the Atlantic, hindering the flow of food. Fewer ships could reach Britain – so each had to brim with readily obtainable, compact, nutrient-dense foodstuffs. The public had to eat unfamiliar items, including much soy protein. Soy flour became a main ingredient in wartime sausages, though the British did not really enjoy them. Britons also ate soy in marzipan, spaghetti and macaroni. The upper and middle classes in particular felt irritated by the new diet, as they were unused to culinary constraints. But ration cards limited even the royal family's meals, and the entire population felt obligated to demonstrate their patriotism stoically.

The British tried growing soy in their empire, experimenting with its cultivation in their African colonies during the war. In Tanzania these efforts failed. In Egypt, Uganda and Southern Rhodesia, where soy was already planted on a small scale, strong wartime demand in the 'mother' country spurred production.[27] But mostly Britain relied on an indirect, brilliant method for growing soy: instead of tending seeds, they cultivated an extraordinarily close relationship with the emerging soy sovereign, the USA. Winston Churchill assiduously courted the Americans, realizing that they would be an indispensable source both of war materiel and food.

And indispensable they were. Once the Soviets joined the Allies, they too turned to the U.S. for help. Together the USSR and Britain requested around 454 million kg (1 billion lb) of fats from the U.S. for margarine and other uses in 1942.[28] Demand fired up production, and American farmers increased their soy harvest by 75 per cent in a single year.[29]

Most of the soy sent overseas did so through a system called Lend-Lease. In early 1941, the U.S. Congress created the programme, authorizing the president to provide allies with urgently needed munitions, industrial goods and food. The Allies, still struggling to repay debts to the U.S. from the previous World War, would not be required to pay for this assistance. Payment would be contemplated later, after the war, to compensate the Americans for damage to borrowed planes, ships and tanks. In return, the Allies would provide Americans with whatever they could: local vegetables for the mess halls of American servicemen in Britain; Australian medical care for Americans injured in New Guinea; and long-term access to British lands in the Western Hemisphere for U.S. military bases. Through Lend-Lease, the U.S. boosted the Allied war effort with enormous quantities of armaments – but also, in its first two years alone, with

$1.6 billion worth of agricultural products (equivalent to over $23 billion in 2017 dollars).[30]

The principal beneficiaries of the food aid were the British and Soviets. Through Lend-Lease, America sent millions of kilograms of soy as oil, flour and grits, plus dehydrated soups (pea-soy and cheese-soy) and cereal concentrates, notably an oat-soy blend.[31] While u.s. foods did not provide the majority of calories in these two countries – in Britain only 10 per cent of food came from the u.s. – the aid did provide missing nutrients, and it reduced hunger. So, too, did the British government's campaign encouraging home vegetable gardens, as well as the more equitable distribution of food built into the rationing system. Together the British and u.s. programmes created a surprising outcome: in 1945 Britain's working-class children were vastly healthier due to their improved wartime diets.[32] Soy oil and soy protein each contributed to this felicitous result.

By contrast, the effort to feed soy to British colonial forces in India was a complete failure. Feeding a wartime army that swelled from 205,000 to over 2.5 million – the largest volunteer force in history, fighting in Africa, the Middle East, Southeast Asia and even Italy – was already challenging. Religion added an explosive dimension. Hindus had religious injunctions against eating beef, Muslims were prohibited from eating pork, neither group accepted meat slaughtered in the manner required by the other, and Sikhs could eat any kind of meat, provided it was slaughtered in the Hindu manner. If pork rations were accidentally mislabelled or sent unmarked to Muslim regiments, or beef rations slaughtered according to Islamic rules were inadvertently sent to the Hindus or even Sikhs, then soldiers could turn against their commanders. Accordingly, Americans sent canned soy chunks, but all the soldiers detested them.[33] The solution instead was canned lamb, slaughtered in the appropriate manner for each regiment and very carefully labelled.

In the u.s., Lend-Lease exports to allies, along with the high food needs of American soldiers and federal price supports for soybeans and other commodities, boosted farmer confidence and revenue: in 1941 their income was higher than at any time since 1929.[34] At last, America's cultivators were leaving the Great Depression behind. Compared to city folk they were still underpaid – but things were looking up.

Before the Second World War, much of the u.s. soybean crop was used for animal forage or as 'green manure' to fertilize the soil. Here Arkansas farmers rake soybean hay in 1938.

During the war, increase in u.s. soybean production came primarily from a new approach to the plant, rather than from any huge increase in acreage. Previously, farmers had often allowed soy to grow for a time and then ploughed it under as soil-enriching 'green manure'. But with the wartime government promising to buy soybeans in great quantities, always at or above a reasonable price, farmers let their soy plants mature to produce beans.

The American farmer thus amply filled the gap caused by Axis domination of Manchuria. In 1942 the u.s. overtook Manchuria as the world's premier producer of soybeans.[35] Crucially, American soy oil also took the place of coconut oil from the Philippines and palm oil from the Netherlands East Indies, unavailable because shipping through the war-torn Pacific was too dangerous.

The Roosevelt administration, acutely aware of farmers' roles, assiduously drew them into the war effort. Face to face, agricultural extension agents entreated farmers to grow more soy. In early 1942 a usda pamphlet bore the title 'Soybean Oil and the War: Grow More

Soybeans for Victory'. The pamphlet's closing words, 'Remember – when you grow more soybeans, you are helping America to destroy the enemies of freedom', invoked undiluted patriotism to persuade farmers. The Department of War admonished farmers even more emotionally in a 1943 poster. In a muddy battlefield, two soldiers reclined – Caucasians, like most cultivators in the soy-growing Midwest. One aimed a machine gun, while the other, clearly exhausted, cradled a beverage in his hands. The imagery was stark: 'the sacrifice of your sons and brothers', it fairly shouted. In bold white and red the poster exhorted, 'Farmers . . . meet your goals. They'll meet theirs.'

To facilitate productivity, the government brought in combine harvesters in areas lacking these big, efficient machines. The Lincoln soybean – a fattier, higher-yielding variety bred cooperatively by the USDA and state agricultural stations – was made readily available in 1944. Further breeding with Lincoln beans would eventually produce many strains with useful characteristics.[36]

Government posters urged u.s. farmers to participate in the Second World War by vastly expanding their soybean production.

Demand for soy oil during the war was a dynamo pushing U.S. soy expansion.[37] As for the protein meal, it was valued within the U.S. as a replacement for meat in civilian diets, since most meat was reserved for soldiers. Farmers in the U.S. were asked to grow more soy, and the population was asked to eat more. In 1943 the War Food Administration set aside twelve times more soy for non-combatants than had been consumed the year before.[38] And just as government publicity pushed the farmers, federal officials deployed radio, newspapers, pamphlets, press releases and magazines to win Americans' allegiance to soy-consumption goals.

Beyond the capital, California and New York were hubs of soy education. In Los Angeles in 1942, radio host Mildred Lager published *Soy Bean Recipes: 150 Ways to Use Soy Beans as Meat, Milk, Cheese, and Bread*. Lager's personal interest in soy coincided perfectly with the momentum of the times. Her work soon caught the eye of McGraw-Hill; in 1945 it published her *The Useful Soybean: A Plus Factor in Modern Living*.

Meanwhile, soy received much attention in New York. In 1942 the state appointed Cornell University nutritionist Clive McCay as chairman of a wartime bread and soybean committee. Cornell wields Ivy League clout, and McCay was influential. He was especially interested in soy sprouts, explaining:

> Our daily paper would surprise us if it carried an ad: 'WANTED: a vegetable that will grow in any climate, rivals meat in nutritive value, matures in three to five days, may be planted any day in the year, requires neither soil nor sunshine, rivals in vitamin C, has no waste (in preparation), can be cooked with as little fuel and as quickly as pork chop.' The Chinese discovered this vegetable centuries ago in sprouted soy beans.[39]

In 1943 New York governor Thomas Dewey created a state Emergency Food Commission. He placed Jeannette McCay, Clive's wife and fellow nutritionist, in charge of its publications. While Clive worked with Chinese graduate students on an automatic watering device for soy sprouts, Jeannette produced 10,000 leaflets on soy to be distributed in New York City. Next, Dewey hosted a meal for journalists to explain the Emergency Food Commission. The *New York Times* reported that

A war-diet luncheon, dominated by the humble soy bean, was served to 67 guests in the State dining room of the Executive Mansion today in an effort to convince New York's housewives that palatable and nutritious substitutes for the dwindling meat supply are available. The luncheon . . . included soy beans in seven different forms . . . [such as] soy bean sprouts and chicken soufflé, sprouted soy beans and onion, soy bean bread, [served with] assorted unrationed spreads . . . The use of soy beans reduced by 75 per cent the amount of chicken needed for the soufflé. The soy bean bread, developed by Food Commission experts at Cornell, will be placed on the market . . . Governor Dewey told his guests that the State's official family has been using soy beans in increasing quantities . . .[40]

A Food Commission official later asserted that the governor gave 'soybean gingerbread to his children and they did not know the difference'.[41]

Governments and academia thus worked hand-in-glove to win the public over to soy foods. Their flavour and nutritional value were portrayed in a positive light, and the federal government also emphasized their economic value: in the early 1940s, beef protein cost 16.6 times as much as soy flour, and milk protein cost 14.3 times as much.[42]

The media took notice. A month after Dewey's luncheon, *Life* magazine published a piece about the event; *Reader's Digest* soon followed with the article 'Are You Neglecting the Wonder Bean?' Reporter Jane Holt at the *New York Times* penned articles about soybeans and the Food Commission's work. Before long, Clive McCay left Cornell to assist the u.s. navy with nutrition research – but Jeannette continued at the Food Commission. By war's end the commission had disseminated 935,000 leaflets and bulletins featuring soy recipes.[43]

Soy-processing companies printed their own recipe booklets, tripled production of soy flour in a single year and made sure that the flour appeared in supermarkets nationwide by 1943. School lunch programmes, prisons and restaurants were especially attracted to soy flour as a healthy, cost-cutting ingredient. Soy also gained favour in baked goods and as a meat extender. The Kellogg Company even introduced a breakfast cereal called 'Corn-Soya Shreds' in 1945. Consumption of soy-based vegetarian products, such as a 'Soysage' substitute for breakfast sausage, also increased. People drank more soy milk, too, and used margarine made with soy oil. The nation's pets joined the soy upsurge, as pet food companies made use of the cheap, nutritive bean, even for carnivores like dogs and cats. Jane Holt argued that in the case of the soybean, 'The wallflower became the belle of the ball.'[44]

But fortunes are fickle, and when the war ended soy protein as human food lost prestige. Patriotism found new outlets, incomes were comfortable, rationing ended and Americans were tired of soybeans. While soy remained an invisible ingredient in processed foods, the quantities were reduced and few home cooks continued to purchase it. The country's mood towards soy was illustrated in the 1955 romantic comedy *The Seven-year Itch*. An early scene of this box-office hit took place in a vegetarian restaurant. Reviewing the bill, the waitress enumerates amusingly unappetizing dishes: 'Let's see. We had the number seven special, the soybean hamburger with French-fried soybeans, soybean sherbet and peppermint tea . . . we had the sauerkraut juice on the rocks.' When the main character tries to leave a gratuity, the waitress notes that although the restaurant does not permit tipping, she can put the extra money into 'our nudist camp fund'. By the mid-1950s soy foods were comically lumped together with odd elements of society such as vegetarians, restaurants that refuse tips and nudists. Such associations were a far cry from the years when soy cookery seemed a creative devotion to democracy.

After the war – and even during it, despite all the initiatives spurring Americans to eat soy protein – much of the country's soy meal was a cheap leftover, an excess by-product of oil extraction. What else to do with that part of the bean? How could oilseed processors squeeze not only more oil, but more profit from the plant? The answer came from investigations into making soy meal more digestible for livestock.

Research into the dietary needs of farm animals was already underway in Europe and the u.s. before the Second World War, and for millennia in Asia animals had consumed soybean mash left over after the making of soy oil or soy milk. In the early twentieth century, soy meal was increasingly given to dairy cattle worldwide.

Accordingly, as the *Christian Science Monitor* reported in 1935, the Vermont Soy Bean Association hoped to grow soy locally to spare dairy farmers from depending on soy from distant Iowa.[45] The newspaper sported a cartoon of a cow standing on the Vermont portion of a map and reaching its neck, long as a giraffe's, across to Iowa to eat. Although ultimately the Midwest enjoyed competitive advantages over Vermont in soy agriculture, Vermont farmers' disappointment by no means curtailed soy's ascendancy. By the late 1930s in America, soy had become the top protein in animal feeds.

Beginning in the mid-1930s, scientists overcame obstacles to feeding additional soy to chickens and pigs. Multiple investigations revealed that soy feed worked better if the beans were treated in advance with moistened heat. Through trial and error, researchers deduced how hot, how moist and for how long the soy meal should be 'toasted' for optimal animal nutrition. Later they understood that the raw beans contain compounds interfering with digestion, and that moistened heat inactivated them. Scientists also discovered that fortifying soy with vitamin B12 eliminated any need for animal protein in poultry and swine diets.

The persistent glut of u.s. soy meal motivated continual experimenting; around 1950, researchers dehulled soybeans for feed, rendering it more digestible for poultry. These combined improvements turned soy meal into a keystone of mass poultry production. No longer an overabundant by-product, its value climbed.

The 1940s and '50s also saw advances in the palatability of soy oil for humans. The oil had suffered from 'beany', 'painty' or 'grassy' flavours that quickly developed when it was exposed to oxygen. Frustrated scientists working with soy sometimes called it the Ugly Duckling of agriculture – if only it could truly become a swan! Eventually, as the usda explained,

> Guided by judgments of taste panels . . . researchers identified the source of many of the off-flavors in soybean oil as trace metals, particularly iron and copper. Even extremely small amounts of these contaminants sped oxidation of the oil, shortening its storage life and promoting undesirable flavors. Responding to these findings, industry removed brass valves in refineries and substituted stainless steel for the cold rolled steel in equipment that came in contact with soybean oil.[46]

Another method for eliminating trace metals had come to America through international reconnaissance. The u.s. army had commissioned Warren Goss, a chemical engineer, to follow General Patton's army as it conquered Germany. Goss was charged with studying that country's oilseed industry – especially the rumoured secret German process for making soybean oil more palatable. Notwithstanding the disarray at German oilseed factories, he ascertained their unusually elaborate process for 'deodorizing' the oil, involving multiple washings and arcane applications of chemicals. For the same purpose, in 1945 British Intelligence agents spent a month in Germany, even though, as one expert remarked, 'the destruction suffered by many of the German oil mills is beyond description.'[47]

For his part, Goss returned to America and meticulously tested each step of the coveted procedure, finding nearly all useless. Only one did the trick: citric acid, added to the oil during processing, deactivated trace metals. Soy-processing companies quickly adopted the technique.

During the war, soy growers and crushers had worried about the post-war market for their products. Now the anxiety slipped away, as soy oil acquired a desired blandness, and soy protein meal became digestible for legions of farm animals. The purveyors of soy were delighted.

Yet for hundreds of millions of people worldwide, post-war existence was anything but delightful. The Russians, though victorious in conflict, were beggared; soy was sometimes one of the few things keeping them alive. Even four years after the Germans had left the town of Rostov, for instance, one man found his aunt subsisting only on 'maize bread and soya bean soup, a little cabbage, potatoes, tea and sugar'.[48] For many, soy provided the only affordable protein.

In Western Europe, agricultural fields and machinery had been destroyed, farmers had died in the war or been too maimed to resume cultivating and the populace could not afford agricultural inputs such as fertilizer. America responded from 1948 to 1952 with the Marshall Plan, pumping $17 billion (some $160 billion in today's dollars) into the crippled economies of the uk, France, West Germany and fifteen other lands.[49] The plan provided subsidies to u.s. soy farmers, encouraging them to continue growing surpluses.

Exporters who shipped soy flour, soy oil and animal feed to those countries also received subsidies. Even small relief organizations sending care packages to Europe obtained Marshall funds for freight costs. Thus philanthropists and the American public donated to the Meals for Millions charity, which between 1946 and 1955 shipped 36 million dried, soy-based 'Multi-Purpose Food' packets to the needy overseas.[50]

In Japan, war deprivation led people to cherish soy foods all the more. In 1946 a delegation of women newly elected to the Japanese Diet – the first females ever to serve in that legislative body – came to their American occupiers, pleading for resumed soybean imports. The women stressed the nutritional value of miso, particularly for nursing mothers.

War had caused changes in how Japanese soy foods were made. Shurtleff and Aoyagi explain that after the Americans allowed resumption of trade, makers of *shoyu* – soy sauce – found themselves dependent on beans imported from the u.s. An official named Miss Appleton, in charge of allotting the beans, wished

> to produce a low-cost product quickly . . . she recommended that all producers make quick . . . (chemical) soy sauce instead of the higher-quality fermented product, which would not be ready for a year or more. In 1945 she issued an order that all of Japan's 8,000 shoyu makers should do as she said or forego their quota of soybeans. The producers objected and, fortunately, in 1948 Noda Shoyu Co. announced the development of their patented . . . [hybrid technique], which they . . . agreed to share with all makers free of charge.[51]

The new process was fairly rapid, yet acceptably tasty, and won Miss Appleton's approval. She permitted all businesses using it to obtain a full share of American beans.

During the war and the decade after, Japanese tofu-making changed, too – 'more', Shurtleff and Aoyagi assert, 'than it had in the previous thousand years'.[52] Prior to the conflict, tofu makers had curdled soy milk with *nigari*, a coagulant consisting mostly of magnesium chloride. To make nigari, producers partially evaporated seawater in sunny fields and then, from the derived brine, precipitated out the salt. But during the war, the Japanese government monopolized nigari in order to extract its magnesium for aircraft construction. Tofu makers had instead to use calcium sulphate from mined gypsum. Even though the resultant tofu lacked a certain delicate sweetness that the public preferred, utilization of calcium sulphate continued after the war. The new coagulant provided calcium to the Japanese diet, and it was easier and speedier for tofu manufacturers to use.

Tofu underwent another shift as well. Super-soft, 'silken' tofu was a rare luxury before the war, as it was difficult to ship and expensive to make. But the advent of calcium sulphate in the Japanese tofu industry made silken tofu both more affordable and firm enough for transport. Silken tofu rapidly became a food of the masses. Silken tofu's melt-in-your-mouth feel became something for everyone to savour in miso soup or, in the summer months, as a chilled treat.

The war modified ancient culinary processes throughout the industrialized world. Items beginning as wartime necessities – notably ingredients dried for transport to far-flung battlegrounds – became norms. Wartime food scientists finely cleaved plants and animals into concentrated substances with desired characteristics. The mid-twentieth century witnessed not only the splitting of the atom, but advanced splitting and transforming of soybeans into constituent parts: lecithin (an emulsifier and texture improver for baked goods); bleached, deodorized and often hydrogenated (solidified) oil; protein of varying levels of purity; soy cotyledons (embryonic leaves in the seed, occasionally used in baking and in ready-to-drink powdered beverages); soy hulls (sometimes included in animal feeds, and very occasionally in human foods for fibre); and even pectin (a gelling agent) further extracted from the hulls. Consumers became accustomed to the resulting 'convenience foods', simple to prepare at home.

Soy's nutrients, fed to soldiers and malnourished populations during the conflict, also became post-war cornerstones of relief efforts in areas of poverty or crisis. Ever since the war, soy protein has in varying contexts been mixed with powdered bananas, corn, wheat and many other ingredients to provide rescue meals or to ameliorate diets.

Because of soy's utility, one way or another later wars would also be linked to it. Some argue that soybeans provide a clue that

Chinese leader Chiang Kai-shek had advance knowledge of North Korea's 1950 invasion of the South. Just before that aggression, Chiang's close associates speculated in u.s. soy futures contracts; after war broke out, they garnered $30 million profit. Had they known hostilities were imminent and surmised that military needs and disrupted agriculture would cause soy prices to rise? The answer remains shrouded, but Chiang's associates were quite possibly tipped off.[53]

The Vietnamese, too, found that soy and warfare intertwined. During the Vietnam War, artists working for the North produced a colourful poster showing farm workers and a pretty young woman pouring harvested soybeans into a large sack. Paralleling u.s. propaganda from the 1940s, the caption exhorted farmers, 'Plant many soybeans.'

Tragically, Vietnam was also brutally connected to soy because of how 1940s soy research had advanced scientific understandings of plant biology. In 1943 the American botanist Arthur Galston finished a study on how triiodobenzoic acid could be used to speed up soy flowering. The chemical could make soy more viable at higher latitudes and elevations where the growing season is shorter. Galston discovered that in excess, however, the chemical had a catastrophic effect: total defoliation. This research aimed at augmenting soy production for food was later used to create herbicides. Later still, triiodobenzoic acid was turned into the defoliating weapon of war, Agent Orange.

Horrified, Galston crusaded against using Agent Orange in Vietnam, lecturing widely about its devastating effect on mangrove trees anchoring riverine ecosystems. He further argued that Agent Orange could harm humans, pushing the Department of Defense to conduct experiments. Laboratory work revealed a link between Agent Orange and birth defects in rats; President Nixon soon halted its use. Galston had journeyed far from his days as a soy researcher, never losing faith in science but rather insisting that it be used ethically.

soy's role during the Second World War thus had far-reaching effects. Total war had required the total bean – both oil and protein – to nourish soldiers, citizens, prisoners, royalty, babies, torpedo men and civilians under siege. The war set in motion numerous agricultural and culinary trends, with soy at the heart of one of the most important, the rising worldwide consumption of meat. The complex relationship between meat and soy concerns us next.

FIVE

FATTENING WITH FEED

For millennia, humans and their domestic animals have led exquisitely intertwined lives. Along with the domestication of plants, the introduction of livestock into human society has arguably been the most consequential event in our history. It is not truly surprising, then, that chickens dramatically changed the destiny of a rural woman, thirty-year-old Amal Ismail, as well as the lives of millions of her fellow Egyptians. Her story and its aftermath illuminate the contemporary importance both of domestic animals and of inexpensive soy meal used to nourish them. Since the 1950s, both beneficial and injurious aspects of the mass feeding of soy to animals have powerfully shaped our world, thanks to the export of American techniques for livestock production. Mrs Ismail and her chickens serve as a humble yet revealing entry into a far larger story. Our survey of soy and livestock will include a chicken-blood cookbook, giant economic aid programmes, airlifted hogs, corporate treatment of animals, antibiotics, wild-bird diseases, obesity, faecal river pollution, drowned hogs and more.

In 2006 Mrs Ismail was one of an estimated 5 million Egyptian women of modest means tending flocks in their gardens and on rooftops.[1] Her birds shared living space with wild birds; as part of two major flyways, Egypt's skies host 318 migrating species.[2] The migrators tend not to favour Mrs Ismail's Nile Delta region as a stopover point – but because a billion or so birds pass through Egypt every year, some inevitably do alight near her home. In addition, Egyptian hunters on the Mediterranean coast annually kill at least 5.7 million migrating birds, and maybe far more;[3] these hunters then sometimes sell their quarries elsewhere. So Mrs Ismail and her chickens had opportunities to come into contact with wild birds, both living and dead.

Early in 2006, Mrs Ismail's flock suddenly fell ill; some died. Protecting her investment, she killed the chickens that were not yet visibly sick – or at least not too far gone – and fed them to her family. She slaughtered and cleaned the poultry herself. Within days, she suffered flu-like symptoms, and then high fever, aching bones and chest pains. According to the World Health Organization (WHO), Mrs Ismail did not tell her doctors that she had come into contact with diseased chickens until it was too late to give her optimal treatment. She died on 17 March. Tests later confirmed that this was Egypt's first fatality from the H5N1 'bird flu' virus – transmitted from wild birds to domestic poultry and then to humans.

Before Mrs Ismail's death, H5N1 had been detected in dozens of Egyptian birds, and the government had disseminated TV, radio and print ads warning the public to avoid contact with sick birds. The government also began insisting on its ban against household poultry raising. But low education levels, and among the poor a high need not to waste the poultry, caused warnings and orders to fall on confused and sceptical ears. Mrs Ismail died in part because of her conflicting needs.

Her demise was a microcosm of Egypt's difficult decisions in the face of H5N1. With wrenching regret, the central government systematically killed and disposed of 30 million chickens and other poultry in an attempt to stop the virus's spread;[4] more mass culls followed. The results were far from perfect. During the nine years following the first cull, tests would confirm that 111 more people had died from H5N1 in Egypt anyway.[5] How do you halt a disease that travels along migratory flyways? One cannot quarantine the sky! Even mass vaccination of poultry hatchlings failed to stop the disease's spread, and more virulent forms of the virus have emerged, endemic to Egypt.

The consequences of the mass culling were long term. Large chicken farms, feed distributors, food processors and chicken owners endured bitter financial losses, amounting to $1 billion; the incomes of 1.5 million Egyptians employed in the poultry industry were severely curtailed.[6] Egypt's poor experienced a decline in dietary nutrients. By 2009 undernutrition among Egypt's children had risen 6 per cent; the nation's proportion of stunted toddlers had risen to nearly one-third.[7] Previously inadequate diets among children were exacerbated by the disappearance in their homes of poultry meat and eggs to eat. Poultry is the main source of animal protein in Egypt; among the poor it is usually the only such source.

The WHO recommends animal protein, eaten in modest quantities, in the human diet.[8] Meat provides a dense 'package' of nutrients that enhance brain, muscle and skeletal health. Although it is quite feasible to obtain these nutrients from a vegetarian diet, feeding a little bit of egg or meat to children is a direct, concentrated and often relatively simple way to provide nutrition to growing young bodies.

Egypt's difficulties with avian flu and its nutritional consequences demonstrate that meat, specifically poultry, matters. True, meat in the quantities consumed in rich countries is too much of a good thing. But for most of the world's undernourished, meat and eggs remain cherished godsends. A chicken-based 'formula' has even been developed for severely malnourished, hospitalized children, as it is more affordable and readily available than fancier formulas.[9]

Cheap chicken abounds around the globe in significant measure because poultry is easily fattened on low-cost, abundant grain and soy protein. Enhancing chicken feed with protein significantly increases the amount of muscle meat that each bird develops. The most common protein in commercial animal feeds worldwide is soy meal, with around 70 per cent of market share.[10]

Although poultry raised in Egyptian households are fed table scraps and allowed to search for insects on their own, families do also invest in commercial feed – and soy meal is absolutely crucial to the large farms that raise more than 70 per cent of the country's chickens.[11] Egypt is among the many countries where the regimen of feeding grain and soy in large poultry operations became important to national nutrition in the years following the Second World War. As a result, the nation's domestic birds eat over 1 million metric tons of soy meal yearly.[12] The largest share of imported soy meal comes from Argentina, followed by the U.S. Thanks to the efforts of the American Soybean Association (ASA) and private companies, the largest share of imported whole soybeans (that the Egyptians crush into oil and meal themselves) comes from the U.S. Chickens are vitally important to Egypt, and because of how humans raise their birds, soy is vitally important to chickens. Soy is a central product

Poultry, often fattened with soybean meal, are a mainstay of working-class Egyptian diets.

in Egyptian agricultural trade, and indirectly also in Egyptians' nutritional status.[13]

The feeding of low-cost grain and soy to livestock provides much of the world with affordable animal protein. The percentage of protein-energy malnourished people in developing countries has been shrinking since the latter part of the twentieth century; the UN reports that the number of the destitute fell by almost half between 1990 and 2015.[14] Although meat is not critical for people to rise out of chronic hunger, far more people do receive vital nutrients from animals now than ever before – most notably, iron. Noting this trend, the UN's Food and Agriculture Organization has argued that intensive livestock production is one long-term key to feeding the world's growing cities.

The value for the poor of consuming a modicum of animal products was resoundingly demonstrated by the anti-anaemia efforts in Peru of the World Food Programme (WFP). In 2003 half of Peru's children suffered from iron-deficiency anaemia, with rates of over 70 per cent in some areas. Anaemia can lead to infections, lack of energy, shortness of breath and heart palpitations. In growing bodies it can cause permanent damage such as mental impairment. Recognizing the dangers to Peru's children, the WFP launched a project in 2004 in a town outside Lima. The project promoted iron-rich foods such as *sangrecita*, which is seasoned chicken-blood pudding.

In just three years, children's anaemia rates in the town dropped from 70 to 18 per cent. The WFP then brought a thousand local mothers and two prominent Peruvian chefs together to create a user-friendly, budget-conscious cookbook of forty-plus sangrecita recipes for distribution in poor areas all over the country.[15] In Peru, sangrecita, an inexpensive by-product of chicken consumption among the wealthier classes, is proving a godsend to the poor. Here we see genuine health reasons why people with rising incomes want animal products – reasons that people in overfed, industrialized nations may not always appreciate.

Beyond human access to iron lies another positive aspect of using cheap soy to produce meat. The paramount animal consumers of soy – chicken and pigs – are also, kilo-for-kilo, among the least problematic as regards climate change. Chicken and pigs furnish a higher return in meat, per quantity of feed they consume, than do commercially raised cattle, sheep or goats. Chicken and pigs also do not directly release as much methane – a very damaging greenhouse gas – as those ruminant animals do.[16] Methane is expelled both in the course of digestion and when manure decomposes, and cattle in particular produce worrisomely large amounts of it.

In recent years around 70 per cent of the world's soy protein has gone towards feeding poultry and pigs; almost all the rest feeds cattle, sheep, horses, farmed fish, other livestock and pets.[17] After the

An Iowa pig farm includes soy fields producing beans for feed.

Second World War, soy protein was transformed into a ubiquitous, lucrative agricultural commodity earmarked principally for animal growth.

What ignited this volcanic rise? How did this soy-feed regimen take shape globally? Substantial credit for exporting the system jointly belongs to two growers' organizations, the ever-vibrant ASA and the now-defunct Soybean Council of America. Two governmental bodies also contributed greatly: the USDA and the framers of America's 'Food for Peace' legislation, formally known as Public Law 480.

The ASA was founded in 1920. In its early years it focused on educating cultivators and the public about how to grow and use soy. In 1928, however, the ASA waded into politics, successfully supporting passage of a tariff on inexpensive soy meal imported from Manchuria. The ASA and sister organizations then continued to work hand-in-hand with government, providing mutual support for a variety of projects.

The projects included the 1936 establishment in Illinois of a federal centre researching new uses for agricultural products, including soy components in many applications. In such endeavours, partnership with the government was extremely helpful to the soy industry in its early years, even though farmers and processors did sometimes regard their regulators and taxers warily.

Then the Second World War recast u.s. agriculture, with farmers greatly increasing their soybean production. After the war, soy farmers constantly worried that demand would drop and the resulting oversupply would ruin soy's market price. Proactively, in 1949 the ASA suggested that George Strayer, a soy farmer who had become their first employee, join a technical assistance trip to Europe for the Marshall Plan. Trip participants explored the possibilities for soybean agriculture and processing in Europe, especially Germany. The fact-finders concluded that Western Europe's environment truly was sub-optimal for growing soy, but that the continent's potential for renewed soybean processing held promise. Such processing would require soybean imports into Europe, and Manchuria's economy was in such disarray that beans no longer flowed from there. Strayer honed a detailed understanding of the logistics of soy export from the u.s. to Europe during that trip and later ones. His influence was prominent in expanding America's soy exports.

The ASA originally thought the protein portion of the beans would go continuously towards human nutrition in Europe. But with their economies recovering, the Europeans tapped into American research on processing soy meal for animal feed. The soy-meal-for-animal-nutrition model took hold firmly there. Thus – partly due to Strayer's unflagging labours – meat eating in Europe skyrocketed, as in other industrialized regions after the Second World War, including by 1973 an almost 400 per cent increase in European consumption of chicken.[18]

In 1955 the single biggest importer of U.S. soybeans was not in Europe, however, but rather in Asia. U.S.-occupied Japan became very dependent on American beans, despite problems and puzzlement during the importing process. Japanese importers frowned on the levels of extraneous matter in the sacks of beans they received – bits of leaves, insect parts, dust and tiny pebbles. The Japanese also felt confused about which U.S. soybean varieties would be suitable for their traditional soy foods. As Shurtleff and Aoyagi explain, the Japanese further

> did not understand U.S. methods of mechanical handling and grading; Americans did not understand Japan's soybean needs and utilization. Recognizing that Japan could be a much larger U.S. customer if the problems were solved, the U.S. Agricultural Attaché in Tokyo asked ASA to send a representative to Japan. So in late 1955, with funding from the Oils and Fats Division of [the] USDA's Foreign Agricultural Service, George Strayer spent 6½ weeks in Japan talking to producers of tofu, miso, and shoyu, soy oil/meal processors, and government officials.[19]

During this journey Strayer organized the Japanese American Soybean Institute (JASI) in Tokyo, which served as the ASA's de facto first overseas office and was a harbinger of much international activity. JASI was created with the joint funding of the ASA, the U.S. government and Japanese soy businessmen. Its goal was promotion of U.S. soy for Japanese products; the Japanese soy processors benefited from a stable supply of beans. JASI vigorously endorsed U.S. soy not only for humans but for livestock. Meanwhile, the ASA provided technical expertise for Japanese soy-oil factories to prepare leftover soy meal for the feed market. The ASA also hired animal nutritionists to assist the Japanese in preparing feeds containing American soy. These efforts more than doubled the percentage of soy in Japanese animal feeds between 1956 and 2005. The ASA and its JASI wing celebrated smashing successes: within 25 years, Japanese consumers were eating four times more edible oil – nearly half from soybeans – and far more meat, much of it raised on soy.[20]

Japanese consumption of chickens – those feathered, grand devourers of soy meal – rose more steeply after a U.S. team hired a Japanese agent, Katzi Toyoda, to entice the Japanese public into purchasing imported American 'broiler' birds shipped frozen across the Pacific. Katzi had studied in the U.S. and parlayed his understanding of American products and Japanese consumer culture to suggest just the right venue for introducing American chicken to the public: the Daimaru department store chain in Osaka. Katzi organized an all-day meeting with the company's food sector managers, which led to an on-the-spot initial order for $10,000 worth of assorted frozen poultry. The shocked but delighted Americans agreed – and then scrambled to find an actual supplier for the order. Fortunately, an Arkansas poultry farmer was quickly on board. In this way, the Japanese populace was introduced to whole and cut up chicken with bones, in contrast to the thin boneless strips they had known from Japanese suppliers.[21]

The Japanese suppliers watched the Daimaru experiment closely and soon competed with parallel products. The net result was that although the Daimaru stores continued to sell imported birds, considering it a badge of honour to purvey such fine comestibles, the Japanese market for imported poultry did not expand significantly. In synch with the post-war 'economic miracle' taking place throughout Japan, the Japanese themselves took over this market niche. The long-term U.S. benefit went instead to soy and feed wholesalers, who now found eager buyers for U.S. soybeans and soy meal among Japanese poultry farmers. The farmers wanted to plump up their chickens the way the Americans did. As Japanese businessmen everywhere embraced economies of scale in order to enhance profits, chicken farmers too saw the value in mass production. Low-cost soy and grain from the U.S. were keys to their flock expansion. The Japanese diet registered the impact: chicken consumption was 22 times higher in 1984 than in 1960, and egg consumption was three times higher. Imports of U.S. soybeans had grown by approximately 600 per cent.[22]

Similar events took place among Japan's hog farmers. In the late 1950s the Japanese fattened hogs on expensive fishmeal protein. In the autumn of 1959, two typhoons struck the agricultural region of Yamanashi, decimating its livestock and crops. Hearing of the destruction, Master Sergeant Richard Thomas, who was stationed with the u.s. air force in Tokyo, conceived of donating hogs from his home state of Iowa. Espying a potential new market for u.s. feed grains and soy, the u.s. agricultural attaché seized on the idea. A deal was worked out whereby Iowa hog farmers donated 36 animals, the u.s. government contributed 80,000 bushels of corn for feed, the air force provided the transport and the delighted governor of Yamanashi agreed to have his agricultural employees prepare the feed to American specifications, including the use of soy meal instead of fish. Three Iowa farmers flew with the airlifted pigs to Japan and remained for two months to show the Japanese the American method of artificial insemination. By mid-1962 the original animals had multiplied to 500. Meanwhile, the Japanese had purchased many other Iowa breeder pigs, much u.s. swine equipment and vast quantities of American feedstuffs, including hefty quantities of soy. Not only piglets, but a market had been born.[23]

Elsewhere, globally, after the Second World War the adoption of soy for animal feed grew rapidly. In Washington, DC, policy-makers were collaborating with farmers' organizations to craft Public Law (PL) 480. The legislation directed the u.s. government to purchase surplus American crops and then export them to countries with debt problems. Those countries would not have to pay for the crops with internationally valuable currencies, instead paying with their own weak currencies. The u.s. agents would then use those weak currencies within the struggling countries to undertake projects, especially market development for u.s. agricultural products.

The policy-makers had multiple goals: relieving the u.s. of price-depressing surplus crops; feeding a hungry world; undermining communism through economic diplomacy; creating public demand abroad for u.s. crops; and strengthening trade ties so that as economically distressed countries became strong enough to pay for imported crops in hard currency, the u.s. would be positioned to benefit. In the law's passage and implementation, idealism has always been present – but so too have geopolitical goals and the capitalist imperative to seek profit. At times the various strains of the law's intent have been in conflict, as for instance when cheap PL 480 imports flood a developing country with so much food that prices for local crops are undercut, and local farmers fall deeper into poverty. Fortunately, at other times PL 480 administrators have managed to work *with* local farmers, rather than in spite of them.

The edible oil and animal feed markets of Spain provide striking examples of PL 480 in action, in tandem with the U.S. industry group called the Soybean Council – despite early challenges that Spain posed for American exporters. In the 1950s the Spanish produced insufficient fat for their population; inexpensive U.S. soy oil seemed to offer a solution. But the Spanish public balked: soy oil definitely did not taste like the olive oil they preferred. A large cartoon in a Spanish humour magazine summed up their opinion. The sketch showed the defenders of a besieged castle pouring oil from a tower onto attackers below. The caption proclaimed, 'There is no need that the oil be boiling – if it is soybean oil, that is enough.'[24]

But America's Soybean Council did not lose heart. They convinced oil companies that if they blended just enough olive oil into imported U.S. soy oil, the Spanish public would accept the mixture. The Council further suggested that whatever olive oil the Spanish processors no longer needed for their own population, they could export for higher prices. The Council then sent experts to Spain to help processors work out technical details of the blending, and they sponsored U.S. trips for Spaniards to visit American refineries. The Council also provided expertise on building Spanish port facilities that could handle large quantities of soy oil. The final piece of the puzzle, help with financing the imports, came through PL 480.

Phase Two of the Council's endeavours involved soy meal. As Spanish post-war incomes rose, so too did the nation's demand for meat. Spanish livestock farmers strained to keep up with demand, providing the Council with an opportunity. They began publicizing in Spain the utility of soy protein for animal growth. Their basic message was simple: more soy yields more meat. They organized seminars for Spanish agricultural educators, teaching the teachers the virtues of U.S. soy. Owners of large farms and feed companies also heard from the Council, and exhibits at Spanish trade fairs reached an even larger audience. Spanish feed technicians and animal nutritionists were flown to the U.S. to discuss soy with their American counterparts, and once again U.S. experts visited Spain to offer guidance.

As a result of these many efforts, during the 1960s the value of Spanish imports of u.s. soy oil, soy meal and eventually soybeans that the Spanish crushed themselves rose from $2.2 million to nearly $100 million.[25] Moreover, by the early 1960s, Spain no longer needed PL 480 concessions; the Spanish could pay on the open market.

During its thirteen years of existence, the Soybean Council operated in countries as varied as Spain, West Germany, Colombia, Morocco, Israel, Egypt, Iran, Turkey, India and Pakistan, and soybeans became the clear leader among the USDA's internationally promoted commodities. But after accusations of mismanagement and fraud, the Council folded, its work taken over by the ASA.

The ASA's efforts to promote u.s. soybeans everywhere on earth, with heavy emphasis on extracting the oil and then using the meal in animal feeds, helped u.s. farmers manage overproduction without as high a level of domestic price supports as farmers obtained for other crops. Like the drafters of PL 480, the ASA addressed the problem of super-abundance, which threatened to depress u.s. prices. The ASA sought government funding to help convince the world to buy America's soy surpluses. The world was the ASA's – and indeed the entire soy industry's – target.

The USDA too set its sights on opening global markets to private American enterprises, assisting not only the ASA but companies such as Cargill Incorporated, a giant American processor and trader of soy and other agricultural commodities. Together Cargill and the USDA helped establish poultry industries and fast-food chains in Asia during the 1960s. Strengthening the u.s. economy was the USDA's goal, and the world was the playing field.

The world responded favourably to the astute, relentless marketing of meat. The stupendous success of the chicken nugget is illustrative. In the late 1970s McDonald's wanted a chicken product pleasing to children: finger food, small and easy to hold, lacking in troublesome bones or gristle, easy to chew, mild in flavour and simple to dip into sauce if desired. McDonald's introduced their chicken nuggets throughout the u.s. in 1982. They were an immediate sensation. By 1986, 10 per cent of America's broiler chicken meat was destined for nuggets.[26] By 2003 the *Wall Street Journal* would write of a national 'chicken nugget boom'.[27] Paralleling the way chickens gobble up bite-size, processed morsels of soybeans with grain, humans now gobble up bite-size, processed morsels of chicken with breading. As McDonald's has spread around the globe, so too have the nuggets. Today billions of breaded nuggets, chicken 'strips' and chicken 'fingers' are sold – in virtually every nation, proffered by many different companies.

But the world is a big, complex place, and despite the U.S. soybean industry's many triumphs, in 2005 the ASA decided that marketing soy internationally required a focused daughter organization. Today the task of globally promoting U.S. soy, primarily for animal feed, rests with the U.S. Soybean Export Council (USSEC), which has offices in more than seventy nations. The USSEC's promotion of soy can be quite indirect; it has, for example, assisted Honduran shrimp farmers with combating the shellfish disease vibriosis, thereby helping these soy customers keep their businesses viable. In Europe, where sustainability is a hot topic, the USSEC gives presentations on sustainability in U.S. soy agriculture. Meanwhile, as the USSEC works the foreign markets, the ASA labours on the home front by lobbying the U.S. government for policies favourable to soy growers. Soy is well represented in Washington – and just about everywhere else.

Unquestionably, propagation of the American model for feeding livestock benefits many. Large soy farmers in the U.S. and South America thrive. So, too, do oilseed processors; agricultural trading companies; meat producers; meat wholesalers and retailers; companies producing farm inputs such as fertilizer, seed, pesticides, livestock vitamins and animal medications; agricultural shipping companies; feed retailers; crop and animal husbandry scientists; veterinarians; marketing specialists; and the countless individuals whose ancillary jobs are created or preserved – teachers, librarians, nurses, hardware shop owners, road crews, electricians, plumbers, recreation employees and so on – because soy farming and export bring money to rural communities. Across the planet, the mass production of livestock, including 21 *billion* chickens and nearly 1 billion pigs per year – collectively eating 216 million metric tons of soy meal in 2016 – provides many individuals with livelihoods.[28]

Yet the proliferation of soy-fed meat worldwide is hardly an unequivocal blessing. Problems abound. Animal feed is cheap in part because enormous livestock operations procure it in bulk; today over half the globe's chicken and pork are produced on concentrated, confining farms. Although some farmers and food companies seek to make such farms more humane, the fact remains that intensive raising of animals on a mass scale treats them less as sentient creatures than as meat- or egg-producers that only incidentally happen to be alive. Herein lies a darker side to the feeding and raising of animals on an industrial scale.

Modernizing the beloved folk tale known as 'Henny Penny' or 'Chicken Little' illustrates the grim lives that mass-produced creatures endure. In usual versions of the story, a chicken overreacts when an acorn drops from an oak tree onto her head: she believes the sky is falling. She runs around the barnyard warning other animals of disaster. In some renditions the animals set out to warn the king; in many variants, a falsely helpful fox eventually eats them. Occasionally, the animals all escape and converse with the king.

Consider, then, how differently Henny Penny's life unfolds at a giant, 'factory'-style egg farm. Henny Penny hatches and, because she is female and destined to lay eggs for corporate owners, she is spared the fate of her brother hatchlings; they are disposed of by electrocution, gassing or grinding in a machine. When Henny Penny is a day old, a hot blade sears off a portion of her beak. This procedure prevents her from excessively pecking her cage-mates or even eating them – stress behaviours she might otherwise engage in. Her beak is naturally filled with nerves, so the beak trim is painful.

In the months following, she eats a carefully formulated, yet fairly inexpensive, soy-enhanced diet to promote growth and egg laying. As she matures, she and seven other hens fill their cage; each occupies a space only slightly bigger than a sheet of letter paper. Henny Penny is constantly crammed against the cage's wires, and to the extent that she can move around at all, her feet must grapple with wires at the cage's bottom, causing her foot injuries. There is no acorn falling onto her head, because she has never been near a tree. Rather, she is the one with something from her body falling off: so much contact with wire causes abnormal loss of feathers. She will never travel to see the king; she cannot move more than a few centimetres within her cage. She will not be tricked and eaten by a seemingly helpful fox because seemingly helpful humans shelter her from foxes – and will be the ones to kill her when she is too old to lay eggs.

Fortunately, by law in the EU and California, 'layer' chickens receive somewhat roomier enclosures; a few other U.S. states and companies have passed or are considering similar rules. The announcement by McDonald's in 2015 and Wal-Mart in 2016 that they would gradually phase out eggs from tightly caged hens may also transform supply chains.

Henny Penny's cousins, the 'broiler' chickens raised for meat, live in large indoor structures – often 20,000 together – where each bird grows rather tightly into the 742 sq. cm (115 sq. in.) allotted to it. The broilers' bodies expand so fast that their skeletons, hearts and respiratory systems barely support their weight; many birds struggle to walk, and others develop heart failure and breathing problems. The floors of their 'growout houses' are sometimes covered with the droppings of tens of thousands of birds before they are cleaned; the stench is overpowering.

Poultry are not the only soy-fed animals to live in unnatural conditions. Swine, too, are mass-produced and confined even though they are clever, social animals – less distant from the personifications in stories than one might think. As a 2009 article in the *New York Times* noted, pigs rank among 'the quickest of animals to learn a new routine' and can perform 'a circus's worth of tricks: jump hoops, bow and stand, spin and make wordlike sounds on command, roll out rugs, herd sheep, close and open cages, [and] play videogames with joysticks'.[29]

Inexpensive soy meal feed is an important component in the 'factory farming' of chickens.

Soy-fattened pigs are tightly confined on 'factory farms'.

In many factory farms, the breeding female of this gregarious species is pent up in a 'gestation crate' – 2 m x 60 cm for a sow weighing up to 408 kg (that is, 6½ x 2 ft for an animal bulking up to 900 lb). The crate's floor is slatted to allow most of her excretions, like those of the nearly 2,000 other sows in the same large shed, to fall into a pit below.[30] As she grows, the pregnant sow is so squeezed that she cannot turn around, or sleep on her side as pigs normally do. She cannot express the natural pig behaviours of foraging, inquisitively exploring an extensive environment, participating in a complex social life or nest building prior to giving birth. The pork industry points out that crates protect sows from each other, as they can injure one another when tussling over social dominance. The farmers provide the sows with water and soy-enriched food, a temperature-controlled environment, protection from harsh weather and ventilation to counteract the toxic (and otherwise potentially fatal) fumes emanating from the waste pit.

Responding to critiques of these conditions, which are likely immensely frustrating for the pigs, some in the pork industry have searched for alternatives. It turns out that with careful management, gestation crates are not truly necessary to prevent injuries from sow-on-sow aggression; there are other, less confining solutions. It is not a given that cheap, industrial pork derived from cheap soy and corn must profoundly cheapen the quality of the animals' existence.

Fortunately, the hog industry is evolving. Particularly heartening was the July 2015 decision by the world's largest pork producer, Smithfield Foods, to phase out gestation crates on all of its affiliated farms worldwide by 2022.

But the model of soy-plus-grains to make meat in mammoth quantities leads to other problems, too. This system can have serious consequences not only for animal welfare, but for human well-being, for long-term resource management and for the natural environment.

Inexpensive meat has a role to play in world nutrition, yet iron-ically growing crops to feed livestock can reduce the health of the less fortunate. In parts of Brazil, the presence of soy, the quin-tessential protein-rich plant, paradoxically has negatively affected the protein intake of the poor. This is because in recent decades rich farmers have converted lands to soy cultivation that were pre-viously devoted to traditional Brazilian food crops. The soy has been exported for animal feed rather than eaten locally. Devoting fewer hectares to traditional food-bean crops has at times led to price spikes for local beans. The poor have been less able to afford the beans they need for protein.

Yet the case of southern Bangladesh provides a partial contrast: there, an expanding animal feed market has provided small soy farmers with a remunerative outlet for their crop. Their ability to stay financially afloat cultivating soy has enabled them to provide their communities with roasted soybeans for local consumption. The major difference between the two cases lies in who controls the soy. Animal feed markets have differing effects on the nutrition of the poor, depending on specific circumstances.

The 'hourglass' structure of crop production, processing and trade generally determines who has the largest control over soy. Although in recent decades fewer and fewer farmers have been tend-ing larger and larger farms within the major soy-producing countries, there are still far more soy *farmers* than soy processing-and-trading companies. Most of the processing and export is controlled by four international enterprises: Archer, Daniels, Midland (ADM); Bunge Ltd; Cargill Inc.; and Louis-Dreyfus Commodities (yes, actor Julia Louis-Dreyfus hails from the French-Alsatian family that controls the company). Because these corporations share similar business characteristics, analysts sometimes refer to them as a block: the

ABCD companies, after the first names of three of them and the second name of the last one. They stand between the farmers and consumers as if occupying the narrowest point of an hourglass, and they exercise a commanding influence.

A 2012 Oxfam report explains that 'the ABCD companies are so dominant in the bulk commodities sector that – especially in soy and palm oil – they play a central role in the decisions that producers make about what to grow, where, how, in what quantities, and for which markets.'[31] These muscular corporations find the present worldwide system of feeding animals quite profitable. Concentrated livestock production goes hand-in-hand with their concentrated wealth and power. The very fact of so much control in so few hands (Cargill and Louis-Dreyfus are privately owned) gives pause for thought, and perhaps for alarm.

The agribusiness chain leading to an ordinary dinner is long, with many controversial business methods. Some of the ABCD's soy customers are themselves huge corporations whose conduct consistently gives them the upper hand in relation to livestock farmers. The top countries for mass-produced chicken meat – the U.S., China and Brazil – provide hungry consumers with nearly half the chicken on the planet.[32] In those three nations, the vast majority of meat chickens are raised through special contracts between, on the one hand, giant corporations that own the birds, and on the other hand farmer-growers who provide the birds with housing and care.[33] This system protects growers from the short-term risks of fluctuating prices both for their inputs (since the corporations give them feed, bedding and medication for the chickens) and for their end products (since they have a guaranteed purchaser for the finished birds).

But because the specialized chicken houses that corporations require growers to build each cost some $200,000,[34] and because a grower needs at least four such houses to make a good profit, growers are severely exposed to long-term risk. If for any reason the corporation becomes dissatisfied with growers, the growers can fail to have their contracts renewed yet still remain terribly in debt to lending banks for the housing costs – a too-frequent occurrence leaving many growers sour on the contract system. Yet the market is now so dominated by such arrangements that an independent grower has difficulty competing with it; banks, for one, rarely provide loans for the chicken housing unless the grower already has a corporate contract. The problem is extending to swine farming, too, as corporate processors adopt the poultry industry's business practices.

Once the animal has been fattened on soy and grain, it is taken to a slaughterhouse, where working conditions are even less desirable – so undesirable that in the U.S., even though the pay is generally higher than minimum wage, only low-income individuals take such jobs. Labourers at U.S. slaughterhouses each learn one task for an assembly-line process, which they repeat as fast as possible for eight hours in a row. The work is tedious even as it demands concentration – a single slip of a sharp tool, or inattention to a hulking machine, can cause serious injury. Repetitive motions, sometimes in awkward body positions, damage workers' limbs, joints and muscles. Slaughterhouse labour, in fact, ranks among the more dangerous of America's occupations. The stench, incessant loud noise, blood and viscera, harsh cleansing chemicals and psychological pressure to perform with little job security also take a toll on employees. The turnover rate among workers approaches 100 per cent per year.[35]

Mass producing meat with cheap soy and grain also has health implications for the general public. Infections spread with lightning speed among animals in crowded conditions, which factory farms address by pumping the creatures up with antibiotics. Johns Hopkins University researchers reported that in 2011, 80 per cent of antimicrobial drugs administered in the U.S. were for agricultural purposes, mostly for animals in crowded housing.[36] Mass producers of livestock and their government regulators are beginning to limit use of antimicrobials, but progress is too slow.

Meanwhile, the microbes vigorously adapt to their environments. The constant presence of antibiotics favours reproduction of bacteria that have evolved to resist those very drugs. Unfortunately, the drugs are often similar to ones needed for humans. Public health officials are perturbed that factory farms breed not only livestock, but also pathogens infectious to humans and resistant to our best medications. In 2015 EU scientists lamented finding *Salmonella* resistant to multiple drugs in the live animals or meat of 37.9 per cent of the EU's fattening pigs, 56 per cent of broiler chickens and a whopping 73 per cent of farm turkeys.[37] Not surprisingly, since the same microbes infect humans, 31.8 per cent of European patients suffering from *Salmonella* infection also harboured multi-drug resistant strains. Fortunately, companies are beginning to respond to consumer concern about this issue. McDonald's, for example, announced in 2015 that its u.s. chicken suppliers would soon stop using antibiotics that are important in human medicine.

Unfortunately, however, when factory farms are not producing germs with drug resistance, their confinement systems still encourage proliferation of the more ordinary forms of *Salmonella*, toxic *E. coli*, *Listeria* and other menacing germs that, unless farms and abattoirs are extremely vigilant, enter the food supply. The u.s. Centers for Disease Control and Prevention estimated that nearly 110,000 individuals in the u.s. contracted *Salmonella* illness from eggs in 2007.[38] Proper cooking protects consumers, but people do make mistakes, especially when they fail to realize how contaminated their foods are. Factory farming contributes to this problem. The system transforms grains and soy into meat – and sometimes into illness.

The 2015 epidemic of bird flu among u.s. turkeys and egg-laying hens – mass-produced thanks to the soy-and-corn regimen – further illuminated the risks of factory farming. This epidemic greatly upset farmers because by mid-year, nearly 50 million birds had either died from the sickness or had had to be destroyed in order to halt the disease's spread. Handling the rapid destruction of so many birds proved extremely challenging. By permeating poultry houses with carbon dioxide, farm workers could kill 100,000 birds a day – but more than that was infeasible because the daily colossal piles of dead birds, of contaminated soy and corn feed and of manure were already nearly unmanageable. Dr John Clifford of the usda reported at a Senate hearing:

> You're talking about manure and birds and product that can be literally miles long and 4 or 5 feet wide and 6 or 8 feet tall. This is not an easy task. Some of these pits underneath some of the layer houses have not been—the manure has not been removed out of there for years, and it's massive.[39]

Workers would dehydrate quickly in stifling protective clothes; they had to take frequent breaks. Space in landfills to receive so many carcasses was limited. And yet, whenever an owner was mandated to sacrifice all of the chickens on a multi-million-bird farm, the faster the workers could do so, the less likely the flu would spread to other farms. Speed in destruction and removal is key, and at the same time, hardly possible. Soy-enhanced mass production creates enormous efficiencies – until it leads to enormous difficulties.

Officials worried that this flu could mutate to become highly infectious in swine. In such an eventuality, not only would mass pork producers suffer economically, but the swine version of the virus could further mutate to become deadly to humans.

One might imagine these risks would markedly discourage world meat consumption, but that would be a mistaken conclusion. The cheap, mass production of soy-fed animals still manages to encourage overnutrition, a grave problem not only in industrial-ized countries but also increasingly among the wealthier classes in developing nations. Americans typically eat well beyond their gov-ernment's recommendations for meat; many Australians, Spanish, New Zealanders, Canadians, French, British, Italians and Argentines also eat more than they need. Is it any surprise that among countries with populations over 100 million, the two with the highest rates of obesity – the u.s. and Mexico – are located in or right next to the vast soy- and corn-producing regions of North America? North Americans unquestionably consume too much corn syrup and fatty, soy-fed meats.

Even as the presence of so many farm animals affects human well-being, it has long-term effects on natural resources too – and therefore on economic health. The gargantuan amounts of water needed to grow the planet's corn and soy for livestock, the water the animals in turn drink as they mature and are fattened, and the water used in slaughterhouses every day, all constitute a significant threat to freshwater availability in the future. Currently livestock production accounts for one-third of the world's fresh-water con-sumption. Nearly 6,000 litres of water (1,320 gallons) are needed to produce just 1 kg (a little over 2 lb) of mass-produced pork, and over 4,000 litres (880 gallons) are needed to make a single kilogram of chicken.[40] Agriculture is by far the most water-depleting activity that humans engage in, and the production of beef, pork, poultry, eggs and milk are the most water-intensive of all agricultural activities.

The land devoted to cultivating feed crops could be used differ-ently – for instance as forest to absorb more of the planet's carbon dioxide, or as fields devoted to soy for direct human consumption, a more land-efficient way to deliver protein to the world's people.

It takes 0.9 kg (2 lb) of feed to produce just 0.45 kg (1 lb) of chicken meat, and a little over 1.4 kg (3 lb) of feed for each 0.45 kg of pork.[41] In other words, in equivalent protein, soy fed directly to humans takes far less land to produce than meat does.

This is no trivial issue: while earth's population continues increasing, our supply of arable land is shrinking by 10 million hectares (nearly 25 million acres) yearly.[42] The shrinkage often stems from deforestation and from unsustainable agricultural practices. Worldwide, production of soy to feed livestock is implicated in both of these processes. In Brazil alone, in the early 2000s incautious soy cultivation for feeding animals led to the loss of 55 million metric tons of topsoil every year through erosion.[43] As fresh water, available arable land and a carbon-stable atmosphere dissipate, we must consider whether we really need to eat so much meat. In the long run, can our economies endure the loss of so many resources?

For families unfortunate enough to live near factory farms, a more urgent question is how to endure their most repugnant problem: vast quantities of bodily waste. Not all the grain and soy the animals eat becomes meat; plenty becomes excrement. Industrial hog operations generally 'dispose of' the waste either in open-air lagoons or else on nearby cropland, where it is spread in solid form or mixed with water and sprayed. But there are not enough appropriate fields for all the manure produced, so often the amount applied exceeds what crops can handle. The terrain is really just a repository for dung. Ammonia emanates from that terrain and, from the lagoons, hydrogen sulphide, causing headaches, respiratory difficulty and eye irritation in workers and nearby residents – not to mention a stench so fierce that local property values drop, and in some places residents defensively closet themselves indoors nearly all the time.

The u.s. state of Iowa alone produces 45 million metric tons of hog excrement annually.[44] Sometimes the faecal lagoons leak, spilling their foul contents. The group Iowa Citizens for Community Improvement has documented 800 manure spills from the state's factory farms since 1995.[45] Of particular concern is how spilled manure washes into streams and rivers. This run-off is a significant reason why 751 Iowa waterways were officially classified as 'impaired' in 2014, meaning they suffered from pollution serious enough to threaten humans and wildlife.[46]

Iowa is not alone. North Carolina had particular trouble with animal waste in the summer of 1995, when in three separate disasters, well over 12 million litres (2,640,000 gallons) of pig and chicken waste burst out of lagoons and into river systems. Millions of fish and other aquatic animals were poisoned. Then, in 1999, Hurricane Floyd overwhelmed factory farms with flooding, drowning thousands of trapped pigs and unleashing millions more litres of lagoon excrement.[47]

These are merely the most egregious of North Carolina's animal waste crises, and North Carolina's are merely among the most internationally publicized of the world's factory-farm faeces problems. China, the Philippines and many other countries have experienced messes in conjunction with livestock so profitably raised on cheap grain and soy. Even farmed fish produce dung hazards. Thus the waste from tilapia – a fish whose growth on a corn-and-soy diet is so speedy and efficient that it is often considered an ideal source of animal protein – is polluting fresh water in developing nations like Honduras.

Globally, regulations to improve the handling of animal waste are gradually being enacted, but enforcement often lags. There is a bright spot in this murky picture, however: 'biogas', produced by the fermenting of manure (or other organic matter). The fermentation produces methane, which is captured and used for energy. In countries as varied as the u.s., Germany, Austria, Sweden, India and China, biogas is used for cooking and home heating, for generating electricity, or even for vehicle fuel.

Using manure for biogas reduces odours in waste lagoon communities, is a renewable system as long as humans continue to raise abundant livestock and is relatively clean. It retrieves some of the energy put into raising grain, soy and then animals in the meat production chain. The major problem with biogas is that, despite sophisticated fermentation and methane-capture technologies in some locations (notably 88 Smithfield manure lagoons in Missouri), at present biogas costs more than other fuels. But as countries focus on environmental concerns and seek independence from foreign energy, investing in biogas technologies becomes more attractive.

THE COST–BENEFIT ANALYSES for biogas are complex, as are the costs and benefits of the entire chain that takes soy and corn, turns them into confined animals and heaped up manure, turns the animals into cuts of meat and finally turns the meat into human nutrition. The model has spread globally since the Second World War, bringing in its wake improved iron levels in children, tasty meat dishes, factory-farm and abattoir jobs, infections, pollution, scientific research and international trade. The American Soybean Association, the USDA and their partners in industry and government have worked diligently to forge this multifaceted reality. Unfortunately for U.S. interests, other countries also jumped deeply into the game; their story is next.

SIX

SOY SWOOPS SOUTH

In 2012 a Brazilian photojournalist, Ueslei Marcelino, visited the Xingu Indigenous Park, a protected area in Brazil's central state of Mato Grosso. Mato Grosso provides headwaters for Amazon tributaries, and it contains three major ecosystems – the most biodiverse tropical savannah in the world, the planet's largest tropical wetland and Amazonian rainforest – as well as transitional zones among them. Xingu lies in a transitional area between the savannah and rainforest and thus harbours a wide variety of wildlife and natural landscapes.

In the Xingu community of the Yawalapiti people, Marcelino witnessed grand preparations for a multi-tribal ceremony celebrating life, death and rebirth. Young Yawalapiti men participated in wrestling matches to see who would later compete against members of other indigenous groups in the park. The haunting, rhythmic sounds of giant bamboo flutes animated dances. Elders chanted prayers to honour the dead. People painted elaborate, bright designs on each other's bodies using seeds and natural oils. Men waded into a river, catching fish to dry and store. Children gleefully jumped off trees into the river's refreshing waters below, and everyone participated in growing and processing cassava. Although Yawalapiti leaders expressed concern to Marcelino about environmental threats to their beautiful home and way of life, what struck the journalist most, and what comes through in his photos for the Reuters news agency, was the delight the Yawalapiti experience in their lifestyle. He nicknamed their home 'the village of joy'.[1]

Almost completely encircling Xingu park are cattle farms and tidy fields brimming with flourishing green soy plants. Ranchers and then soy farmers from southern Brazil tore out the natural vegetation around Xingu in order to create profitable enterprises. The farmers laboured arduously to prepare their land for soy, and they continue working hard to bring ever more modern, cost-effective agricultural techniques to their fields. They study the land and plan carefully, investing in excellent fertilizers, pesticides, herbicides, equipment and seeds. They farm on an immense scale, and because they have prospered, they have been able to build their own schools, churches, courthouses, hospitals and roads. They are proud of their pioneering lifestyle; they are high achievers, resourceful, dynamic. Their communities and properties bring them joy.

Lamentably, these two rewarding ways of life, each with its own virtues, exist side-by-side in anxious tension. Each lays claim

Combine harvesters in Mato Grosso, Brazil, bring in the soybeans.

to large swathes of land, and the two types of people must share the air and water that circulate from farms to wilder regions and back. What happens to one group affects the other, and not always in ways that are fair. Xingu peoples are troubled, for example, by changes in the park's water quality. In the past 25 years their rivers have become warmer and more clouded with silt – qualities that threaten the populations of fish, the residents' main source of protein. Scientific research confirms what Xingu inhabitants had already deduced: deforestation at the rivers' headwaters is to blame. At times, deforestation has poured so much eroding mud into the region's river systems that the water has been constantly dark. It has been impossible to hunt fish with traditional bows and arrows, since no one can actually see the fish. The residents of Xingu also worry that pesticides sprayed on nearby soy fields are contaminating their water supply.

The tension in the region around Xingu is just one example of a process occurring over and over again, since the 1980s in Brazil first, and then in Argentina, Paraguay, Bolivia and Uruguay. Soy plantings have hurtled into wilderness areas with accelerating speed that only began to slow down in 2006. Conflicts among interested parties, often profoundly at cross-purposes, have at times been severe. On one side, standing together cheering on what they see as the march of progress, are many government agencies, multinational soy-processing firms and owners of huge, productive soy farms. Opposing them, sometimes vehemently, are other government agencies, indigenous peoples, rural smallholders and environmentalists – who denounce, litigate and negotiate. They seek, often desperately, to protect ecosystems, livelihoods and cultures. Each side accuses the other of engaging in unjust invasions. Each side has broken laws, and there have been murders, solved and unsolved, of key actors. The Wild West is now south of the equator.

Earth's burgeoning population and passion for meat would probably have pushed expansion of soy into South America at some point no matter what. The actual trigger came with the sea and the wind – or rather, lack of wind. Winds off the western coast of South America blow from east to west in an oscillating pattern of intensity – some years they are stronger, some years weaker. In strong years, the winds push warm surface water westward to Indonesia and New Guinea, where it sits like a giant tepid pool within the Pacific

Ocean. Meanwhile, along the western coast of South America, cold, deep-sea currents gain the space to rise upwards, bringing with them nutrients nourishing a plethora of fish. Fishermen depend on this cold water. When the winds weaken, as they do periodically, the warm surface water remains near South America, and in fact warm water begins to spread eastward from the warm pool in Asia. The cold, nourishing water stays trapped down below, the fish are less plentiful and the fishermen have much less to sell. So it happened in 1972–3, when Peru's anchovy harvest dropped by nearly 90 per cent.[2]

The anchovies had been expected on the world market for animal feed. When the fishery collapsed, global prices for feed proteins jumped upwards, including prices for soy. Aggravating the loss of anchovies was the failure of West Africa's peanut crop due to severe drought; peanuts are also used in animal feed. In the U.S., the Nixon administration feared that rising soy prices would cause domestic inflation. They reasoned that they should keep soy cheap to keep the cost of meat down – after all, it seemed that the American public expected, even demanded, cheap meat. Keep the soy at home, they thought, and it won't become too scarce, and then too expensive. So the U.S. government temporarily halted soy exports.

The Japanese, largely dependent on the U.S. for soy, saw the writing on the wall. Panicked, they lost no time in searching for a new supplier. But who? Where? No other very large supplier existed. All right then, they decided, they would simply have to help create one. Thus began decades of Japanese investment in Brazilian soybean agriculture and research. Japanese immigrants had introduced soy cultivation to Brazil decades earlier, and farmers in Brazil's southeast were already growing some soy and exporting it to Japan. But now Japanese officials partnered with the Brazilian government in much more ambitious plans. These efforts would eventually swell Brazil's soy output from 1.5 million metric tons in 1970 to nearly 100 million metric tons in the 2015–16 growing season.[3]

In 1973 the Brazilian government formed a forward-thinking agronomic agency, EMBRAPA. Brazilian functionaries realized how appropriately soy had been called 'the magic bean' during the Second World War and hoped their country could become, like Jack with his beanstalk, rich from that magic. Accordingly, EMBRAPA devoted considerable resources to studying soy. In the agency's early years,

A cascade of soybeans in Mato Grosso being transferred for export.

Japan helped fund their experimentation with the plant in unfamiliar soils, latitudes and climates.

Soon EMBRAPA set their sights on the 'empty' centre of the country, where they hoped soy agriculture could somehow take hold. That vast region, virtually untouched at the time, is more than eight times the size of the UK, considerably larger than all the named deserts in Australia put together, and nearly as big as the entire U.S. Midwest. Brazilians call this savannah the *Cerrado*, which literally means 'closed' – a region long perceived as impenetrable to agriculture, a useless wasteland. There were good reasons for the label. Cerrado soils lacked important nutrients, were highly acidic and were laced with toxic levels of aluminium; conventional crops such as soy barely tolerated them. To make matters worse, the unvarying day length of the Cerrado's low latitudes was a poor fit for soy.

Solutions were sought, and found. New soy varieties had to be developed, a feat that EMBRAPA scientists pulled off through long, painstaking research, breeding over forty new cultivars suitable for tropical latitudes. As for the Cerrado's abysmal soil quality, in the 1950s an American scientist, Colin McClung, had demonstrated that application of dolomitic lime to those soils would correct the worst problems. EMBRAPA experts built on this knowledge, pinpointing precisely how to fertilize cerrado soils to transform them into prime cropland. For their accomplishments in opening what had been closed, turning the Cerrado into a realm of soy, the 2006 World Food Prize – agriculture's equivalent of a Nobel – was jointly awarded to an indefatigable EMBRAPA soil specialist, Edson Lobato; a visionary former Brazilian Minister of Agriculture and early shaper of EMBRAPA, Alysson Paolinelli; and the American scientist, Dr McClung.

When McClung made his breakthrough, he worked for a Rockefeller company that sought to make money while solving world problems. Back home in the U.S., soy cultivators resented such efforts. Why, they asked, should American businesses help Brazil become a major rival in global soy production? But the brunt of farmers' ire was reserved for U.S. government departments that also aided Brazil. In the 1960s the U.S. Agency for International Development (USAID) and President Kennedy's 'Alliance for Progress' sent American agronomists to Brazil to assist in setting up a world-class programme of soybean research. Plant geneticists, pathologists and breeders from the U.S. participated, and USAID also provided funding for promising Brazilian crop specialists to be trained at U.S. universities. World Food Prize winner Edson Lobato was, in fact, one of those USAID beneficiaries. Many American soy farmers came to see these international development efforts as an outrageous misuse of their government's resources. They asked, appalled, 'You tax my earnings so you can aid my competitor?'

Some American farmers also wondered why the USDA and U.S. universities – many of whom are taxpayer-funded – were so willing to share thousands of soy samples with EMBRAPA. And why were agricultural universities so happy to enrol and educate Brazilian soy farmers? Whose side were they on, anyway?

Their consternation was understandable, given their circumstances. By the mid-1980s, many American soy farmers were deep in debt. When soy prices had been high in the 1960s and '70s, they had borrowed money to expand their farms and upgrade their machinery. But in the '80s the price of soy dropped, as did the value of u.s. agricultural exports as a whole. Farmers and farm states were mired in budgetary troubles. The federal government began debating major new farm legislation, including financial rescues.

In the midst of this turmoil, the ASA rallied its members against what it saw as government betrayal on behalf of foreigners. It repeatedly asserted this viewpoint to its members, the press and politicians. Senator Dale Bumpers of Arkansas, a significant soy-producing state, shared the ASA's indignation. He successfully pushed through an amendment to the Farm Bill making it illegal for any u.s. agency to fund improved foreign production of an agricultural commodity that would compete with u.s. exports.[4] In explaining the amendment, Senator Bumpers took phrases directly from ASA newsletters and press releases. The ASA and its farmers were in no mood for generosity towards upstart Brazil; u.s. aid programmes would have to stick to helping foreigners understand how to use soy, not how to grow it.

But according to crop scientists, the farmers were short-sighted. Acclaimed soy geneticist Theodore Hymowitz notes that Brazil experienced infestations of a soy-attacking fungus, 'Asian rust', long before the disease reached u.s. fields. Brazilians developed expertise in the organism's life cycle and the optimal times, concentrations and intervals for applying fungicides. Now they can help u.s. farmers understand how to combat this pest. Agricultural assistance is thus a two-way street, Hymowitz argues, and building cooperative relationships with 'competitor' nations can prove highly beneficial in the long run.[5]

Brazil has in fact become a world leader in soy cultivation and research. Interestingly, its government's approach to international aid combines assistance for crop production with production-oriented sales. As EMBRAPA strategist Geraldo Martha Jr and his colleagues explain,

The success of Brazilian tropical agriculture motivates poor countries to seek information and support for technology transfer . . . EMBRAPA decided to have [its own] researchers in less developed countries, creating EMBRAPA Africa, in Accra (Ghana); EMBRAPA Venezuela, in Caracas; and EMBRAPA Americas, in Panama. The goal in this initiative is to transfer knowledge . . . and to look for opportunities in licensing EMBRAPA's technology.[6]

Brazil has chosen to nurture potential competitors since those countries can be present-day customers.

Meanwhile, global changes have continued to drive soy expansion. Europe's 'Mad Cow' crisis spurred production: in 1990 the UK, and then in 1994 the European Commission, banned animal offal as a protein source in feeds for cattle and other ruminants. Soy was a logical replacement, and European demand for soy meal rose. Then, as China's economy has boomed, its population's desire for meat, and therefore indirectly for soy meal in animal feeds, has also fuelled the explosion of soy agriculture in South America.

Back in the Cerrado, these international processes can feel at once very important and absurdly remote. More immediate, insistent concerns claim cultivators' attention. Especially in the early years, their physical survival, the survival of their plants and the solvency of their finances were all very much at stake. The contrasting life stories of two prominent soy farmers show how carefully ambitions had to be shepherded.

The first of Brazil's grand soy farmers, Olacyr de Moraes, was once one of humanity's wealthiest men. In addition to vast soy plantations, at one time de Moraes owned a construction and engineering business, sugar refineries, limestone quarries, a bank and a hydroelectric power company. In the 1970s, in conjunction with a cattle-fattening operation, de Moraes began sowing soybeans in Mato Grosso; at the time, the region offered barely any transportation or communications infrastructure and few human resources. Just to get equipment, people, seeds, supplies and cattle into the area, de Moraes and his business partners paid labourers to hack paths through seemingly endless kilometres of scrubby woods. But the investments paid off; the farming eventually flourished. By the 1980s de Moraes was the largest individual soy farmer in the world. He also tilled corn and cotton. Working with EMBRAPA, he invested in research on developing soy varieties suitable for the Cerrado, earning him the sobriquet 'The King of Soy'. At its height, his empire knitted together forty companies and was valued at $1.2 billion.[7]

But the king overreached. Aware that the price of transporting soy from far-inland Mato Grosso to Brazil's Atlantic harbours was a major obstacle in lowering the price of Brazilian soy on the world market, in the 1990s he poured $200 million into building a railway to connect his farms to the port of Santos, southeast of São Paulo. He dreamed of a 4,800-km (3,000-mile) rail network that would even reach a port on the Amazon River. Unfortunately, a deal with the State of São Paulo to build a bridge over the Paraná River suffered long delays. The rail construction proved more difficult and costly than expected. Creditors came hounding, and in 2006 de Moraes sold the company at great loss. Today the rail system is operational, but only in the southern half of the network that de Moraes envisioned. Completion of the northern segments is still under discussion. Journalist Pat Joseph summarized de Moraes's saga in the *Virginia Quarterly Review*:

> In trying to transform the region through privately financed infrastructure, de Moraes bet everything and lost his shirt . . . [In 2006] he met with President da Silva and, in what must have seemed a very rich twist of fate for both men, the once-mighty empire-builder begged assistance from the former union radical turned head-of-state. A tearful supplicant, de Moraes reportedly exclaimed in anguish, 'I paid the price of pioneering.'[8]

In his later years, de Moraes rebuilt some of his fortune with mining investments; his company had the good fortune in 2011 to discover thallium in northeast Brazil. This was a valuable find, as thallium is uncommon around the world and has many uses in industry and medicine. De Moraes saw a chance to, as he put it, 'make in the mining area a "replay" of what I did in the soybean business'.[9] In 2015, when at age 84 he succumbed to pancreatic cancer, his tattered finances were on the mend.

But he was no longer the King of Soy. That title passed to a man who, in 2002, had begun renting a soy farm from the floundering de

Moraes. The new titan, Blairo Maggi, had worked for decades with his mother, four sisters, brothers-in-law and a handful of long-time, trusted employees in the family business, building on his father's legacy of colonizing the Cerrado. Purchasing and leasing more and more land (in Mato Grosso, land rent is often paid in sacks of soy), they created a Maggi domain that harvests some 400,000 metric tons of soybeans a year,[10] as well as cotton and corn in rotation with dominant soy. The magic bean became the Maggi bean. The family's network of agricultural and energy companies, the Amaggi Group, is now worth over $6 billion, with soybeans at its heart.[11] Controlling multiple links in the chain of how soy is produced, transported and used, Amaggi works in seed production, forestry, livestock, fertilizer sales, warehousing, soybean crushing, power generation, port management, river transport, export and import.

Along the way Mr Maggi has had his ups and downs. He has lost millions of dollars and made billions more. In 2002, the same year he leased the de Moraes property, he entered politics to fulfil a religious promise to help people: one of his daughters had been cured of lymphatic cancer. Elected governor of Mato Grosso, he was later re-elected and held the position until 2010. During his tenure, the state's economy grew at the average speed of the 'Asian tiger' nations, around 10 per cent per year, even while the administration managed to reduce local tax rates. The phenomenal growth enabled the state to construct over 68,000 homes for Mato Grosso's poor, along with hundreds of modern, well-furnished schools.[12]

But nothing comes without a price, and it was the natural environment that paid for improvements in people's lives. Soy farmers wishing to expand offered Mato Grosso cattle ranchers handsome prices for cleared pastures. As the ranchers sold those properties, they were tempted to snap up cheap, virgin jungle and raze it to create new pastures, sometimes with legal permission, and sometimes not. At alarming rates, the soy boom indirectly – yet relentlessly, ruthlessly – pushed the frontier of eco-destruction. The year 2002 saw a 40 per cent jump in the rate of Amazon deforestation,[13] much along its southern border where Cerrado farmers were increasing their soy holdings. Fire was a favourite method for removing trees, and in that unusually dry year the flames sometimes burned out of control. Smoke was so thick that some airline flights had to be cancelled.

Yet Maggi was unperturbed. In 2003 he asserted to the *New York Times*:

> To me, a 40 percent increase in deforestation doesn't mean anything at all, and I don't feel the slightest guilt over what we are doing here. We're talking about an area larger than Europe that has barely been touched, so there is nothing at all to get worried about.[14]

In a 2004 interview he further argued:

> It's very easy to defend the Amazon on the beaches of Rio or in the offices of Washington or London. But our families need jobs and homes. Do you know how many poor people there are in Brazil? Soy will raise people's standards of living.[15]

He also accused Europeans and Americans of crying 'when we cut a tree, but they don't cry when children die or do not have an education'.[16]

The activist group Greenpeace vociferously disagreed that destruction of the natural world is the only solution to poverty. In 2005 they 'awarded' Maggi a 'Golden Chainsaw' prize for having an unconscionably detrimental impact on the Amazon. Ironically, Maggi had already been in secret talks with conservationists about possible systems to compensate farmers and ranchers for not cutting down trees. But because the talks had not yet yielded results, in the public sphere shaming was the order of the day.

Next Greenpeace targeted Cargill, which sold Brazilian soy to many businesses in Europe. They did so with well-publicized denunciations of Cargill, and also by pressuring the company's customers. In 2006 Greenpeace's public-relations campaign convinced McDonald's to reject chicken raised on soy from newly deforested areas of the Brazilian Amazon. Greenpeace dubbed this their 'McVictory' and helped McDonald's convince other food businesses making purchases benefiting Cargill to sign a 'no new deforestation' policy – in Europe notably Marks & Spencer, Tesco, Sainsbury's, ASDA, Waitrose and Carrefour, and in the U.S., Wal-Mart. Soy traders and planters got the message. Failing to take deforestation seriously was becoming an economic liability for Mato Grosso's most lucrative

In Brazil, cattle ranchers have often cleared Amazon forest; later they sell the land profitably to soybean farmers and then deforest a new area for their herds.

economic sector. All of the giant soy-shipping companies in Brazil – Cargill, ADM, Bunge, Dreyfus and Amaggi – agreed to a limited two-year 'Soy Moratorium' on buying beans from newly deforested areas.

Still, back in Mato Grosso Governor Maggi focused on his self-styled role of providing people with jobs and more affordable food. Unabashed, in 2007 he forcefully challenged his critics with the pointed query, 'Do you want trees and hunger?'[17]

But by 2008 he'd had a change of heart. Concluding that he needed to take environmentalist views more into account, he found ways to compromise so that his business, his state and his country could make money even as Amazon and Cerrado ecosystems were preserved. He also got the environmentalists to take him seriously in negotiations, rather than just try to tar and feather him. As governor, he had the state of Mato Grosso invest $2.3 million in satellite imagery analyses to help catch illegal loggers.[18] In November 2009 he offered amnesty to farmers operating their farms with an illegally low level of land set aside for conservation, but he insisted that within four years they would have to bring their properties up to the federally mandated level (which varies depending on the type of ecosystem).

Maggi also began a dialogue with leaders of the new UN initiative on Reducing Emissions from Deforestation and Forest

Degradation (REDD). REDD offers financial incentives for ranchers, farmers, loggers and indigenous peoples to leave forests intact. Recognizing that REDD payments could be much more remunerative for the state of Mato Grosso than selling soy, beef or timber, Maggi began exploring precisely how wealthier nations might demonstrate their valuation of Brazilian wilderness in monetary terms. As of early 2017, Brazil had not yet joined the UN in an official REDD partnership – many Brazilians doubt that the world community would ever stick to their commitments – but Maggi, for one, has shown himself willing to study the possibilities.

Maggi also worked with the World Wildlife Fund and other organizations on certifying soy grown according to basic environmental standards. Participants in this initiative set up an international organization, the Round Table for Responsible Soy (RTRS), to hammer out guidelines for production that would be acceptable both to environmentalists and to agro-capitalists. The Amaggi Group became the first soy-farming enterprise in the world to gain RTRS certification, a distinction that allows its soybeans to fetch a higher price from consumer goods companies seeking a 'greener' profile. The most prominent such company is the colossal food, soap and cosmetics firm Unilever, whose brands include Hellmann's, Amora, Dove, Knorr, Lipton, Bertolli, Magnum, Marmite, Carte d'Or, Cif, Omo, Vaseline, Pond's and over two hundred more.

In his many complex endeavours, then, Blairo Maggi has exerted undeniable influence. In 2009 *Forbes* magazine listed him as one of the planet's most powerful people, citing his massive soy empire and his imprints on the natural world, both negative and positive.[19] With his clout ever-transcendent, in 2011 he was elected to the Brazilian senate for an eight-year term, and in 2013 that body chose him to head their Environmental Commission. People concerned about Brazil's natural wonders then debated – was this the chainsaw guarding the tree, or was this an open-minded leader uniquely positioned to broker responsible, workable deals? Maggi was regularly seen cooperating in public with international environmental groups such as the Nature Conservancy, the Environmental Defense Fund and the World Wildlife Fund. Yet he has also argued in the Brazilian Senate against large fines for soy farmers who have broken environmental laws, and against any abrupt banning of pesticides sprayed from aeroplanes onto soy fields.

In 2016 Maggi became Brazil's Minister of Agriculture, Livestock and Supply. Balancing many competing interests, he manages to stay aloft on a pinnacle of prominence and prosperity. It appears that there will, in the end, be a striking contrast between his destiny in agribusiness and that of Olacyr de Moraes – though, of course, as de Moraes himself showed, destinies can be fickle.

Yet in terms of soybean production, Blairo Maggi is actually no longer Brazil's King of Soy. That distinction passed to his first cousin, Eraí Maggi Scheffer, whose nearly 225,000 hectares (approximately 555,000 acres) of Mato Grosso soy fields made him the largest individual soy farmer in the world.[20] Although the net worth of Scheffer's enterprise, Bom Futuro ('Good Future'), is far less than that of Amaggi because its auxiliary businesses are smaller, it is still an economic force to be reckoned with.

It has, alas, also been embroiled in controversy, despite engaging in some appropriate ecological practices and despite the business community's respect for its successes. The company has good procedures for reducing soil erosion, and it maintains the legally required amount of woodland reserves – but to the consternation of environmentalists, like many Brazilian farm managers those at Bom Futuro use paraquat, a weedkiller that withers green plants indiscriminately and can be toxic to humans and animals. The EU banned this herbicide in 2007 because of correlations between paraquat exposure and Parkinson's disease, a progressive, devastating disorder of the human nervous system.

Moreover, Bom Futuro has in the past been found irresponsible in relation to worker exposure to pesticides: in 2008 the Brazilian Ministry of Labour freed 41 workers on a Bom Futuro farm who had been subjected to degrading conditions and inadequate protection from chemicals. The labourers had at times been required to work twelve-hour shifts with only the woods as a toilet, no toilet paper, no gloves for handling pesticides, no way to wash their hands, no clean place to eat and a tiny fetid shack for ten men to sleep in together on rotting mattresses. The company argued that this was an isolated mistake – inappropriate behaviour on the part of that particular farm's managers. In response to this incident, a court indicted Eraí Scheffer in 2010 for the crime of using slave labour; in 2013 he and three co-defendants were acquitted. The presiding judge argued that although the work conditions had been harsh and inappropriate, the labourers had not endured them for long enough – only weeks or months, not years and years – to be truly akin to slaves.[21]

Sadly, degrading labour, heavy use of chemicals and deforestation are common in Mato Grosso and other cerrado states. The soy industry is a significant source of such woes. Worse yet, bloodshed has often accompanied soy expansion. Two common forms of violence have been the predation of bandits on soy farmers, and the assassination of environmentalists trying to impede soy-spurred deforestation. In Mato Grosso the soy farmers are now well established, and such lawlessness is largely a thing of the past. But in the neighbouring state of Pará, where property claims are not yet as well delineated as in Mato Grosso, frequent bloodshed continues. In May 2011, a husband and wife in Pará – Brazilian activists who had long fought illegal logging pushed into their area by the burgeoning soy frontier – were murdered. Just six months earlier the husband, José Cláudio Ribeiro da Silva, had noted in a TED talk that he regularly received death threats but would not give up defending the ecology of his state. He stood up for the sustainable harvesting of rainforest products as an alternative to massive ranching and farming, and he paid with his life. The murders capped a decade that saw 448 Brazilian land and environmental activists killed.[22] Hardly any of these crimes have been solved or punished. In the Wild West of South America, intimidation and outright violence lurk behind the bucolic juxtaposition of verdant fields and luxuriant forests.

Yet the picture is not all bleak. The Round Table, the Brazilian government's efforts to halt deforestation, the improved use of satellite technology to catch illegal loggers, and especially the Soy Moratorium, have all significantly decreased destruction of the Amazon for soy plantings. A 2014 report in the journal *Science* found that before the moratorium, 30 per cent of Brazil's soy expansion came through Amazon deforestation, whereas after the voluntary measure, almost none did.[23] True, some landowners simply used previously denuded pastures for soy and then cleared new land for pasture (sometimes in flagrant violation of Brazilian law). This destruction unfortunately did not officially count as a violation of the moratorium. Nor did clearing land for rice or corn production, and then after a few years quietly changing it over to soy. Moreover, Cerrado areas were not included in the moratorium and so were not spared, prompting the report's authors to call for more stringent protections for the savannah. Still, the overall effect of this partnership between private companies and environmentalist groups has been quite positive. Because of its public-relations impact on the soy market, the moratorium has been more effective at stopping deforestation than any of the Brazilian government's efforts. Brazilian forest rangers strive heroically to save the wilderness; they endure kidnappings, vandalism and death threats in the course of their work. But their enforcement units are woefully underfunded and understaffed. The moratorium has the weight of the international market to bolster it, and that has made all the difference.

Statistics from EMBRAPA show that much of the recent increase in soy production has been due to improved yields rather than hectare expansion. Amazon deforestation dropped dramatically from its highs of 1995 and 2004 (with woodland losses, respectively, of 29,059 and 27,772 sq. km / 11,220 and 10,723 sq. miles) to the much smaller 4,571 sq. km (1,765 sq. miles) of 2012.[24] Strategists at EMBRAPA trumpet that about '85 per cent of the Amazon Biome and [approximately] 55 per cent of the *Cerrado* Biome are still covered with the original vegetation!' and reassure the world that 'The Brazilian agriculture transformation – predominantly based on productivity gains – is proof that it is possible to have an efficient and competitive agriculture in the tropics.'[25]

But an upswing in deforestation in 2013,[26] probably prompted by the effects of the 2012 U.S. drought in raising world soy prices, had environmentalists worried that EMBRAPA was too optimistic. Then, when Amazon losses suddenly spiked in early 2014, activists became truly alarmed. The Soy Moratorium had been repeatedly extended, and they called for it to be prolonged yet again; to their delight in 2016 it was indeed extended, 'indefinitely'. The activists also urged that loopholes in the moratorium be closed and that monitoring for compliance be more thorough.

For its part, EMBRAPA is an agricultural agency, and it continues to tout beneficial aspects of the Brazilian agricultural miracle. Its employees like to note that the real price of food in Brazil has declined drastically since the 1970s. Strategist Martha notes that the real cost of a typical food 'basket' in São Paulo is now only half of what it cost in 1975.[27] Some 40 million Brazilians were lifted out of abject poverty over the past ten years alone, in part because of lower food prices and the jobs available through agribusiness and corollary enterprises.[28]

Brazilians can eat more chicken, pork and edible oil than ever before. The Brazilian public has little interest in eating soy protein; they mostly see it as food for animals or the poor. But even though soy protein is a 'lowly' product, the poor have in fact benefited from it, as federal and state government programmes provide flavoured soy milks to children at schools in distressed neighbourhoods and sometimes to pregnant women needing assistance.

Brazil's transportation infrastructure has also improved in the past two decades in no small part because of soy agriculture. Although better infrastructure crushes natural landscapes and sometimes even the livelihoods of local people, it also makes a wide variety of other economic activities feasible. Towns and jobs spring up. Improved health care becomes available. Schools open. Many Brazilians applaud soy as the bestower of these benefits.

Brazil's infrastructure is still inadequate, however. Transportation is the country's biggest headache in exporting soy from the Centre-West interior. The town of Sorriso, in the middle of Mato Grosso's soy region, is nearly 2,200 km (1,367 miles) from the agricultural port of Paranaguá on the Atlantic coast. In Europe, this is even farther than the distance from London to Kiev, or in Australia, from Sydney to Alice Springs. It is farther than the corresponding soy transit route from Des Moines, Iowa, to the port of New Orleans. There is a big distinction between the U.S. and Brazilian examples, moreover: on the journey soy makes from Mato Grosso southward, there is no river comparable to the Mississippi for ease of transport.

On the contrary, Brazilian transport is notoriously difficult. Trucks piled high with soybeans on Mato Grosso roads have to muddle through a legion of potholes; with each bounce, beans trickle out of the trucks. In 2010 a local farm organization estimated that 47,500 tons of soy are lost in this manner annually.[29] Trucking routes in Brazil are also often extremely clogged with traffic, especially near the Atlantic ports. Some Cerrado farmers have found alternate routes north, creatively cobbling together paths using various river and land systems. But for those options to be more cost-effective, much infrastructure is still needed.

These problems put Brazil at a disadvantage in exporting soy compared to its principal South American rival, Argentina. That country's soy agriculture mirrors Brazil's in many ways – the combination of development, economic benefit, environmental degradation and flashpoints of social conflict – yet Argentina has also danced its own particular tango with soy.

In the 1970s small, left-wing guerrilla groups carried out bombings and assassinations in a campaign against the Argentine government. In response, agitated federal authorities increasingly favoured the business class and brutalized opponents of their regimes. Especially between 1976 and 1983, when a military dictatorship held power, the government kidnapped, imprisoned, tortured, murdered or permanently 'disappeared' tens of thousands of Argentine citizens – a traumatic period known as the Dirty War. Many prisoners were drugged into a stupor and thrown alive out of aeroplanes into the Atlantic Ocean. Thankfully, the government's colossal failure to wrest the Falkland Islands from Great Britain in 1982, and the war's high financial costs – including for the agricultural elite, who were served up new export taxes to finance the conflict – finally forced the military from power in 1983.

During the Dirty War, smallholders and indigenous peoples stood little chance of protecting their land claims against the encroachments of well-connected elites seeking to enlarge their properties. Predations especially took place where hunters, small farmers or small ranchers lacked clear legal title to the territories they worked, even though they had often productively used the land for generations. Although Argentina's Civil Code grants ownership of previously underutilized lands to anyone occupying and usefully working them for twenty years or more, rural people with little schooling were unaware of their rights. Many elite encroachers managed to convince – or bribe – local authorities into approving their access to such plots, to be used for a variety of purposes. As waves of soy swelled throughout Argentina from the 1990s forward, predictably much of this land was converted to producing the profitable bean.

According to Argentine activists for environmental and social justice, land usurpations have been notably harsh in the northwest corner of the country, where from the 1970s to the present the police, military and pro-elite vigilantes have used bulldozers, tear gas, beatings, threatening gunshots, gunfire from helicopters, legal trickery, kidnappings, torture, murder, fire, theft and death threats to expel long-time smallholder residents.

Members of a Guaraní-Kaiowá community walk through soy fields that took over territory they claim in Mato Grosso do Sul, Brazil. In 2016 this dispute turned violent, with multiple casualties among the indigenous people as farmers shot those trying to occupy the land. South America has experienced numerous conflicts between soy farmers and First Nations.

In this area, the lands taken have mostly been forests whose natural products were being sustainably harvested. In fact, the government of Salta Province rushed to issue as many deforestation permits as possible before Argentina's 2007 Forest Law made granting such permission more difficult. Bureaucrats issued permits to soy farmers as well as to loggers and road builders for the petroleum industry. Many of the permits were based on shockingly sloppy – even farcical – environmental impact statements. Moreover, the rule stipulating that affected communities be consulted in advance of any deforestation was shirked through sneaky means, such as failing to notify community members of impact hearings, or holding the hearings in locations to which it was far too distant for community members to travel. The resultant loss of forests has hurt the tree-dependent livelihoods of the Wichí and Guaraní peoples, among others. As one Wichí woman explained to an activist, 'Soya is like a big whirlwind that consumes the mountain, the land and our history. It leaves us chewing on nothing but air and bitterness.'[30]

The loss of vegetation has made it more difficult for soils to absorb rainwater, or even to stay in place: in some areas of northwest Argentina, erosion has become a significant problem. These side effects of tree-cutting no doubt contributed to the 2006 and 2009 overflows of the Tartagal River at the city of the same name, causing landslides that destroyed first a road bridge and then a railway overpass, killing three people and bringing mayhem to the lives of another 10,000. During the floods of 2006, the National University of Salta decried 'the irrational management of natural resources and the absence of the State [in regulating their use] . . . the small producers are ruined, the indigenous communities have been devastated and their rights to the land violated.' The National Forest director dryly made his own statement: 'The price of soy doesn't include its environmental impact.'[31]

Deforestation for soy and other purposes probably also contributed to the 2009 regional outbreak of dengue fever – an illness with no specific cure and no vaccine – that made 26,000 people sick and killed six.[32] Lack of trees for shade increases air temperature, which in turn favours the longevity and abundant reproduction of mosquitoes carrying the dengue virus. Areas near deforestation have also seen a rise in leishmaniasis, a parasitic skin disease transmitted by sandflies. This infection can be difficult to treat, terribly disfiguring and sometimes fatal. Although soybeans are nutritious and can promote human health, their uncontrolled cultivation can set up unhealthy conditions.

By contrast with the pattern of usurping lands and felling trees, in other areas of Argentina sophisticated soy enterprises have dutifully rented agricultural plots from small farmers, particularly in the central Pampas region. Most of Argentina's rented fields are cultivated with soy, as soy enterprises are constantly hungry for more terrain. Partly because of soy agriculture, the price of Argentina's arable land rose dramatically – often 500 per cent – in the first decade of this century.[33] Soy is much valued in Argentina because it brings in foreign currency that Argentines use to shop in international markets. This 'green gold' accounts for over one-quarter of Argentina's exports and is the single biggest source of foreign currency.[34]

Yet soy cultivation also has negative economic impacts. Although Argentines consume large amounts of soy oil per capita, soy farming undermines other aspects of the country's food self-sufficiency. Many small farmers find it more profitable to lease their plots to soy growers than to cultivate the fruits, vegetables and grain that the population eats. The 'soyization' of Argentina has in recent years also influenced thousands of small dairy farms to close: the profitability of soy drives land rents too high for them, or the dairy farmers simply switch to growing soy themselves. Prices of important foods such as cheese, tomatoes and potatoes have risen. Of course, many varied factors influence Argentina's inflation, but to the extent that crops destined for human food are planted less and less, both food-price inflation and dependence on foreign food suppliers increase. Soy expansion, land values and the local costs of food are inextricably linked.

Besides the renting of many small plots, another creative feature of the soy business in Argentina is the presence of 'sowing pools', which are consortia of shareholders pooling their capital to farm on a very large scale. Because the profit margin for soy farming can be very thin for each bag harvested, mass production, reduced labour costs and economies of scale can spell the difference between a farm's financial survival and its demise. But this style of farming inevitably entails huge investments in land and high-tech farm equipment – hence group funding is essential for mid-size investors to join the game.

Whatever the context of Argentine soy cultivation – on land that was legitimately purchased, was seized, is rented, is farmed individually or is managed by a consortium – in Argentina virtually 100 per cent of planted soy is genetically engineered (GE).[35] In 1996, just after the Monsanto Company began marketing GE soy – discussed in Chapter Seven – Argentina authorized its cultivation. As in the U.S., Argentina's soy farmers quickly adopted the new seeds. Monsanto found Argentina's alacrity troubling, however, because the country's intellectual property laws contradicted the company's business model. Elsewhere in the world, Monsanto successfully prohibited farmers from saving any of their harvested Monsanto-patented seeds for use in later plantings, requiring them to sign a contract to this effect. The company thus obliged farmers wishing to use Monsanto seeds to repurchase them each season. In this manner, the company collected recurring royalties on its biotechnology, which it considered entirely justified because of its enormous expenditures in creating the novel seeds. This business model was repeatedly thwarted in Argentina, as the country's laws granted farmers the right to save *any* harvested seeds for later sowing and prevented Monsanto from suing them for doing so. Argentina's farmers have loved Monsanto's seeds but feel they should only have to pay for them once.

Monsanto was also alarmed that between 1998 and 2005, a thriving network smuggled bootleg Monsanto seeds into Brazil; at the time, most GE plantings were officially illegal in Brazil. As in Argentina, these farmer-saved seeds brought no profit to Monsanto. Then in the mid-2000s, even though cultivating certain GE seeds became legal in Brazil, Monsanto again faced an unfavourable legal environment, similar to the one it had encountered in Argentina. South America frustrated Monsanto: bean counting did not go well there. Once Monsanto's patent on its original GE soy technology expired in 2015, it was too late to recoup the revenues it had failed to garner on that continent.

But bean counting has gone just fine for the nation of Argentina. In 1991 President Carlos Menem's government instituted major agricultural reforms, reducing the power of government monopolies that had stultified farmer initiative. Farmers and soy processors may have looked askance at Menem's flamboyant, playboy shenanigans and public spats with his wife, but they gleefully cheered his agricultural policies. They paid particular attention to the elimination of taxes on exporting processed soy; by contrast, a 3.5 per cent tax on exports of whole, unrefined soybeans remained. The government had structured the taxes to spur more local soy processing, as it wanted the added value of refining the beans to bring further income to the country. The plan worked. The building of soy-processing plants proceeded apace: the industry sank $1 billion into new factories from 1997 to 2001.[36] In 1995 Argentina became the world's primary exporter of soy oil, and in 1997, its top exporter of soy meal, positions it has maintained since then.[37] A country lauded for refined architecture, wines and literature had found powerful economic reasons to refine an Asian bean.

In 2008 the honeymoon between the central government and Argentina's soy farmers soured. President Cristina Fernández de Kirchner's administration had decided that since world prices of soybeans and sunflowers were rising, it would be reasonable to raise taxes on oilseed exports. The government wished both to raise funds for increased public services, and to encourage farmers to switch to producing more staple foods. But the plan created a political crisis. Soy farmers, along with owners and workers in the many collateral businesses that serve soy agriculture, protested the new taxes, with weeks of roadblocks all over the country. Thousands of massed demonstrators pounded pots and pans in the capital in a type of noisy Latin American dissent called a *cacerolazo* ('casserole banging'). Counter-demonstrators, frustrated that the soy interests balked at contributing more to the general welfare via taxes, also took to the streets. Brawls ensued between the two groups. Professional truckers, meanwhile, were furious about the roadblocks and sometimes tried to remove the farmers and their heavy equipment forcibly.

The attempted dip into soy farmers' profits thus generated economic and political turmoil. Stymied transportation led to shortages of meat and dairy products in urban markets, and agricultural exporters had to renege on some of their contracts with Chinese buyers. Kirchner's political fortunes roiled. The Economy minister was forced to resign. Four months after the crisis began, the Senate sat for seventeen confrontational hours debating the tax, with such gridlock that the vice president was called to cast a tie-breaking vote; he voted against the president's policy. The government had backed down. The soy farmers had won.

But taxes have hardly been the only spark for outrage in Argentina's countryside. The cultivation and careful processing of beans have not always been accomplished via careful business practices. Landowners have sometimes failed to issue adequate protective gear to workers applying farm chemicals, and empty pesticide containers have sometimes been left lying around, inadequately decontaminated. Indignation has swirled around the poor training of certain pilots who sprayed fields with agricultural chemicals. Unfamiliar with their planes' GPS systems, and not being sure from the air where a particular farmer's lands began and ended, some of the hired pilots stationed children around field edges to wave their arms overhead, indicating property lines. These 'human flags'

Battling weeds, insects and fungi to produce our food, farmers strategically spray soy plants with pesticides. In South America, careless spraying near homes has sometimes led to protests and legal action.

were exposed to dangerous levels of chemicals (a problem in other soy-producing regions of South America as well). At other times, prosperous landowners or their employees have done slipshod work with truck sprayers nicknamed 'mosquitoes' because of their long, latticed booms resembling insect wings. Individuals doing the spraying have gone beyond permitted areas, or have sprayed during windy conditions, so that the fields of local smallholders have been doused with herbicides toxic to their crops. Occasionally, searing chemicals have coated villagers' skin, with dire consequences.

Although such offences are not normal in Argentina, they have occurred too often and have rarely been penalized. At last, in 2012, an Argentine court sentenced a farmer and a pesticide pilot for inappropriately spraying chemicals, including a Monsanto herbicide very commonly applied to soy fields. The spraying had occurred around a working-class neighbourhood on the edge of Córdoba, a city in Argentina's central farming belt where controversy about the increasing use of agrochemicals has simmered for years. The neighbourhood, Ituzaingó, lies surrounded on three sides by soy plantations. 'Mosquito' and aerial sprayers had veered much too close to human habitations. The two men were spared prison, instead being sentenced to years of community service. They were also banned from applying agrochemicals for eight to ten years.

A few months after the trial, Córdoba once again was a maelstrom of news, as crowds demonstrated against Monsanto's effort to build a giant facility in the suburb of Malvinas. The company envisioned a factory for GE corn that farmers could plant in rotation with Monsanto's GE soy, to diversify their harvests with conveniently similar production methods for the two crops. For months, protests, blockades, vandalism, threats, scuffles and military protection ensued at the construction site. In 2013 the National Congress granted the demonstrators an audience. In 2014 a provincial court

A poster in Argentina begs Little Cowboy Gil, a local folk saint, to 'save us from the soy farmers'.

proclaimed Monsanto's environmental impact study inadequate and ordered the company to stop construction. Monsanto vigorously denied the allegation, appealed the decision twice, and lost both times. The company's next step is to prepare a fresh environmental assessment, which according to a new law must include a public hearing and potentially even a local referendum. The outcome in Malvinas appears far from settled.

Meanwhile, the off-and-on issue of taxes on oilseed exports was far from decided either, with new tensions mounting in the countryside. Farmers saw their profits eroded because of a combination of inflation and their government's requirement that revenue from exports be converted into the local currency at the official rate, which is artificially low and financially draining. Cultivators became even less tolerant of the oilseed export tax; in their minds, not only should the tax never be raised, it should actually be lowered.

Realizing that the Kirchner administration would never agree to reduce the tax, farmers embraced an alternative strategy: save the beans until Kirchner reached her term limit in December 2015. Soybeans can be stored in dry, sealed silo bags for up to three years. The earthworm-shaped bags – enormous at 60 m (200 ft) long or more – can each hold at least 250 metric tons of beans. They represent a kind of savings account: the farmer hopes to sell the soy when prices are high and government policies have become more favourable. But for every filled bag that is stored for later sale, the government loses export tax money in the present, a situation prompting Kirchner's administration to accuse the farmers of hoarding and speculation. In 2015 the government began requiring that all sales of empty silo bags be registered, to 'collect information about the universe of buyers of silo-bags, to have buyers clearly identified', according to the tax agency managing the registry.[38] Farmers found to be holding on to their soy became ineligible for federal loans. Kirchner's administration argued that this was only fair, as the farmers had benefited from those loans in the past, and therefore should reciprocate by sharing more of their profits in the form of taxes on sold beans.

The accusation of hoarding hurt. Farmers protested that lack of infrastructure meant sometimes they waited weeks for trucks to pick up their crops; during the delay, silo bags were simply the best way to protect the beans from pests. They downplayed the rising rate of silo-bag storage. Instead, they took offence at the government's very public characterization of them as selfish and greedy, which they complained fanned flames of resentment against them. In part they blamed the Kirchner administration for a spate of night-time attacks on their filled silo bags, citing as evidence the nasty political graffiti on a wall north of Buenos Aires: 'Be a patriot, destroy a silo bag.'[39]

Thirty silo bags were vandalized throughout the soy belt in 2014.[40] When bags are cut, the farmer must sell the soy right away, even if the current market price is very low. Worse yet, some of the spilled beans spoil. Not only bags and profits are slashed – so also is the farmers' sense of security on their own properties. They deride the federal government for doing little to protect them. They appreciate instead the government of Córdoba Province, which announced in February 2015 a plan for drones to detect crimes in fields and identify perpetrators. The system will include high fences around fields and, on field gates, padlocks enhanced with GPS sensors and alarms. Any tampering with a lock will trigger an alarm that will, in turn, automatically send out a drone to take footage of whatever happens next in the field. The farmers are eager to get this system in place, as in May 2015, in an isolated area of Córdoba, fifty silo bags were attacked in a single night.[41] In Argentina, it seems a new type of 'bean field war' has begun.

To the northeast, Paraguay, too, has seen tremendous stress over burgeoning soy production. In the 1990s Brazilian farmers moved in growing numbers to Paraguay, becoming immigrants popularly known as *brasiguayos*. They purchased land legally, and sometimes illegally with the complicity of corrupt Paraguayan officials. They planted soy, soy and more soy. Reliable statistics are scarce, but estimates suggest that absentee Brazilian citizens and brasiguayos control between 50 and 80 per cent of Paraguay's soy production chain.[42] This dominance is reflected in the landscape. Researcher Mariano Turzi remarked in the *Yale Journal of International Affairs* that currently 'it is hard to discern the frontier between Paraguay and Brazil, and some parts of the border are just one green ocean of soybeans.'[43] Soy farming is also often undertaken by the descendants of German and Japanese immigrants, as well as Mennonites whose forebears settled in Paraguay in the twentieth century to escape religious conflicts with the governments of Canada and the Soviet Union.

In Argentina, the equivalent of the Boston Tea Party was a Soy 'Party'. Enraged during a national dispute over wealth and economic responsibility, vandals who felt that farmers did not pay enough taxes slashed dozens of silo bags full of soybeans in 2014–15. Once the beans have been exposed to the weather and animals, it is very hard to recuperate their value.

Over time, cattle ranchers displaced by soy farming, and the soy farmers themselves, have cut down vast tracts of Paraguay's Interior Atlantic Forest. Other agriculture had already threatened this ecosystem before soy came to Paraguay, but soy's advent accelerated the destruction. Today only 7 per cent of the multi-country Atlantic Forest remains.[44] For millennia the forest had flourished with extraordinarily rich wildlife, but now many of its treasures are vulnerable to extinction, including the bright-red-capped 'helmeted' woodpecker and the 'dwarf brocket' deer, with its lush russet fur.

More recently under attack lies the Gran Chaco forest to the west – Latin America's second-largest woodland and home to jaguars, tapirs, armadillos and many, many other creatures threatened by human development. As in the eastern part of the country, deforestation in Paraguay's Gran Chaco is relentless, stripping down 610 hectares (about 1,500 acres) *per day* in January 2015.[45] The brasiguayos and other 'outsider' farmers have coaxed hot, dry-forest terrains previously deemed inarable into agricultural bounty, but the lands end up showered in pesticides. Soy farmers have prospered, propelling Paraguay to number four among soy-exporting nations and shooting its gross domestic product upwards.

According to the World Bank, in 2013 Paraguay boasted the globe's second-fastest-growing economy; the annual rate was a whopping 14.2 per cent.[46]

Lamentably, the soy farmers' practices have led to severe clashes with local small farmers, indigenous peoples and the landless. In recent years Paraguay, a country with a 40 per cent poverty rate and quite possibly the most unequal land distribution in the world, has also been a very violent soy-conflict zone.[47] The soy boom is not only failing to benefit a large swathe of society, it is actively hurting many people. Tens of thousands of small farmers have been displaced from lands they cultivated; they now languish in urban slums. Careless use of pesticides has endangered the health of poor people unable to escape the most heavily affected rural areas. Activists have been arrested, injured and slain.

The tense relationship between the brasiguayos and Paraguayan smallholders boiled over in 2004–5 in the settlement of Tekojoja, a place whose poignantly hopeful name means 'equal terms' or 'equality' in the indigenous Guaraní language. At issue were opposing ideas about land ownership, as well as contradictory aspects of Paraguay's legal system. Founded in 1976, Tekojoja developed during a period of agrarian reform in which the landless often began acquiring legal rights to the soil by settling on and farming the uncultivated lands of big property owners. The government supported this form of land appropriation in order to redistribute wealth, to make terrains more agriculturally productive and to win popular support. Landless individuals in such situations were often the young adult children of smallholders; they sought land in order to set up their own economically viable households. Over time, gradually, they obtained greater and greater rights to the plots they settled, and in this endeavour they were backed by a special government agency. They were also protected by laws disallowing foreigners from purchasing lands within agrarian-reform settlements. But eventually this pro-smallholder system would forcefully collide with the manifold manoeuvres of soy barons seeking to expand their properties.

In the early 2000s, brasiguayo soy farmer Ademir Opperman found ten Tekojoja families willing to sell their properties; he offered alluring prices. Most of these transactions were illegal, and a group of about 150 people from a nearby community – landless men and women who had hoped to acquire those lands but could not possibly outbid the wealthy brasiguayo – protested with their presence and their labour, setting up simple shelters on the plots and farming them. Petitioning various government agencies, the settlers and Opperman contested each other's claims to the land. After an internal review, the agrarian-reform agency concluded that it should never have given occupancy permits to the brasiguayo. It revoked them. Opperman appealed. Over the course of three years, the case made its way to the Paraguayan Supreme Court. Meanwhile, Opperman twice convinced regional law enforcers to evict the 'squatters', burn down their houses and destroy their crops. Determined to hold on to the land, and to keep soy and its hated pesticides out of their community as much as possible, the evicted residents returned, rebuilt and replanted. Authorities ruled the evictions and destruction illegal, but each time they happened, the number of struggling individuals willing to continue building and farming on the sites shrank. The brasiguayo was slowly winning a war of attrition.

But a war of attrition requires patience, and patience was not Opperman's strong suit. At his behest, two truckloads of riot police arrived in Tekojoja at 5 a.m. on 24 June 2005, hauling 130 residents – the majority children – to the local jail. Opperman then had his 'private security guards', riding tractors, tear through dozens of houses and set them aflame. As Opperman himself was leaving the community, he spied a group of about fifty residents who had been hiding during the evictions or who lived on undisputed plots but wished to show solidarity with their abused neighbours. Apparently mistaking two men in the crowd for anti-soy activists he despised, Opperman and his henchmen fired guns, killing both men and seriously wounding another. Ángel Cristaldo, in his early twenties and engaged to be married, had just completed the home he had planned to live in with his bride. Instead of her wedding, his fiancée endured the agony of his funeral.

Wishing to make these murders count, unlike many before them, the leading popular activist in the area called in journalists, who released photos from a Canadian anthropologist who had been present that day. The photos showed that the smallholders had been unarmed when they were attacked. The national reaction was swift and quite unsympathetic to the soy grower. Opperman was arrested. In 2006 the Supreme Court ruled mostly in favour of the smallholders, and the president of the Republic even promised them brick homes paid for by the central government. By 2009 the community indeed sported 48 new brick houses, complete with the luxury of toilets and sinks – but no water.

In the aftermath of the murders, the people of Tekojoja still felt beleaguered by agrochemicals wafting towards them from large-scale soy plantations. They still felt vulnerable. They watched while, like a slap in the face against their longing for justice, soy magnate Opperman, the razer of houses, was sentenced to a comfortable house arrest. He then managed to escape, and has not been seen in the area since.

The saga of Paraguay's landless was far from over. In April 2008 the nation's voters elected a former Roman Catholic bishop, Fernando Lugo, as the head of a left-leaning government championing the rural poor. After Lugo's victory, all over the country elated landless citizens appropriated patches from large estates, setting up camps and planting subsistence crops. The soy elite was thoroughly alarmed. Might this signal the beginning of a more extensive and effective land redistribution? They remonstrated against Lugo's politicking, which they said encouraged incursions that should instead be stamped out. Perhaps taking a cue from the big soy owners' roadblocks in Argentina a few months earlier, by December Paraguay's soy farmers had organized their own protest, albeit a far less disruptive one than Argentina's. Thousands of large farmers staged a *tractorazo* on the shoulders of the nation's highways – parades of tractors, trucks and other farm equipment, many sporting the national flag – to signal their distress over rural conflict at the time of the soy harvest, and their disapproval of the government's attitude towards soy growers. They called for peace and productivity, by which they implied their own continuing control of properties. But their protest had little immediate effect on their fortunes. Tensions over land kept increasing. The landless were not persuaded by the elite's view of productivity; from their point of view, that kind of productivity only abandoned them to grinding poverty.

Meanwhile, announcing worries about a violent (but very small) radical guerrilla group, the Lugo government twice declared a state of emergency in various provinces. The measures included bans on political meetings. Many rural activists resented the bans as stymieing their work; Lugo was betraying them. The president's political fortunes were now precarious both among the soy barons to his right and the peasant leaders to his left.

Conservatives controlling the federal legislature were ready to pounce against Lugo as soon as a politically feasible opportunity presented itself – one that might seem legally justifiable that the voters might accede to. The events of June 2012 gave them the opening they needed.

In the country's east, a 2,000-hectare (about 5,000-acre) piece of land was for years a navy training site. Despite being landlocked, Paraguay has a strong naval tradition because of its connection to the Atlantic Ocean through the Paraguay-Paraná river system. Accordingly, the piece of land came to be called 'Marina Kue' in the Guaraní language (meaning 'place that was the navy's') – but due to bureaucratic error, its transfer from a private company to the military was never fully formalized. In 1999 the navy abandoned the tract for a more convenient location, and another private company, owned by the extremely wealthy soy producer, businessman and leading politician Blas Riquelme, began using a portion of Marina Kue. Because the site had earlier been occupied by the military, however, in 2004 it was transferred to another arm of Paraguay's government, the land reform agency.

Encouraged by this turn of affairs, subsistence farmers began occupying parts of Marina Kue – parts that Riquelme's company claimed. The farming families argued that the land reform laws empowered them to cultivate exactly this type of tract. The company pointedly disagreed, arguing that the land never formally belonged to the central government in the first place and therefore was not legitimately agrarian-reform property after all. Over several years Riquelme's company repeatedly carried out evictions while the subsistence farmers struggled to obtain official titles to the land. The company had the support of the country's elite and of the local police, while the family farmers had the support of the land reform agency, rural activists and various courts.

By 2012 there were three footpaths leading into and out of a remote little subsistence settlement at Marina Kue. On 15 June at 7 a.m., at the behest of Riquelme's soy company, 295 police officers in columns blocked two of the paths. Many wore riot gear; some carried assault rifles. Twenty-nine officers on horseback were poised to pursue any smallholders attempting to leave via the third path, which passed through a company soy field towards the main highway, an hour's walk away. The 64 residents – including young children, pregnant women and senior citizens – were cornered, facing highly armed opponents. This eviction had trapped them in a vice. They picked up their few rickety guns, which the police saw as evidence of violent intent. Residents testified later that they hoped for peaceful negotiations but were fearful. The police testified that, on the contrary, the residents were aggressive militants – ready to ambush them and merely using women and children as 'cover'.

Exactly what happened next is hotly contested. A helicopter swooped so low over the smallholders that they could hear nothing else. Someone fired first shots; the volley was returned. Before long, six police and eleven smallholders were dead. Eighty people were injured. According to the police, all the casualties occurred very quickly. According to the smallholders, those among them holding guns were executed, but not before one of them had managed to kill the police leaders at the front of one column. These events, Marina Kue's former residents say, constituted only the beginning of the confrontation. They say that enraged police next went on a rampage, shooting people as they fled, as they lay wounded, or even many minutes later, after they turned themselves in.

Within a few days, the government had charged dozens of smallholders with various offences. Twelve, already in detention, were charged with invading private property, organized crime and collaborating in homicides. Eventually the adults in detention were ordered to prison, while two teens were sentenced to house arrest; most of the other accused smallholders remained insecurely at large. Despite reports of police misconduct, no officers have been disciplined, or even investigated, for the loss of life. In 2013 the UN Human Rights Committee responded to this judicial imbalance, expressing concern about a lack of impartiality and due process of law in the investigation.[48]

Instead of discipline for the police, it was Lugo's government that was disciplined. Conservatives' reactions to the police deaths were swift and vociferous. Attempting to placate his critics on the right, Lugo dismissed his Interior minister, appointing a conservative to take his place. He also promoted the very police commissioner who had been in charge of the Marina Kue operation to the rank of National Director of Police. These actions infuriated the political left. Little more than a week after the tragedy at Marina Kue, a strange alliance of conservatives and leftists impeached Lugo and removed him from office. His vice president, a conservative, assumed the presidency.

The families directly traumatized at Marina Kue abandoned the site. Not long afterwards, Blas Riquelme died of a stroke at age 83. But protests against landlessness and the expansion of soy have continued in the area. By 2014 Riquelme's company was renting Marina Kue to other soy growers. Meanwhile, some landless survivors of the violence created a precarious encampment on the property's edge and continued to denounce the use of pesticides on nearby soy. Eventually the contested terrain was designated a protected wildlife preserve, a manoeuvre the landless considered thoroughly unjust. Sorrows over Marina Kue thus continue and are, unfortunately, but one of many conflicts over land tenure and soy agriculture plaguing Paraguay today.

The landscapes of Bolivia and Uruguay also evince expanding soy agriculture. In Uruguay, production is concentrated in the northwest, in the Uruguay River basin bordering Argentina's most soy-laden area. In Bolivia, production is along the frontier with Brazil. In the 1970s the World Bank supported soy cultivation there to compensate for troubles in Bolivia's tin and cotton industries. Soy is now Bolivia's most important crop, accounting for 45 per cent of agricultural land nationwide and 10 per cent of total exports.[49] In contrast to other South American countries, in Bolivia soy producers are mainly small farmers, who together have made their country a primary exporter of soybeans to fellow member countries of the Andean Pact Community trading bloc. About half of Bolivia's soy exports go to Pact nations without added tariffs, making their price favourable compared to Brazilian soy. The other half of the exports passes through the Uruguayan port of Nueva Palmira via a concessionary arrangement with that country. But the cost of hauling the beans so far away and the congestion at that port pose serious logistical and economic problems for Bolivian farmers, hampering the increase of Bolivia's soy exports to European markets. As a result of these transportation difficulties, and of Bolivian farmers' insufficient income for purchasing the best farm equipment and chemicals, Bolivia produces less than 1 per cent of the world's soybeans.

In Uruguay, soy became the top exported crop in 2008, though Uruguay is a very small player in international soy markets.[50] Its beans are shipped primarily to China and Europe. The pattern for soy in Uruguay has many similarities with that of Paraguay: recent, rapidly mounting production (beginning in the early 2000s for Uruguay); displacement of other crops and livestock; heavy investment and land ownership by foreigners (in Uruguay's case, mostly Argentines); increasing concentration of land in the hands of elites; very little refining of soy until recently; and local consumption of soy meal for animals and soy oil for humans, but few soy protein products as human food. As in Argentina, the soy boom has raised land values in a way that squeezes out dairy farming. Fortunately, however, Uruguay has not experienced as much social conflict surrounding soy cultivation as other South American nations.

Uruguay is joined to its soy-producing neighbours by farmer migration, capital flows and shared transport systems. It also participates in South America's MERCOSUR (Mercado Común del Sur, or Southern Common market), which includes soy producers Argentina, Brazil, Paraguay and Bolivia. Together, these nations constitute an emerging, shadowy 'United Republic of Soy'.

In 2003 the seed and agrochemical company Syngenta placed a startling advertisement in rural editions of two Argentine newspapers. The advertisement promoted Syngenta's 'Centinela' service for soy farmers. Centinela ('sentinel') was a new, high-tech system of monitoring field conditions unfavourable to soy. A network of Syngenta laboratories could quickly analyse plant samples and climatic conditions from throughout southern South America. The advertisement showed a map of the continent's southern cone, with the soy-cultivating areas shaded as a single green surface. In Spanish, that space bore the label 'United Republic of Soy', and next to the map, bold letters proclaimed, 'Soy knows no borders; neither does information from Centinela.' Presumably the intent was to indicate that if a soy-infecting fungus or other disease had been detected anywhere in the region, Syngenta would distribute that information to farmers subscribing to their service, regardless of national boundaries. A Paraguayan landowner could thus quickly protect himself against an infection coming from northern Argentina, and a cultivator in southern Brazil could become aware that Uruguayan weather conditions adversely affecting soy were heading his way.

The advertisement provoked outrage among activists objecting to the agribusiness model for soy. They did not disagree with the premise that soy was dominant in the large region shown on the map. Indeed, they had already been arguing for several years that multinational companies, big landowners (often foreigners) and the various governments 'in cahoots' with them were abetting the creation of a pro-business soy zone – a power bloc that regularly disrespected national frontiers, ecological balances and the rights of smallholders and indigenous peoples. What incensed the activists was their sense that this advertisement *celebrated* the calamitous appropriation of a large territory. Some felt that use of the word 'republic' to denote a process that they saw as undemocratic was nothing short of a cynical lie. They responded over the next decade with articles and even an ebook denouncing this 'United Republic of Soybeans'.[51]

What nobody disputed was that the elites of this multinational soy zone wield unmistakable influence. While not always united among themselves, they nevertheless frequently engage in parallel activities, stamping their world with their common interests. Economically, they have created empires encompassing not only soy cultivation but transportation, crop processing, energy production, construction, real estate, lumber and many other fields; in some places they have turned their product, soy, into a kind of currency for land rentals; they have built entire towns; they have sponsored construction of schools, hospitals and low-income housing; and they have caused complex shifts in food prices. Environmentally, they have brought agriculture to regions where no one had thought it possible; they have funded development of new crops; they have denuded forests; they have generated significant pollution; they have contributed to soil erosion and flooding; they have influenced the evolution of pests in multiple ecosystems; they have sponsored or pushed for massive infrastructure projects; and they have studied and begun to implement systems to mitigate their own enormous 'footprint' on the land. Politically, they have sent some of their most successful members to high government or political-party office in several countries; they have lobbied hard for their own views on intellectual property law; they have negotiated directly with international environmental groups, as if creating treaties or a foreign policy; they have engaged in a simmering war with activists and country folk seeking land reform; their actions have changed tax policies; and they have helped to topple government ministers and even a president. Their dealings are often akin to those of a nation-state, and so the expression 'United Republic of Soy' persists.

THOSE WHO OPPOSE this 'republic' have also had successes, piece-meal though they have often been. Deforestation has slowed in some places; lands have occasionally been awarded to impoverished rural families; laws have been enacted to improve pesticide application; eco-reserves have been set aside; and multinational companies have sometimes been held to higher levels of social and environmental responsibility. The agribusiness interests have faced the intense interests of other social actors, and sometimes the soy aristocrats have had to modify their plans. There is a contest afoot in South America, and the playing fields are covered, end to end, with soy.

SEVEN

MOULDING OUR WORLD

A t sunset, two does watched their massive, shaggy cousins roam the ridges, their fur billowing in the wind as if in concert with the tall grasses. Wild shoots, nourished by thick organic matter deposited over 10,000 years, swayed all around a tranquil herd 300,000-strong. The two deer were less calm. Their alert ears twitched, straining to detect movement beyond the burble of a stream, the rustling of elm leaves and the croaking of leopard frogs in the marsh past the copse. Only the melody of a piping plover calling to its mate and the flutters of woodland bats caught the deer's attention. The does carefully scanned the night air with their noses. Good, no wolves. No scent of humans, either – no need to fear arrows shredding flesh. Cautiously the deer stepped out onto the prairie, joining the open sea of life before them.

This was the world – the deer's luxuriant world, with all its raw beauty and danger – that would one day become western Iowa. By the twenty-first century, that prairie habitat would be 98 per cent destroyed, replaced by endless neat rows of soybeans and corn.[1] The bison and wolves would be gone, the piping plovers and bats scarcer and scarcer and almost all the wetlands and riverside woodlands supplanted by farming. A world of extreme, untamed abundance and subtle biodiversity would become a zone of near-uniformity.

In North America, tallgrass prairie was replaced first by corn (maize) and other crops, and then by corn and soy. Hardly any of that ecosystem exists today. The entrenched presence of corn and soy in the u.s. Midwest blocks the prairie from being restored to its magnificent native state. This is the price the planet paid for crops that humans deem valuable. How easily we forget.

153

Humans' most destructive activity – overall more damaging to other life forms than our firebombing of cities, toxic nuclear wastes, landfills brimming with plastics that will remain for four hundred years, ocean oil spills, clouds of urban smog, strip mining or factory sludge leaking into rivers – is ordinary agriculture. Today, the farming of crops and animals is responsible for some 80 per cent of continuing deforestation, and the fossil record indicates that agriculture has always been the major human despoiler of the land.[2] Now, with agrochemicals running off the land into the oceans, and with pollution emanating from seaside fish pens, farming even harms the seas.

Humans must eat to survive, and the size of earth's population demands more than just hunting and gathering. Agriculture is unavoidable. But farming is so dangerous to the other species with whom we share the planet that it behoves us to do it as responsibly as possible. We need to feed our own cherished species well, and at the same time respect the intricate, wondrous, vulnerable miracles of life around us. With this dual perspective we consider the environmental effects of soybean cultivation.

As we have seen, both growing soy and feeding it to 'factory'-raised animals exact serious environmental costs. So too does moving beans over long distances. The Brazilian town of Santarém, and the highway being paved to reach it, particularly illuminate habitat

Tens of millions of bison, like these from an 1855 lithograph, once roamed prairie now occupied by maize, soy and other crops in North America.

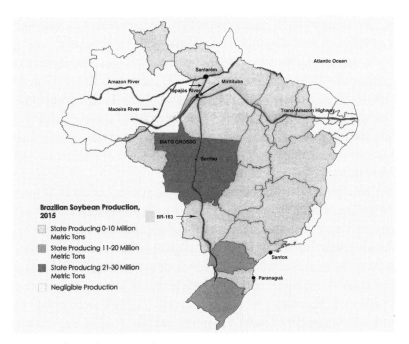

Map of Brazilian soybean production, 2015.

loss resulting from transportation – especially transport spurred by giant governmental ambition and corporate thirst for profits. But although it is too late to save the expanses of American tallgrass prairie, it is perhaps not so for the wilderness around the road to Santarém. With stringent laws and enforcement, there could be hope. It remains to be seen whether the soy kingpins will promote destructive processes there, or whether instead they can sustain a more careful, sophisticated relationship with the environment than the commandeering that ravaged the u.s. prairie.

At Santarém, the *café au lait* Amazon River, churning silt carried from the Andes, meets the crystal blue waters of the Tapajós River. Just before the rivers meet, along a bank of the Tapajós stands a state-of-the-art grain terminal operated by Cargill, the privately owned agricultural conglomerate. In 2015 the terminal's massive pulleys transferred 1.7 million metric tons of soybeans and maize from barges onto larger, seaworthy vessels bound for Europe and Egypt.[3]

Cargill built the terminal around the turn of the millennium with dubious legality. In 1999 and again in 2003 Brazilian courts ordered the company to stop work until they had submitted a complete environmental impact statement and the authorities had approved it. The company continued construction and export activities anyway, arguing each time that this was legitimate since they were appealing the court decisions. The terminal was inaugurated for exports in 2003 while an appeal to the Supreme Court was still pending. All this activity was rather like a child saying, 'Even though my babysitter told me to stop trampling the neighbour's flowerbed, I'm not going to stop because I'm waiting to hear what my mum says,' and then when the mother says to stop, 'well now I'm waiting to hear what dad says.'

Meanwhile, with a ready way to get their crop to market, farmers dreaming of riches hacked and burned down thousands of hectares of forest near the new port. Soy farming mushroomed. Eco-activists roundly denounced Cargill as the instigator of environmental havoc. In 2007 Brazil's Supreme Court concluded that Cargill's behaviour had indeed been illegal and closed the terminal down. Under intense pressure from upset soy farmers, Cargill pledged to complete an impact assessment within six months, and the terminal was allowed to reopen after twenty days, although a formal permit from the Brazilian State of Pará did not come until 2012.

Greenpeace's 2006 call for a boycott of Cargill products, along with the 2007 shutdown, showed the company the writing on the wall. Brazilian law had to be fully complied with. But Cargill had not been as remiss as media portrayed: since 2004 they had been in talks with The Nature Conservancy (TNC) about how to reduce deforestation around Santarém. In 2005 they financed a database with detailed maps of all farms in the region, which made it more possible to keep track of deforestation. TNC provided the expertise. At the same time, Cargill and TNC provided very low-cost technical assistance for cultivators to help them understand Brazil's strict Forest Code and succeed as farmers even while complying with it. Previously, farmers in the area often worked multiple low-yielding soy fields; their approach to increasing their harvest was simply to cut down more forest to create more fields. Now they received aid to take a different tack: stop clearing land for new fields, and instead coax existing fields to yield more.

Cargill next insisted that anyone selling them beans would have to prove their compliance with the law, which made farmers *want* to obey it. Further, Cargill promised to buy all beans grown in accord with the Forest Code; environmental compliance became the ticket to a reliable income. The Brazilian government also motivated farmers by denying loans to cultivators in areas blacklisted for lack of compliance. Thus, in partnership with an environmental organization and Brazilian authorities, Cargill evolved into a corporation promoting sustainable development.

But another controversy pertaining to Santarém brews, as it has for decades. In the early 1970s Brazil began carving a road out of the Cerrado and jungle to stretch nearly straight north from Cuiabá, the capital of Mato Grosso, up to Santarém. Although largely unpaved, the road eventually added 1,756 km (1,091 miles) to highway BR-163 and contributed significantly to the growth of Santarém. Under the pressures of a tropical climate, however, the route quickly deteriorated; by the mid-1980s long portions had become impassable. In some places, the potholes were so huge they could 'eat' the wheel of a large truck.

But the dream of efficient transport to Santarém did not fade. It persisted because, without a genuinely passable highway north, Mato Grosso's soy farmers are beset by high transportation costs. Most of their soy is trucked to clogged, distant ports to the southeast. Some is brought to Santarém and other river ports in a roundabout way, travelling by truck to the Madeira River to the west (that is, the opposite direction from the Atlantic), then by barge up the Madeira to the Amazon River, and only then down the Amazon. Understandably, Mato Grosso farmers covet a better route to the Atlantic.

Because BR-163 provides a straight shot north from Mato Grosso, experts estimate that paving it could save soy farmers 442 million U.S. dollars over twenty years. The cost to the Brazilian government of paving and maintaining the road would, in theory, be only $256 million. Thus the net benefit to Brazilian society, from a conventional economic perspective, could be substantial at $186 million.[4] But the project has been plagued by legal and engineering challenges, cost overruns and delay, after delay, after delay. Although currently some 80 per cent of BR-163 is paved, the unpaved gaps are a muddy, axle-breaking impediment. Soy growers' enthusiasm, and their exasperated impatience, have not been enough to get the road finished in a timely manner. The road is slated for completion in 2018 – but no one is holding their breath.

For environmentalists, and the unwitting wildlife whose existence is on the line, the more delays the better! They feel no desire to see the 'Arc of Deforestation' along Brazil's Amazon Basin – an arc nearly the size of France and Spain combined, or of Texas plus California – expand any further.[5] A report from Tufts University explains, 'more than two-thirds of Amazon deforestation takes place within 50 km [31 miles] of major paved roads, where agriculture, cattle ranching and logging activities become economically feasible.'[6] Pioneers in the jungle soon require schools, clinics, post offices, petrol stations, supermarkets, clothing and hardware stores, electrical and water lines, construction workers and skilled tradesmen, handymen, feed stores, churches and clergy, motels and on and on. Towns spring up; forests fall down.

If one transcends conventional economics by factoring in the value of rainforests as sources of sustainable timber; as carbon sequesters; as homes for plants and animals which, through low-impact harvesting, could provide food and medicines; as protectors against fire and erosion; as magnets for responsible tourism and recreation; and as regulators of helpful rainfall patterns – then the cost–benefit analysis of development shifts dramatically. The Tufts study found that, taking such value into account, the completed paving of BR-163 would generate a *loss* to Brazilian society of between $762 million and $1.9 billion over twenty years. This conclusion roughly matched that of a group of Brazilian conservation economists.[7] But the Brazilian government continues ploughing ahead, believing that it can tame the forces of development along BR-163. Improved satellite mapping of deforestation in real time, along with TNC's database of land usage, make enforcement of environmental laws more possible than before. All the same, Brazil's poor record of preventing forest decimation along roadsides gives great cause for concern.

BR-163 is hardly the only soy infrastructure project that threatens Brazilian ecosystems. Part way up the Tapajós River as it flows towards Santarém lies the river port of Miritituba. The port is a budding hub of soybean transportation, as it is close to the intersection of BR-163 with the east–west Trans-Amazon highway and is a convenient port for soybeans travelling northward on the Tapajós. The giant grain-trading corporation Bunge has opened a terminal there, the Brazilian company Cianport is constructing port facilities and Cargill has applied for construction permits. Other ports along Brazil's rivers and coast – ten in the state of Pará alone – are also being developed. Bridges, highways and waterways are being built or improved.

Elsewhere in Brazil, rock blasting, dredging and straightening of the Paraguay River, all to enhance the transport of soy, threaten to upset the ecological balance of the Pantanal. The Pantanal is a massive wetland of profound significance as a regulator of regional water flows and home to marvellously diverse flora and fauna. It is so rich in wildlife that UNESCO declared it a 'Natural Heritage of Humanity' area, and tour guides sometimes declare, 'If you want to see animals, forget the Amazon; go to the Pantanal.' But despite the great value of protecting the Pantanal, the plans of soybean exporters for the region's waters put it at risk.

We saw in the previous chapter that Brazil is not the only South American country where soy farming causes ecological damage. It can be easy to judge all these South Americans as environmentally irresponsible. But many in the world's South pointedly question the right of the North to pass judgement. When in 1989 a U.S. senator asserted that 'Contrary to what Brazilians think, the Amazon is not their property: it belongs to all of us', many Brazilians were incensed at the hypocrisy and arrogance they perceived in the remark (which U.S. senator made it is disputed). How would U.S. citizens feel if a Brazilian senator announced that all states bordering the Mississippi were not actually U.S. property, but instead belonged to the world to manage?

South Americans working in agribusiness wonder, what gives permission to Europe and North America to condemn modern agriculture in the Southern Hemisphere, when so much of *their* prairie, forests and wetlands were long ago destroyed? Northerners wreaked havoc on their own natural worlds and now blithely tell the South to save their environments. Even if the North really means, 'Learn from our mistakes', on what authority do they speak? The authority of historic plunderers and despoilers? And when the North protests that their past plundering is irrelevant today, South Americans want to know, why should the North tolerate its own large-scale farming in the many ecosystems where it succeeds, whereas they condemn the South for wanting the same? Is this just a strategy to keep Southern countries from succeeding as the North's business competitors?

Sometimes South Americans ask the North, if you really care so much about the environment, why don't you replant your own forests, restore your own wetlands and bring back the wild abundance of your own prairies? Let the land revert back to native grasses and millions of bison in Midwestern North America. Let the bulk of Europe return to towering forests. *Then*, these South Americans feel, the North will have the moral standing to question others' behaviour. Meanwhile, soybeans and other crops bring profits. Many South Americans deem that fine for farmers and entrepreneurs anywhere.

Unfortunately, modern agriculture poses another problem besides direct habitat loss. Such agriculture is not merely large and technology-driven. It is also monoculture – that is, a single crop is planted over vast expanses. Monoculture puts agriculture itself at risk; the presence of one type of plant everywhere on large tracts means that any pest adapted to attack that plant can proliferate like wildfire through the fields. From the viewpoint of a pest, mono-culture offers a colossal, all-you-can-eat buffet. To protect crops against such epidemics, farmers must vigilantly pursue pest control, whether through chemicals, genetic engineering or organic methods (although organic farmers often strive to avoid monoculture in the first place). Monoculture is efficient and therefore profitable, but it is also dicey.

Soybean monoculture subjects fields to limited diversity even within the species. In the U.S., for example, there are many sub-types ('cultivars') of soy grown commercially, but on the whole they are not very genetically different from one another. Breeders have used a few preferred cultivars as the parenting sources for many others, and not only the strengths but also the weaknesses of those parent lines have been passed on. As in a small, isolated town where everyone is descended from the same original handful of settlers, health problems can arise. Although seed repositories safeguard non-preferred varieties for future use – the Chinese Academy of Agricultural Science has about 26,000 soy varieties, the USDA's collection has nearly 22,000,[8] and several other countries each have well over 10,000[9] – the fact is that in farmers' fields today, mostly just the few favourites are grown. Thanks to the work of Dorsett, Morse and others discussed in Chapter Three, some cultivars have been bred to resist pests – but in the endless war between plants and pests, having a really big mix of genes is a major asset. As Purdue University researchers explain, 'Limited genetic diversity for the modern cultivated soybean is . . . making the crop vulnerable to rapidly evolving . . . pests and pathogens.'[10]

Many environmental activists are concerned about another aspect of soybean uniformity: the beans are usually genetically engineered. Of all crops, soy has the largest percentage of its land planted in GE varieties (some 80 per cent of world soy hectares in 2016). Soy also fills the largest proportion of GE hectares worldwide – 50 per cent in 2016. The next closest contender is maize (corn), which occupied only 33 per cent of the planet's GE-cultivated lands in that year.[11] Soy's GE predominance arose in part because Roundup Ready (RR) soy, introduced to farmers in 1996, was the first GE crop to reach widespread commercial success. Soy had a head start as a GE product that conventional farmers love.

Monsanto created RR soy to help farmers with weed control. The company was already selling Roundup, their brand name for glyphosate, which kills by interrupting a metabolic pathway found only in plants and microorganisms. Glyphosate is fabulous at destroying weeds. Not only that, but once applied it breaks down fairly soon into relatively harmless substances, so it is less toxic to humans and non-plant wildlife than many other herbicides. But Roundup had a problem. Because it kills plants so well, farmers had to apply it very carefully only to weeds, lest they accidentally kill their crops as well. This caveat limited Roundup's convenience and therefore profitability. Monsanto realized that if they could create a crop that flourished despite coming into contact with glyphosate – a crop whose metabolism would not be affected – then farmers could spray the chemical broadly over their fields, killing weeds efficiently with only their healthy crop left standing. A previously effective but inconvenient chemical would suddenly, when paired with the special crop, become a very convenient product for farmers. The system would be quite enticing, worth some extra cost for the fancy new seeds – which themselves would become a money-maker for the company, too.

Monsanto searched and searched for a gene that would protect a plant from glyphosate, finally finding it in a Roundup factory's waste pond, where bacteria were thriving. The bacteria had just the gene the company wanted. They engineered it into soy plants, creating a blockbuster product. By 2014 all the soybeans planted in Argentina, 94 per cent of those in the u.s. and 93 per cent of those in Brazil were glyphosate-tolerant.[12]

Not to be outdone, the Swiss chemical company Syngenta eventually devised their own glyphosate-tolerant soybean, which they market in Brazil under the name VMAX. Glyphosate-tolerant soybeans are still vastly more economically weighty at present than other forms of GE soy, but GE beans with other traits are gaining in importance. Bayer Crop Science launched a GE soybean called Liberty Link that is tolerant of the herbicide glufosinate. The government of Brazil partnered with the German chemical company BASF to produce GE soy able to withstand imazapyr, also a weedkiller.

Anticipating expiration of their RR patent, Monsanto prepared new types of soybeans, currently in various stages of development, regulatory approval and marketing. First they created 'Genuity' Roundup Ready 2 Yield soy, which as well as tolerating glyphosate also produces more three-, four- and five-bean pods than the older RR soy now off-patent. Monsanto next 'stacked' more GE traits into the Genuity beans to make daughter varieties. Some of the new beans tolerate not only glyphosate, but the herbicide dicamba. Yet already the company faces lawsuits from farmers contending that dicamba has inappropriately drifted over from their neighbours' farms, harming non-GE crops.

Other Genuity cultivars produce oil with healthier characteristics. Another Monsanto Genuity line is engineered to include not only higher pod yields but also further yield-improving qualities. Still others resist attack by parasites: caterpillars in Brazil, or aphids ('plant lice'), or fungi, or parasitic roundworms that lower soy yields worldwide. A tiny roundworm, the soybean cyst nematode, is a particularly grave problem for farmers. Farmers are certain to cheer – and buy – high-yield beans with greater resistance to these nematodes.

Still more qualities have been added to soy genetics. Argentine scientists, alive to their country's drought risks, have transferred a drought-tolerant gene from sunflowers into soybeans. A joint venture between an Argentine and a U.S. company implemented promising field trials with these soy seeds, and the Argentine government approved them for commercial planting. South African researchers have similarly tested GE drought-tolerant soybeans, as has a Japanese government agency that aids developing countries. Several studies have explored making GE soybeans that cope better with salty soils, useful because worldwide the area of salt-affected lands is expected to double in the next 35 years.[13] It should be noted, however, that the 2014 discovery of a natural soy gene conferring salt tolerance has given hope to anti-GE activists for tackling this problem through conventional breeding.[14]

While companies were busy experimenting, the U.S. government and a consortium of research laboratories were sequencing the soy genome. The data, published in 2010 and available through an open USDA database, facilitate not only conventional breeding, but also genetic engineering. Still more types of GE soy can be expected as scientists learn where to insert additional genes.

These developments have engendered many arguments over GE soy. Nutrition questions appear in Chapter Eight; economic implications in Chapter Nine. Here the issue is how GE soy affects ecosystems and agriculture itself, and there are multiple concerns – genetic 'superweeds', excess pesticide use, the breaking of intricate chains connecting different creatures, soil health and the effects of glyphosate exposure on people in farming communities.

Anti-GE activists worry about the alien genes in GE crops 'jumping' to weeds. Gene jumping is real, occurring from time to time in nature; it is one driver of evolution. The transfer of a novel gene from soy to a wild plant – a gene that enhanced the weed's survival – could create more resilient, and therefore more troublesome, weeds.

A worrisome situation with a plant other than soy was the 2003 'escape' of RR 'creeping bentgrass' (for golf courses) from an experimental field in Oregon. Then in 2010, a nearby farmer encountered a further set of escapees when his Roundup was unable to kill bentgrass in an irrigation ditch. This RR bentgrass is now found several kilometres beyond the experimental plots, growing wild. Worse, its easily wind-blown pollen enables it to breed with wild relatives up to 16 km (10 miles) from test areas; this creeping bentgrass really is genetically creeping outwards. There is justifiable concern that it will pass its glyphosate-tolerant gene on to the wild weeds.

But concern need not morph into panic. A glyphosate tolerance gene turns a plant into a 'superweed' only in the sense that the weed can no longer be eliminated with glyphosate. Other weedkillers can still eliminate it. Besides, herbicide tolerance routinely develops in weeds when fields are repeatedly doused with chemicals, whether or not there are GE crops in those fields and whether or not any genes have jumped. 'Superweeds' are nothing new, and so far are under control.

With soy we should also add that, except in the far Eastern Hemisphere, gene jumping is unlikely. Commercial soy is almost entirely self-pollinating: pollination from one plant to another occurs well under 1 per cent of the time.[15] Not only that, but in the Western Hemisphere GE soy does not have wild relatives that could successfully breed with it. What the U.S. National Park Service has affirmed for Colorado is true elsewhere in the Americas – that GE soybeans are 'likely of no threat . . . They are not closely related to wild species occurring [here] . . . the chances of gene flow occurring between distantly related species of higher plants and animals is very small.'[16]

Gene jumping from GE soy to another plant is more possible in Asia and Australia, however, where soy does have reproductively compatible wild relatives. It is reasonable to be concerned, particularly in China, about a potential scenario posited by environmental microbiologist Charles Hagedorn:

> a gene changing the oil composition . . . might move into nearby weedy relatives in which the new oil composition would enable the seeds to survive the winter. Overwintering might allow the plant to become a weed or might intensify weedy properties it already possesses.[17]

Cultivating GE soy in the Eastern Hemisphere therefore requires special care.

The contrast between bentgrass and soybeans illustrates a crucial dimension of genetic modification. Each situation is different. Pronouncements that genetic engineering is or is not environmentally safe cannot be taken out of the context of the particular crop being grown, with its particular genetic alteration, using particular farming techniques, in particular locations. A wide array of possibilities is available to genetic engineers, and each case must be rigorously evaluated on its own terms. True, detailed study is complex and time-consuming, but the stakes are high enough – the potential of genetic engineering for great good or serious harm – that societies must make the effort.

Beyond gene jumping, some worry about how cultivation of GE soy promotes pesticide use. Application of glyphosate has skyrocketed worldwide since the introduction of RR crops. But after 1996 use of other, quite toxic herbicides correspondingly decreased. Recently, though, sales of other herbicides are rising as farmers combat mounting glyphosate-resistant weeds.

In 2014 Dow AgroSciences won qualified approval from the U.S. Environmental Protection Agency (EPA) for a weedkiller containing both glyphosate and, against glyphosate-resistant plants, the common herbicide '2,4-D'. Dow began selling this mixture, brand-named Enlist Duo, for soy and other crops genetically engineered to tolerate both chemicals. The EPA approval contained restrictions on how and where Enlist Duo could be applied and was predicated on Dow's research showing that the two chemicals did not interact with each other to cause any toxicity greater than their sum – no synergy of effects.

Aware of Dow's plans, the Natural Resources Defense Council (NRDC) had already gone to court to try to ban 2,4-D, which was a component of the notorious chemical cocktail Agent Orange, used by the U.S. government during the Vietnam War to defoliate the jungle hiding places of the Viet Cong. Agent Orange turned out to be carcinogenic and associated with many other health problems. Although 2,4-D has not been found central to the health problems – the chief culprit was an Agent Orange chemical called dioxin – all the same, Dow's plans horrified environmental activists. They worried about possible synergistic effects of combining 2,4-D with glyphosate, and also about the tendency of 2,4-D to drift in the air when sprayed, contaminating non-target sites. They feared that soybeans and other crops designed to tolerate Enlist Duo could become alarmingly popular among farmers, leading to a massive increase in pesticide spraying. They noted that 2,4-D is not without negative health effects of its own. Seeking funds for a lawsuit against the EPA, various environmental organizations sent dramatic letters to supporters about the dangers of Dow's chemicals and 'Agent Orange' crops. In 2014 the Center for Food Safety and several other groups joined the NRDC's legal actions.

In a surprise twist, in the autumn of 2015 the EPA discovered that Dow had told the U.S. Patent Office the opposite of what they had told them. To the Patent Office, Dow had declared Enlist Duo deserving of patent protection because their joining of glyphosate and 2,4-D had created an innovative synergistic effect! The EPA promptly demanded that Dow explain themselves and petitioned a u.s. Court of Appeals temporarily to revoke Enlist Duo's legal registration. Environmental organizations delighted in this turn of events. By 2017, however, the EPA had decided in favour of the product and had even expanded the scope of its permitted use.

Environmental organizations have other worries, too, about GE crop systems. They are concerned that wildlife near GE plants could be physically harmed or have their life cycles disturbed, warping the intricate tapestries of ecosystems. In 1999 this worry erupted in controversy over the most cultivated kind of GE corn, which has a pesticide built right into the plant. People chafed at this corn's possible effects on monarch butterfly larvae. Yet many studies suggest that while one kind of rarely planted GE corn can indeed be toxic to monarchs, most GE corn seems not to hurt them.

This can also be said for the more recent engineering of soybeans to include this same built-in pesticide. The modified plants are called 'Bt' after the soil bacterium from which the gene was taken. Bt soybeans have not yet been commercialized, since many countries are still evaluating their safety. Ironically, the Bt bacterium is routinely applied in organic farming as a natural tropical pesticide. When its insecticidal gene is inserted *inside* crops, however, more misgivings and more regulation ensue.

As for the monarch butterflies, oddly enough it is the RR crops, of which the most prevalent is soy, that may be the most detrimental. Glyphosate tolerance does not have a pesticide effect – but glyphosate is better than most herbicides at killing the monarchs' food, milkweed. Many factors have contributed to the steep decline in monarch populations over the last twenty years, including logging in their overwintering areas in Mexico, so glyphosate is surely not the sole, and perhaps not even a major, cause. But it is probably also not innocent in its effects on these winged gems. A field that is thoroughly 'cleaned' from weeds may be too clean for the creatures accustomed to living there.

There is also the possibility that if GE nematode-resistant soy were to become a commercial reality, as various companies are working to accomplish, the anti-nematode toxin in the plants could be ingested by other bugs, which are in turn eaten by *beneficial* nematodes. Susceptible to the toxin in their food supply, the 'good' nematodes would die off, leaving pest insects with one less predator to control them. Governments must require rigorous testing for this risk, and citizens must demand it.

Of course, citizens should likewise demand that agricultural chemicals *not* associated with GE technology be used more judiciously – notably the 'neonic' insecticides that apparently harm not only pests but also the bees we need for crop pollination. EPA research shows that neonics rarely improve U.S. soy yields or offer any profit to farmers. They simply do not work against the most important insect pests for U.S. soy.[18] Neonics, however, are marketed and used on U.S. soybeans – an unreflective practice that is both useless and noxious.

Yet another area of concern about GE crops is how they affect soil health. Microscopically, dirt – especially the dirt around plant roots – is an astonishingly vast ecosystem, comprising complex interactions among tens of thousands of species of bacteria, fungi, algae and protozoa. It is possible to obtain a PhD in soil science, and very technical studies examine how geologic, climatic, farming and chemical conditions alter the web of life in soil. This research matters, since many microorganisms are helpful to humans and other life forms, others are not, and some are both helpful and hurtful in differing ways.

A few soil studies have found that plants sprayed with glyphosate can emit the toxin from their roots.[19] When fields with RR crops receive wide applications of the chemical, microorganisms nearest the roots can die off, changing the soil environment. Other microorganisms appear actually to benefit from glyphosate. It is not clear at this time what the long-term effects might be from repeated alterations to the balance among these many tiny creatures. A great deal remains unknown. Glyphosate is hardly alone, however, as a cause for concern; studies also show other herbicides affecting the soil's community of organisms.

Finally, there is the matter of how glyphosate exposure affects farming communities. Thanks to the advent of RR crops, by volume glyphosate is the world's most widely applied weedkiller today.[20] It is a component of more than 750 herbicidal products worldwide,[21] and trace amounts of it have been found in human urine, breast milk, bread and other foods. Between 2002 and 2012, its use in U.S. agriculture more than doubled, rising to over 128,000 metric tons.[22] Globally, farmers applied 747,000 metric tons of glyphosate in 2014.[23]

For years, accusations were levelled against glyphosate as being the cause of various sicknesses, and for years study after study found the chemical safe for humans. Illness among those exposed to high levels of Roundup appeared to be caused not by its glyphosate, but rather by the surfactant chemicals added to make glyphosate stick better to plants. Some surfactants are also detrimental to amphibians and fish. For these reasons alone, workers spraying glyphosate-based mixtures need to wear protective gear, and if they are using certain formulas, they should avoid spraying near lakes and rivers. They should, of course, avoid dousing human habitations.

Those who espouse genetic engineering vigorously counter their opponents' misgivings about GE products. They note environmental benefits, actual and potential, of GE crops. (Potential benefits for human health are addressed in the next chapter.) For one, glyphosate-tolerant soy makes low-till or no-till farming more feasible. With RR soy, a farmer generally need not break up the land by tilling in order to remove weeds; after successful glyphosate applications, there are simply few to no weeds left.

Tilling loosens the soil so much that it is a major cause of erosion worldwide. The no-till farming encouraged by glyphosate-tolerant crops can thus help reduce the grave global problem of lost topsoil. Robust soil is basically a non-renewable resource, as it takes hundreds of years to form. Some scientists predict that most of the planet's useful topsoil could either be too degraded for farming – or simply gone, washed into the sea – within sixty years.[24] Although there are other methods besides GE crops for success in no-till farming and soil protection, GE advocates argue that this biotechnology is an important resource in the battle to save the soil we need to feed humanity.

GE advocates also point out that non-GE conventional farming often requires even more toxic weedkillers and pesticides than GE agriculture. Critics respond that organic farming is the way to address that problem, but there is significant debate among agricultural experts about whether organic farming is possible on a large-enough scale worldwide to feed the planet's burgeoning human population.

Moreover, Oxford University scientists found in 2012 that, per unit of product, organic farming tends to emit more greenhouse gases than non-organic farming. This is partly because organic farms have somewhat lower crop yields, so to grow the same amount of food, more land must be used for agriculture rather than left as forest. Organic farming can also require more fossil fuel than other cultivation systems because it often uses powered machines intensively to remove weeds. Organic soy farmers are also much more likely than GE farmers to use tilling to disrupt weed growth. Tilling releases carbon from the soil into the air. As the Oxford researchers noted, however, there are wide variations in both organic and conventional farming methods. They advocate moving beyond rigid categories of 'organic' versus 'conventional' to incorporate the best environmental practices from any approach.[25]

Best environmental practices include optimal management of fresh water. Around 70 per cent of the fresh water humans use goes towards producing food, including vast amounts for the soy-eating farm animals that provide us with meat.[26] Fresh water makes up only 3 per cent of the world's water supply,[27] yet compared to a hundred years ago, we irrigate five times more land and have intentionally dried up over half the world's wetlands or lost them through climate change.[28] If we continue our carelessness with water, analysts predict that within a few decades we could suffer falling crop yields, rising food prices, malnutrition and wars over access to fresh water.

Luckily for South Americans, the Guaraní Aquifer, an enormous natural reservoir, lies underneath soy-producing regions in Argentina, Brazil, Paraguay and Uruguay. Wherever this aquifer is 'recharged' with new surface water, the underground supply needs protection from contaminating agrochemicals. In the early 2000s, a multilateral consortium began studying how best to manage the aquifer. Today the four nations involved continue research, negotiations and clean-up efforts to keep soy production and other processes from polluting their water.

The availability of fresh water in South America matters not only to that region, but also to the Chinese. Researchers from the Virginia Polytechnic Institute explain:

China began looking overseas for soy in the mid-1990s when it became clear that its . . . production capacity was insufficient to meet rising demand for this water-hungry crop, so it now imports most of the soybeans it needs and thereby imports 14 per cent of its annual water.[29]

Importing soybeans and other crops brings 'virtual water' into dry countries; the water is imported in the form of plants that received rain or irrigation elsewhere. The largest vehicle of this virtual water trade is cotton, followed by soy. Worldwide, about one-fifth of all such traded water comes in the form of soybeans.[30]

But exported virtual water sometimes comes from a region that is itself dry, or at risk of becoming so. Aquifers in certain u.s. soy-growing areas show serious depletion – mostly because major cities make so many demands on them, but also in part because of agriculture. American aquifer depletion is exacerbated during drought years when some farmers, who usually grow rain-fed soy, dig wells and install irrigation equipment. Similarly, expanding soy cultivation in Brazil's eastern cerrado could easily stress the subterranean water supply. Short-term profits from exporting soy can imperil long-term access to fresh water.

Yet producing other high-quality proteins puts freshwater supplies in even more peril. Water engineers have reported for the UN that 'the water footprint per gram of protein for milk, eggs and chicken meat is about 1.5 times larger' than for bean crops such as

Maize and soy, globally the two most important crops in commercial animal feed, each require a full gallon of fresh water to produce only a handful of seeds. Scientists are developing soy that requires less water, and when irrigation is needed, more efficient methods of drip-irrigation. Innovative drip-irrigation that includes fertilizers with the water is known as 'fertigation'.

soy.[31] And the water needed to produce beef protein is fully six times more than the water requirement for beans. So although under current farming regimens soy plants do drink substantial precious fresh water, compared to animal proteins it turns out that soybeans – when eaten by humans as a *substitute* for animal products – are a water-conserving choice. (Mycoprotein, a fungal product, might be even more water-saving.)

Water conservation should be improved, however. Drip irrigation and micro-sprinklers, which deliver water drop by drop exactly to where it is needed, can reduce agricultural water needs by 30 to 70 per cent even as crop yields rise. Yet such techniques occupy less than 2 per cent of irrigated land globally.[32] Looking both to present-day profits and future sustainability, agronomists and farmers in Nebraska, South Dakota, India, Chile, northwest China and other water-scarce areas are experimenting with various styles of drip irrigation for soybeans.

The Round Table for Responsible Soy (RTRS) addresses water usage and many other environmental and social impacts of cultivating soy (see Chapter Six). Organized in 2006 by a global consortium of 200 participants – large soy farmers, major processing companies, big traders, financial institutions and environmental organizations – the RTRS certifies entities that meet standards for protecting natural habitats, complying with local labour laws and purchasing soy only from similarly certified entities. Required record-keeping and compliance audits give the RTRS stamp of approval genuine meaning.

The RTRS is controversial, however. Some activists object that voluntary certifications whitewash questionable behaviour and that agribusinesses use them to claim that tough governmental regulations are unnecessary. Besides, as Oxfam noted in 2013, the number of RTRS-certified hectares in, for instance, South America is a tiny proportion of the soy-cultivated hectares there.[33] The RTRS is far from enough.

But it is a start, and its technical standards help farmers, inspectors, processors and even consumers make choices. Paraguay's largest soybean-crushing facility, for example, was built with a loan from the Inter-American Development Bank that stipulated it must adhere to RTRS standards for reducing new deforestation. Hand-in-hand with the bank, the factory's owners also designed it to use soy-meal pellets as its energy source; no fossil fuels are burned. In addition, the plant has a zero-effluent system for keeping waste out of the Paraguay River. More environmentally friendly soy processing and farming are clearly feasible.

Vigilance is key. Ultimately, though, the most responsible approach to soy is to avoid feeding it to animals destined to become meat; we could feed more of it to people. Such dietary change on a large scale could have a huge, positive environmental impact (though a negative economic effect on soy industries) because less soy would be needed. Feeding soy directly to people delivers high-quality protein far more efficiently than first feeding soy to livestock and then feeding the livestock to people. But soy as human food brings up many nutritional questions. The myriad, confusing and frequently exaggerated claims about soy's effect on human bodies are taken up in the next chapter.

GROWING SOYBEANS AND other crops poses many actual and potential challenges to environments, including habitat loss, monoculture, genetic modification, toxic chemicals, climate change, erosion and depletion of fresh water. But fatalism is misguided: the destructive effects of farming *can* be mitigated through careful research and ingenuity. No-till cultivation, pest control through organic methods or chemicals with reduced toxicity, effective penalties for environmental rule-breakers and a reduction in the meat eating that drives so much agriculture can each make a genuine difference. The question is how much effort we will put into protecting our natural world. This is our *only* world. There is no other planet for us. There is no 'escape hatch' from our responsibilities – or from the consequences of our actions.

EIGHT

POISON OR PANACEA?

'Everything should be made as simple as possible, but not simpler.'
Composer Roger Sessions, paraphrasing Albert Einstein[1]

As human food, soybeans have quite the reputation – or rather, multiple conflicting reputations. Depending on what one reads or hears, soy is a wonder substance whose consumption reduces the risks of heart disease, breast and prostate cancers, periodontal disease, osteoporosis, chronic obstructive pulmonary disease, Type 2 diabetes, obesity, menopausal hot flushes, infections, blood clots and maybe even neurodegenerative diseases such as Alzheimer's or Lou Gehrig's disease (ALS). Or, alternatively, consuming soy increases the risks of breast cancer, Alzheimer's disease, male infertility, erectile dysfunction, aggressive behaviour, submissive behaviour, social withdrawal, depression, allergic reactions, menstrual disruption, gastrointestinal disturbances, liver disease, calcium malabsorption and problems for the kidneys, gallbladder, pancreas, thyroid and central nervous system. Soy is depicted with a broad brush either as an ideal food or as a pernicious interloper in our diets. A Google search for 'soy and health' yields nearly 53 million entries. How to interpret such cacophony?

It is useful to step back and take stock of the brouhaha. We start by recalling that humans attach layers and layers of meaning to everything we do, and eating is so basic to our survival that it evokes especially strong opinions. With this perspective in mind, we further note that soy has a long history in Asia and yet is new to many cuisines around the world. An ancient food, it can instinctively be viewed either as ordinary, or nearly in a mystical light as a gift from wise ancestors. A new and often highly processed food, its components can be seen either as miracle ingredients of modern science or as alarming additives foisted on unsuspecting populations. Any food

173

both this ancient and this new is bound to carry a full complement of symbolic associations. The first task in deciding how much soy to eat is to recognize that soy is many things to many people, and that mentally assigning it to a single role – poison or panacea – is an oversimplification, symbolically tidy and satisfying though that may feel.

In evaluating health pronouncements about soy, one must also question the sources. What do the various people, companies, media sources and organizations have at stake in their claims – prestige? Increased membership? Increased sales? Do they relay complete evidence about soy foods? Do they assume that anything their opponents declare is automatically wrong? Do they characterize their opponents' positions in emotion-drenched language? Do they leap to conclusions, or do they instead assess evidence carefully? How much consensus is there around the evidence they cite? Is the 'consensus' really just an echo chamber of people repeating the very same thoughts over and over again?

These are difficult questions because everyone in debates about soy foods marshals some sort of evidence; it can be both time-consuming and confusing to sort out differences in the quality of evidence invoked. And motives can be subtle or intentionally obfuscated. This chapter works to clarify these matters by examining three aspects of soy as human food: the intrinsic qualities of the beans, genetic engineering and soy for the malnourished.

THE BASIC BEANS

Just about everyone agrees that soy contains both nutritive and, when raw, anti-nutritive components. Soybeans are high in protein and fibre. They also contain many essential vitamins and minerals: vitamin B6, vitamin K, folate, thiamin, riboflavin, choline, calcium, potassium, copper, iron, magnesium, phosphorus, selenium and zinc. Soybean oil is fairly heart-healthy. When raw, however, certain soybean compounds bind to our digestive enzyme trypsin and prevent it from breaking down proteins in our food. Thus ironically, although soybeans are themselves rich in protein, when eaten raw they interfere with proper protein absorption. The trypsin inhibitors in soy cause consternation in some circles, but their presence is easily remedied: adequate heating inactivates 90 per cent of the offending compounds, a percentage that is entirely sufficient to transform soybeans into a good source of protein.[2] Cooking, along with removal of the bean's hull, also inactivates soy's phytic acid, a compound that would otherwise interfere with absorption of many of soy's beneficial minerals. Cooking and removal of the hull are routine procedures in preparing soy for animals and people. Additional processing techniques, both traditional and modern, are used to remove other soy compounds that can cause flatulence.

Soybeans also contain isoflavones, compounds that act like weak versions of the hormone oestrogen. Herein lies the lion's share of the controversy about soy that has not been genetically engineered (non-GE). Oestrogen naturally occurs in men's as well as women's bodies but is present at higher levels in pre-menopausal women; it regulates the female reproductive system. Soy's association with the word oestrogen, splashed across the Internet, has given the bean a peculiarly gendered image in recent years. Danger and opportunity are perceived in the notion that when eating soy we are feminized.

It is worth examining three disputes about non-GE soy in some detail before tackling the GE question. First, what are we to make of disconcerting headlines about loss of masculinity?

'Scientists Warn of Sperm Count Crisis:
Biggest-ever Study Confirms Drastic Decline in Male Reproductive Health'

'Men Don't Worry about Their Sperm Count – But They Should'

'Sperm Quality & Quantity Declining, Mounting Evidence Suggests'

'Soy, Sperm Count, and Fertility Problems'

'Soy Foods "Reduce Sperm Numbers"'

'Eating Soya Could Slash Men's Sperm Count'[3]

Men rightly ask if they should they stop eating soy. Some wish to become fathers, and others wonder if a food that could cause sperm to falter might impair other bodily functions.

Before addressing the soy query, one must ask if sperm counts are in fact dropping. As with so much in biology, the answer is complex, and in this case also uncertain. Reviewing data from the 1930s forward, a much-publicized 1992 study sounded the alarm, but doubt was later cast on its conclusions.[4] There were inconsistencies in the ways semen was collected, faults in the statistical analysis and geographical differences among populations that might have skewed the data. Since then, some studies have again found reduced sperm counts; notably, one examining semen from more than 26,000 French men found a substantial decline in sperm counts between 1989 and 2005.[5] A 2017 analysis of four decades' worth of semen samples from Western societies similarly detected a significant drop.

Yet other studies have found no change in sperm counts, and some have even found increased sperm. Apparently, trends in sperm quantity depend on the location. The data suggest, for example, that changes in lifestyles or environment in some areas of France are affecting sperm in ways that do not apply to places like Italy, where sperm counts appear to be rising.[6]

Where sperm counts do seem to be dropping, there are many possible causes. Environmental toxins, the residue of birth control pills in water supplies, changes in diet, consumption of soy foods, sexually transmitted diseases, sedentary lifestyles, tighter clothing, stress and even mobile phones in front trouser pockets have all been suggested as culprits.

The soy food connection is far from solid. It is based on conjecture; on data from some studies (but not all) in which male rodents fed high doses of isoflavones developed reproductive abnormalities; and on a 2008 Harvard study of humans.[7] The latter study found a correlation between soy food consumption and decreased sperm count in small subsets of men; the lead author, Jorge Chavarro, described the results as preliminary. Other experts cautioned that previous, carefully controlled studies in men and primates had not found any link between sperm counts and soy.[8] Moreover, millions of Asian men regularly eat more soy foods than the men in the 2008 study yet have no problem conceiving children. Later studies have suggested that the real problem for sperm counts is excess weight: fat tissue produces oestrogen.[9] Possibly, obese men wishing to conceive children should avoid soy foods so as not to add even a little bit of oestrogen to their already high levels, but even that qualified recommendation is unconfirmed. The only soy that is unequivocally excessive here is that which appears in scaremonger headlines.

The second nutritional debate about soy centres on cardiac health. Because oestrogen in pre-menopausal women's bodies was thought to protect their hearts, researchers investigated whether soy isoflavones might similarly be helpful. After analysing two decades of this research, in 1999 the U.S. Food and Drug Administration (FDA) concluded that consumption of soy could significantly benefit heart health in both men and women. Accordingly, the FDA allowed packaging for soy-rich foods to state that '25 grams of soy protein a day, as part of a diet low in saturated fat and cholesterol, may reduce the risk of heart disease.'[10] But then in 2000 an American Heart Association (AHA) review of the research indicated only a negligible positive effect of soybeans on heart health.[11] The contradiction between these assessments, each from a source that is highly respected worldwide, sparked a new round of research.

In 2006, based on more recent studies, the AHA reiterated that soy seems not to have any grand effect on heart health. But, they added, soy products generally contain fats that are acceptable for the heart as well as vitamins, minerals and fibre. Hence, as a substitute for less healthy foods, soy can be a good choice for hearts – not especially better than other nutrient-dense foods, but much better than the empty calories in treats.[12] Meanwhile, the FDA stands by its earlier ruling, still permitting soy-rich foods to tout the nutrition claim. But the FDA also continues to review the science, allowing for a possible policy reversal.

The third soy food dispute pertains to breast cancer. About 80 per cent of breast cancers are oestrogen-receptor positive,[13] which means that the hormone can latch onto and inside the cancer cells. The cancer cells respond to oestrogen by growing and growing beyond the control mechanisms that normally protect the body. Understandably, scientists and people from all walks of life wish to know what effect the weak oestrogens in soy might have on such processes.

The data so far is ambiguous. Imagine a pre-menopausal woman who, unbeknownst to her, has a very tiny oestrogen-sensitive breast tumour. Fond of soy foods, she eats them almost daily. The weak oestrogens in the food reach her dangerous little tumour and latch onto their oestrogen receptors. This prevents the much stronger oestrogen that her body naturally makes from finding many tumour locations to latch on to. The receptors are already occupied. The cancer therefore receives mostly weak oestrogen and does not have as much stimulation to grow. Perhaps the woman's own immune system even manages to eliminate this stymied little tumour, or perhaps the soy foods simply buy her more time before the cancer becomes a problem. In any case, the soy food has apparently been helpful. This is one theory about the interaction between soy and breast cancer, and some evidence seems to support it. Epidemiological studies show that Japanese and South Korean women – who eat far more soy protein than their counterparts in other industrialized countries – have remarkably low breast cancer rates, the lowest among developed nations.[14]

Now imagine a different woman who also has a tiny, oestrogen-positive breast tumour, only she has already gone through menopause. Her body therefore now makes only limited oestrogen; her tumour does not receive much stimulation from her own natural oestrogen. But, like the younger woman, she too eats soy foods frequently, and her tumour receives oestrogen from that source. A tumour whose growth might have been very sluggish ends up receiving more oestrogen than it otherwise would have. It receives nowhere near as much oestrogen as what circulates naturally in the body of a woman of child-bearing age, but the amount is still more than this woman would have had if she hadn't consumed the weak plant oestrogens. In this scenario, heavy consumption of soy foods is a bad idea for post-menopausal women who are at special risk for breast cancer or who have already been diagnosed with it. Evidence for this theory comes especially from an oft-cited 2004 study.[15] In it, post-menopausal rats with induced breast tumours were fed a type of isoflavone from soybeans. The rats experienced increased tumour weights compared to similar rats not fed the isoflavone.

The picture is even more complex because of the possible role of isoflavones on breast development in young females. Some researchers posit that East Asian women have low breast cancer rates because frequent soy consumption early in life changes their breast architecture; a large study in Shanghai showed that women who ate the most soy both in adolescence and in adulthood had the lowest rates of pre-menopausal breast cancer.[16] Their breasts seemed to grow in ways that protected them from future cancer. Other research suggests that if a woman who ate a lot of soy in adolescence does get breast cancer, her cancer is less severe than that of non-soy eaters.[17]

But some scholars disagree, pointing to studies suggesting, possibly, the opposite conclusions. The scientific validity of *all* the studies is disputed. The controversy is sufficient that the Solae Company, a soy-processing firm now owned by DuPont, petitioned the FDA for the right to put a health claim about cancer reduction on its products and then withdrew the request after a public and scientific outcry. Meanwhile, the FDA has made no official comment on the relationship between soy and various cancers. The research is still too uncertain; definitive pronouncements seem premature.

The same can in fact be said for virtually all of the health pronouncements about soybeans, both positive and negative, that appear in the first paragraph of this chapter. So far, the evidence suggests that dietary soy in non-extreme quantities (that is, soy as a food, not as hyper-concentrated isoflavone pills) neither hurts nor helps the organs and disease processes listed. The exception is allergies; some people – possibly up to 2 per cent of people of European origin, though the proportion is probably far lower – are indeed allergic to the beans.[18] Among the list of health and disease processes attributed to soy consumption, allergy is the one well-documented, scientifically clear phenomenon, albeit only for a very small percentage of the earth's population. For all the other processes, the scientific evidence is scant, unexciting, unclear – or usually, all three – for any effects of soy beyond the basic nutritive value of its protein, oil, fibre, vitamins and minerals. Soy is neither a cure nor a curse; it is simply a food. It is most appropriately associated in our minds neither with 'feared conditions' nor 'fantastic remedy', but rather with 'flavourful cooking'. It is neither 'antidote' nor 'ailment', but instead 'aliment'.

BIOTECH BEANS

What about foods made with genetically engineered soy (or GE soy – also called GMO, for 'genetically modified organism')? Should such foods be feared, or applauded? Prohibited, more tightly regulated, deregulated, funded, labelled? Why or why not? To formulate thoughtful answers to these questions, one must first have a general grasp of genetic engineering. Among scientists, each step has its

Genetically engineered soy seedlings are grown for further testing and breeding.

own, precise terminology – but, as with any field, outsiders can find this jargon a barrier to comprehension, in the same way that people who are not carpenters, plumbers or chefs may be puzzled by all the tool names and terminology in those professions. In layman's language, then, here are common, basic steps that have been used for genetically modifying soybeans:

1. Have a goal for how you want to alter soybeans. Then notice what other living thing has the precise quality you want soy to obtain (for example, which organism produces a certain kind of oil, or is not affected by a particular chemical, or is able to survive with less water, and so on). Figure out which gene enables the organism to have that desired quality.

2. Pull DNA out of that 'donor' organism.

3. Separate out the gene you want from the rest of the 'donor' DNA.

4. Make thousands of copies of the gene you separated out. Do so by producing them inside a fast-growing bacterium such as *E. coli.*

5. Subtract unneeded portions from the many gene copies, and add elements enabling the genes to function optimally inside soy's DNA. Added elements include:

- a second gene that will later make it easy to see if the entire process worked. This extra gene is called the 'selectable marker' because it will eventually mark the soy cells that have been successfully modified. The selectable marker will also enable you to select the successfully modified cells out of a mass of unwanted cells. Commonly, the selectable marker gene will make the desired soy cells respond differently from other soy cells either to an antibiotic or to a herbicide.

- a DNA 'promoter' to stimulate activity of the sought-after gene (the gene from steps 1 and 3). In the engineering of plants, the most common promoter comes from the Cauliflower Mosaic Virus. Other plant viruses have also been used to promote genes added to soy, including Figwort Mosaic Virus. (Crop scientists have cobbled together promoters from the DNA of various other organisms as well. Some promoters have been developed to stimulate a gene only temporarily. Such a promoter is itself designed to be activated only when exposed to a specific molecule – for example, oestradiol, a type of oestrogen that becomes the temporary prodder of the promoter. This kind of layered modification reflects the increasing complexity of engineering soy and other plants. Work that is ever more precise and sophisticated goes hand-in-hand with tools that are ever more tailored to specific molecular tasks.)

The entire set of DNA pieces joined to one another at this stage is referred to as a 'cassette'. Cassettes differ depending on what the engineer is trying to accomplish.

6. Prepare very immature soybean cells to receive the new gene nestled within its cassette.

7. Put the cassette into the immature soy cells carefully, so as not to ruin the cells. This can be done with soy using a molecular-level gene 'gun' that shoots the cassettes into cells. More often, scientists make use of the microorganism *Agrobacterium tumefaciens*'s natural ability to insert DNA into plants. In addition, cassettes have sometimes been inserted into soybean roots using a different *Agrobacterium*. (With other crops, scientists can achieve insertions by other means, including microscopic fibres coated with the designer cassettes to poke them into crop cells – in essence using a needle rather than a gun; and electrical impulses to get tiny pores in the crop cell walls to open, allowing the cassettes to pass inside – in essence an electronic door key. Soy is a notably difficult crop to transform, and these methods have proved less successful for it.)

8. Some of the immature soy cells now contain the new gene and the rest of its cassette. Many do not, and even among those that do, depending on the method you used, the gene may frequently not end up in a good position on the soy DNA in order to be effective. Repeat step 7 several hundred times, so that a few cells will actually both have the cassette *and* have it in the right place for it to be expressed. If you have been able to use one of the newer, more precise gene insertion methods, this repetition step will be more efficient.

9. Using the selectable marker in your cassette, pull out only the successfully marked soy cells from all the others. For example, if cells containing the cassette are marked by their ability to survive a particular herbicide when other cells would die, then expose all the soy cells to that herbicide, and see which ones survive. Those contain your desired gene (the one you obtained in step 3). Discard the other soy cells.

10. In a greenhouse, let the successfully modified soy cells mature into the first generation of your GE soy plants. Collect the seeds they produce, which too have the new gene in their DNA.

11. A regular plant breeder can now use the seeds to grow a second, bigger generation of the new soy plants. These GE plants are mated to traditional soy varieties with their own desirable characteristics (for instance, a particular traditional variety grows well at a certain latitude, another tends to be resistant to a certain pest, and so on). Through many iterations of cross-breeding, new varieties will be formed that include the traditional good characteristics AND the desired new gene.

Scientific articles about this work are daunting for people outside of the field. The work is all done at a microscopic level, with specialized techniques and equipment. Each of the minuscule chemicals has a specific, detailed name, as if all the Lego building projects of an entire city's children were complexly named according to the positions, sizes, shapes and connecting functions of the variable pieces in the creations.

Yet the steps in genetic engineering are not fundamentally exotic – the verbs above indicate basic processes found in many endeavours: finding, separating, copying, marking, stimulating, inserting, cultivating and breeding. To scientists with long years of absorbing the terminology and procedures of their profession, the processes can be challenging the way a top chef might find it challenging to create a very elaborate, original cake as the final exam for a demanding culinary award (the 2009 documentary *Kings of Pastry* illuminates the sustained and intense training, creativity and effort required).[19] To the scientist, genetic engineering does not seem freakish or like 'playing God' any more than making a carefully planned, novel, multi-layered, difficult, complex cake seems to the virtuoso baker.

Genetic engineering is to them, rather, a practical process, similar to genetic modifications that occur all the time in nature and that plant breeders have been using, with less precision, for millennia. A 2007 paper from industry crop scientists Larkin and Harrigan clarifies how genetic engineers view conventional breeding techniques

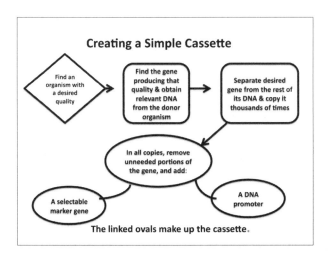

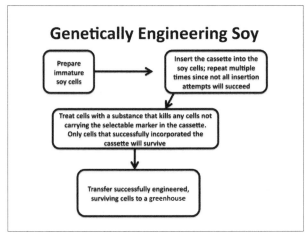

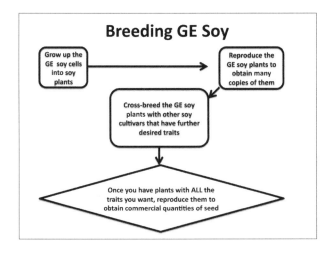

(which, it should be noted, have for many decades included radiation and chemical bombardment of plants in an effort to induce genetic changes 'naturally'). Larkin and Harrigan explain that certain tomatoes have been conventionally bred to resist infection with roundworms. The tomatoes were crossbred with a related poisonous South American plant. This non-GE effort successfully introduced into the tomatoes a roundworm-resistance gene, called *Mi*. But the cross-breeding, because it was necessarily imprecise, also introduced many other genes from the poisonous plant – probably hundreds of genes. Are the new tomatoes safe? We cannot be sure. Yet few countries place any restrictions on the cultivation of this or any other new plants achieved through conventional breeding, even though little is known about their full genetic profiles. New plants formed through conventional breeding rarely have to undergo any testing.

By contrast, genetic engineers have isolated and cloned *Mi* and have been able to insert this gene, and *only* this one of the poisonous cousin's genes, into tomatoes. The resulting GE tomatoes are subject by law to extensive testing. The authors assert:

> Most people given this information arrive at the view that the greater inherent risk resides, not with the GM tomato, but with the conventionally bred tomato, carrying hundreds of unknown genes from a poisonous and inedible plant and not subject to regulatory scrutiny . . . There are risks of unintended consequences associated with both conventional and transgenic modes of plant breeding.[20]

The authors are not arguing that all GE crops are necessarily safe or that regulations should be diminished. They simply assert that

> GM crops should not be considered a single monolithic class that is either good or bad for the economy, agriculture or the environment. Each novel crop [whether GE or conventionally bred] should be considered on its own merits and demerits.[21]

Unfortunately, the straightforward, core aspects of genetic engineering have been inadequately conveyed to the public. Yes, there are mysterious aspects to the process of genetic engineering – why did this experiment turn out *that* way? – but so also there can be mysteries of food chemistry as to why a particular, delicate cake did not turn out as expected. Puzzling out the answers and finding solutions are part of the job. But because the terminology and tools of genetic engineering do not appear in everyday life, the field seems more alien than other endeavours.

Some of the problem of scientific communication has been the presence of poorly explained, scary-sounding words. In the relative absence of clear explanations, guessed-at interpretations circulate instead. In the case of GE soy as human food, concerns have swirled around the steps above that we can label 'find a gene', 'copy in *E. coli*', 'add another gene with resistance', 'add pieces of a virus' and 'make use of *Agrobacterium tumefaciens*'. The most widely publicized of these apprehensions centres around the first, 'find a gene', and we begin there.

In locating a gene to introduce into a crop, scientists often skip far beyond the levels of shared taxonomic genus, family, order, class and phylum, and end up finding the gene they want in a species from an entirely different kingdom or domain in the tree of life. Thus genes from bacteria commonly end up inside plants – especially in cotton, corn and soy. This creativity spurs anti-GE activists to decry the final products as 'Frankenfoods', evoking the murderous monster cobbled together from mismatched, ill-fitting parts.

But is it so strange, really, to add to or subtract from the building blocks of life? The answer depends in part on whether one emphasizes the word 'blocks' in that query, or the word 'life'. Some in the debate focus on genes as blocks whose patterns give instructions to other molecular blocks; they point out that all living things have genes, and a great many genes are shared. For instance, about one-third of the genes in yeast have an equivalent gene in humans,[22] often one so incredibly similar that one can remove a gene from yeast, insert a human gene in its place and cause no ill effects for the yeast. It is possible to create a healthy, normal-acting human-gened yeast.[23] Genes are thus not mystical entities. In fact, their deletions, rearrangements, borrowings, copying, insertions and novel creation are completely ordinary and even necessary for the survival of life in ever-changing environments. Such modifications occur fairly frequently in nature, often quite randomly and also often for some creature's targeted purpose. In particular, certain bacteria and viruses are adept at genetically engineering each other and other organisms across different domains of life.

From this point of view, a bacterial gene added to soybeans is not a dramatically alien insertion. In fact, soybeans' many useful properties derive from the diversity of their unusually large and complex genome. In addition to soy's ancestral DNA from bacteria (which all life forms, including humans, share), it also appears that during soy's evolution, twice in the distant past the plant acquired new sets of genes. In the latter of these incidents, some 13 to 15 million years ago,[24] it seems the second gene set came from another species. Following both events, the second sets gradually underwent an unusually high number of changes. Soy is full of varied genes; that is its normal state of being.

On the other hand, although genes are like ordinary blocks, life processes are nevertheless mysterious. Much is unknown about how genes function in tandem and in relation to non-gene sections of DNA. The fact that we humans share many genes with other organisms (99 per cent with chimpanzees[25]) shows that one does not necessarily have to alter a large percentage of genes in order to create major changes in life forms. So although gene transfer is common in nature and so far has not been terribly problematic in crop engineering, it *can* be powerful. How powerful depends on the specifics of the genetic transfer. Genes are part of life, and living things can have dramatic effects on one another.

Could scientists attempting to change a single gene inadvertently change other genes in ways that are undesirable, yet subtle enough not to be detected until after the plants are widely grown? Could researchers unwittingly change other areas of DNA that do not include genes but could have noxious effects on genes? These outcomes are possible, particularly as scientific techniques and understanding advance, allowing for more precision – but also for greater and greater speed, which could encourage carelessness.

For example, molecules with curious names such as 'zinc-finger nucleases', 'TALENS', 'Crispr-Cas9' and 'Cas9-Guide RNA' have been discovered and modified to function as nanoscopic scissors, quickly targeting specified regions of DNA for cutting and gene insertion. As the ability to place new genes into soy becomes more exact, the very first step in genetic engineering – the finding of useful genes to add, even from very different organisms – becomes at the same time both less and more perilous. Precision reduces risk, but speed – and the decreasing expense of genetic engineering – add hazard as more and more universities, companies and research institutes race to profit from novel techniques and products. This situation applies, of course, not only to agriculture, but also to the industrial and medical applications of genetic engineering.

Beyond worries about what scientists will end up creating when they 'find a gene', a second concern is the use of *E. coli* for copying DNA. The very phrase 'E. coli' strikes fear: after all, toxic *E. coli* on poorly washed vegetables or undercooked meat can kill people. But the strain of *E. coli* used in laboratory work of many kinds, including genetic engineering, is very different from the toxic kind. Among bacteria, there can be vast differences in genetic make-up, even within the same species. In the case of *E. coli*, the species is in reality a continuum of organisms that only have a small core of DNA in common.[26] This variability of *E. coli* is a very good thing, because versions of those bacteria naturally live in the human gut, protecting us from harmful pathogens, aiding us in digesting our food and producing vitamin K for us to use. *E. coli* and other helpful gut bacteria are more truly 'man's best friend' than any dog could ever be.

Not only is laboratory *E. coli* thoroughly non-virulent, but also when a gene that was copied within the *E. coli* is extracted, the bacteria themselves are destroyed. The leftovers are discarded. They are not inserted into any plant and therefore do not end up in our food supply. So worries about *E. coli* in genetic modification are misplaced. In press releases and abstracts, scientific communicators could help the public understand this by regularly referring more fully – and accurately – to the lab strain of *E. coli* as 'beneficial *E. coli*' or some similar phrase.

A third part of genetic modification sparking concern is the procedure to 'add another gene with resistance'. As noted above, resistance to an antibiotic or herbicide functions as a kind of marker – a way of identifying and separately harvesting cells in which the effort to add genetic material actually succeeded. But could a resistance gene eventually cause problems? Doesn't antibiotic resistance compromise the efficacy of some of our most important medicines?

Antibiotic resistance is indeed a worldwide medical problem. Scientists agree that it is provoked by excessive and inappropriate uses of antibiotics in humans and livestock – not by antibiotic-resistance genes in plants. In fact a 2014 UN report on worldwide antimicrobial resistance found no need even to mention crop modification.[27]

While resistance genes in GE crops could conceivably jump to bacteria in the soil, the likelihood that this could create problems is very low. First, in field conditions genes are generally degraded and no longer viable outside the plant. Second, if a soil bacterium were to acquire an antibiotic-resistance gene, it would have no survival advantage over the millions of other microbes around it. It is not in an antibiotic-drenched environment in which it could be the last microbe left, free to multiply without the obstruction of competitor microbes. Third, most soil bacteria have no interest in human bodies; they are far less likely to infect humans than are livestock microbes.

Transfer of genes in the soil is not a significant risk. But does this mean we can serenely *eat* antibiotic-resistance genes that might still be within the modified crops? Could a resistance gene within the plant – one that had originally come from a bacterium – be transferred to bacteria already present in our digestive tracts, giving them dangerous drug-resistance?

In the late 1990s, one research team found that when mice were fed large quantities of viral DNA, that DNA did not transfer to the bacteria that naturally occur in mouse guts.[28] Moreover, later scientific studies found that various farm animals ingesting GE crops did not retain any intact DNA from the plants.[29]

However another, very small study found that under extreme conditions (in people missing large sections of their digestive tracts), about 4 per cent of the herbicide-resistance DNA in GE soy could be found, undigested, in human faeces. Worse, a few microorganisms in the individuals' digestive tracts did incorporate that material into their own genetic codes.[30] Although the gene in question did not code for antibiotic resistance, the study did suggest that under certain very specific, unusual circumstances, genes from GE soy could affect gut flora in an unsought, and conceivably unhealthy, manner.

Typically, the processing that soy undergoes when it is turned into food breaks down the plant's genes. In addition, human digestion breaks down DNA. Moreover, for an extra layer of protection governments regulate which antibiotic-resistance genes GE companies may use. Permitted genes are generally ones conferring resistance to antibiotics little used in human medicine. Thus in the unlikely event that such a gene were to migrate to an infectious microbe, the antibiotic losing potency would be one that doctors rarely prescribe anyway.

A 2008 study published by the UK's Royal Society of Medicine explained that

> the probability of transmission of antibiotic resistance from plants to bacteria is extremely low and . . . the hazard occurring from any such transfer is at worst, slight. Nevertheless, other selection strategies that do not rely on antibiotic resistance have been developed, and procedures to eliminate the selectable marker from the plant genome once its purpose has been fulfilled have also been designed.[31]

All signs are that GE crops with antibiotic-resistance genes are safe to eat, and that they are being phased out anyway.

But then there is the matter of viruses used as 'promoters' to stimulate genes. In the 1980s, scientists discovered that in many plants, genetic instructions from the Cauliflower Mosaic Virus (CAMV) are remarkably effective at activating the host plant's own genes. CAMV has since been extensively used in crop engineering; it has activated many genes – as well as polemics about its safety. Since the late 1990s a few scientists-turned-activists have sounded an alarm about using segments of this virus: they fear they are genetically unstable and too powerful.[32] They worry that GE foods with promoters could stimulate the wrong genes within people eating them. The activists cite a handful of older studies that found CAMV promoter activity in mammalian cells. Later studies, however, have *not* found this promoter compatible with mammalian DNA.[33]

Because it is a plant virus, CAMV has not evolved to infect animals or humans, and in fact humans commonly consume it in ordinary, non-GE foods to no ill effect. For those who doubt, however, the question lingers as to whether the ways in which the virus has been chopped up and modified for GE purposes could render it newly infectious, newly gene-stimulating or allergenic to people. Yet many assessments over many years and in many countries have failed to find any CAMV risk to human health in current GE crops.

We come now to the *Agrobacterium tumefaciens* step in crop engineering. Here again lurks a word that strikes fear. The DNA that this ingenious bacterium inserts into plants causes the plants to develop tumours, which then produce nutrients for the bacterium. Could soybeans that have been modified using *Agrobacterium* therefore cause human tumours – maybe even cancer? The definitive answer is 'no'. Scientists completely remove the piece of *Agrobacterium* DNA that induces tumours long, long before the genetic engineering is finished. The final soy plants do not develop tumours, and no tumours can arise in humans from this technique. The tumour scare here arises from incomplete understanding of the GE process.

Genetic engineering is not as dangerous as some believe: worries about *E. coli*, antibiotic resistance and tumours can be quite overblown. Yet crop modification carries enough risk to warrant rigorous regulation – particularly because scientific understanding of how genes and other parts of DNA function together is still limited. Many studies indicate that our current GE crops are safe to eat – but as more and more GE techniques are invented, are existing regulations sufficient to keep us out of harm's way? In 2004, researchers from twelve European institutes asserted that although many worries could be put to rest,

> The next generation of GM crops is likely to include those with . . . more far reaching effects on metabolic processes, i.e. an increased complexity of the genetic modification . . . This could lead to the occurrence of unpredictable unintended effects . . . not revealed by [the typical] approach [to crop testing].[34]

The tenor of their report is 'proceed, but with meticulous caution.'

The development of RNAi silencing as a GE technique spotlights both the great promise and the unknowns in gene manipulation. This technology harnesses organisms' natural capacity to use short molecules of ribonucleic acid (RNA) to interfere with or 'silence' gene expression. Organisms sometimes use RNAi (the 'i' stands for 'interference') to tamp down expression of their own genes, so that each gene's instructions are used only when and to the extent necessary. At other times, organisms use RNAi to silence the genes of an infecting agent such as a virus, thereby incapacitating it.

Genetic engineers have appropriated each of these RNAi processes to alter crops. In soy, Monsanto used RNAi to develop its

'Vistive Gold' beans; RNAi was adapted to silence the beans' own normal conversion of one fatty acid into another. This modification created beans whose oil had greater levels of the heart-healthier fatty acid. The U.S. government has deemed this crop safe.

Scientists have also used RNAi to help soybeans resist viruses. This technique mimics an ancient biological process conserved throughout evolution. Organisms take advantage of a weakness common in viruses: in order to reproduce, viruses need a kind of RNA that is vulnerable to being 'stolen' by the organism the virus is attacking. The host organism can use this stolen code to launch a counter-attack that targets and then silences the viral RNA. The host thus uses the virus's own RNA code as a weapon against it.

Genetic engineers tap into this natural system: they steal the viral RNA on behalf of the soy plants and insert the code into them. This assistance greatly speeds up the progress of host defences, allowing soy to launch its counter-attack and silence viral reproduction much sooner than in the ordinary unfolding of evolution. A similar technique fights non-viral pests, including the soybean cyst nematode that annually causes hundreds of millions of dollars in damage worldwide.

Crop scientists must be circumspect to ensure that the pest genes they silence are not too similar to genes in higher organisms. That is, RNAi technology must not inadvertently interfere with the host crops' own essential genes or genes in the livestock and humans who eat the crops. Protection from genetic interference is also imperative for non-targeted creatures in the environment that might nibble on or pollinate the crop.

The need for vigilance in searching for unintended effects of RNAi silencing is highlighted by the fact that RNAi silencing itself, like many scientific advances, was a surprise discovery. Scientists altering petunia genetics in the 1990s had a very unexpected outcome from their experiment. A thoroughly unintended change in the petunias' colour led them to detect RNAi silencing, for which they won the Nobel Prize. Of course, surprises are a wellspring of scientific progress. Still, one must assiduously implement rules so as not to release anything potentially injurious outside of laboratories into the wider world. Fortunately, RNAi technology has so far been used responsibly and, as far as testing shows, without adverse impacts. Various RNAi soybeans have been shown equivalent to non-GE soy in amino acid, fatty acid and isoflavone profiles, as well as levels of ash, moisture, carbohydrates and anti-nutrients.[35] Nutritionally, these RNAi-manipulated soybeans are apparently the same as ordinary soybeans.

We have examined the process of genetic engineering – but what of specific GE soybean products? The finding of nutritional equivalence between RNAi-modified soybeans and non-GE varieties holds up for other types of GE soybeans as well. Detailed analyses reveal that the levels of various components, including allergy-provoking proteins, are, on average, the same in commercial GE and non-GE soy. Repeated testing has failed to find any human illness caused by the eating of GE soy.[36] Yes, small studies here and there have found GE soy inferior, but such studies are outliers and often plagued by experimental flaws.

Herbicide residues have prompted concern, as sometimes farmers use glyphosate heavily on their glyphosate-tolerant soybeans, which retain some of the chemical. In 2015 controversy over glyphosate escalated. Researchers routinely assessing its safety for the EU were soon to release their finding that the chemical posed no long-term risks at the exposure rates associated with normal agriculture when their report was 'scooped' by a similar group working for the UN's World Health Organization (WHO). But the WHO group had come to the opposite conclusion. Based on data suggesting that at high doses glyphosate is associated with tumours in laboratory animals and that exposing human cells to glyphosate can damage their DNA, the WHO group classified glyphosate as 'probably carcinogenic' for humans. Monsanto was furious, environmentalists felt vindicated, numerous scientists were sceptical of the WHO's research methods, and many other scientists felt that further analysis was warranted.[37] Then, in 2016 a different WHO analysis determined that the low level of glyphosate in human diets is unlikely to induce cancer.[38] These studies all focused on glyphosate in food. Other types of exposure – for instance among farm workers – need more study.

As for the beans themselves, some GE soy is actually better for human health than non-GE varieties. Certain GE soybeans, for instance, contain oil improved for heart health. Oil from Monsanto's Vistive Gold soybeans is engineered to have a long shelf life without needing hydrogenation; it therefore lacks the artery-clogging trans-fats that hydrogenation produces. Businesses and institutions with large frying operations buy oil in bulk and therefore require long shelf life; this new soy gives them a healthier option than hydrogenation. This soy oil is also quite low in saturated fat. The company is waiting to commercialize the crop until various foreign governments approve it, as they wish to market it heavily for export.

Meanwhile, DuPont has garnered u.s. and Canadian regulatory approval for its own GE soybeans with long-shelf-life oil. Most of the export markets for these beans, called Plenish, have legally approved them, including China, Mexico and Japan. Their oil is high in mono-unsaturated fat, the same ingredient in olive oil that benefits the human cardiovascular system.

Not to be outcompeted, Monsanto has created another soybean with oil engineered to be salutary. This one is high in a fatty acid that the human body naturally converts to be similar to fish oil, providing a boost to heart health. Monsanto argues that marketing this soy could reduce the over-harvesting of wild fisheries. This bean was engineered using a gene from a primula flower, cousin of the primrose, along with a gene from a non-toxic, non-allergenic mould. Government approval in the u.s. is under way.

Research is proceeding on engineering still more soybeans with healthful qualities. Experimenters are making soy with more vita-min E, as well as soy with more of certain amino acids that human bodies use to make proteins. And, since ordinary soy can provoke allergic reactions, beans lacking the allergenic proteins have been a coveted goal. In 2003 a team led by soy-allergen expert Eliot Herman of the USDA published a GE method for creating a soybean lacking its usual major allergen.[39] But consumer distrust of genetic modification made companies leery of commercializing that bean, particularly in the infant formulas for which a low-allergen soy could be most profitable.

Twelve years later, a new team of crop scientists, including Herman, announced that they had screened 16,000 varieties of soy until they found one in which the key allergen was naturally absent. They then bred it with varieties, previously identified by soy geneticist Theodore Hymowitz, that lack two of soy's anti-nutritive properties. Finally, still using conventional breeding, the team spent ten years patiently breeding and cross-breeding the offspring with a commercially successful variety. At last they had developed a new,

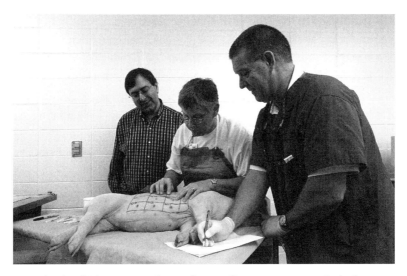

Two University of Arkansas researchers perform an allergy test on an anaesthetized, soy-sensitive pig. Soy allergy expert Eliot Herman of the USDA looks on. Dr Herman has pioneered development of soybeans that do not provoke allergies.

agronomically viable, non-GE, low-allergen, low-antinutrient soybean. They dubbed it 'Triple Null'.[40] The history of these efforts serves as a microcosm of the science and business environment for crop enhancement. It demonstrates that both GE methods and conventional breeding can develop desired crop traits, that the GE method is faster though less commercially acceptable, and that the same individuals can embrace both.

The lead scientist in Triple Null's development, Monica Schmidt, also joined with Herman and a paediatric surgeon-gastroenterologist to develop an unusual, therapeutic GE soybean. This soybean is engineered to produce a protein that speeds development of the digestive tracts of premature infants, thereby helping protect them from a digestive infection that kills about 4,000 U.S. babies yearly. This soy could be used for premature babies in a therapeutic infant formula as an effective, inexpensive way to save lives and prevent tiny babies from needing major rescue surgery.[41]

Other researchers are exploring how to engineer soy so it will grow medicines inside its beans, including:

- antibodies against a herpes virus that attacks the human vagina;

- antibodies to HIV (the virus that causes AIDS);

- standard vaccines, in order to deliver them more quickly and less expensively to needy populations;

- human growth hormone, used to treat genetic diseases and the muscle wasting associated with AIDS;

- insulin for diabetics;

- novokinin, a blood pressure drug;

- a protein used to treat haemophilia; and

- a protein used to test for thyroid disease (at present very expensively obtained from living human thyroid tissue or from cadavers).

When genetically modified, soybeans are particularly good at supplying proteins with medical value, as soy naturally:

- produces high levels of protein in general;

- can generate inserted proteins that are too large and complex to be made via other technologies;

- produces compact beans that are relatively easily transported and stored (unlike traditional vaccines and other medicines, soybeans require no refrigeration);

- is less likely to be contaminated with germs affecting humans than are other organisms used for harvesting medicines;

- is easy to feed people (for example, in flavoured soy milk) to deliver the medication; and

- is inexpensive. As a scientific team explained in 2013, 'a single soybean plant can produce 500 doses of a vaccine' – a $50,000 value.[42]

Soy has great potential, then, to contribute to human health when it has been genetically altered for medical benefits.

But once again, there are risks. There have been near-misses, in which a GE crop could have caused harm if it had been commercially released. Two cases deserve attention. First, in 1995 Pioneer Hi-Bred sought to improve animal feed by inserting a gene for a protein from Brazil nuts into soybeans. Even though Brazil nuts were a known human allergen, based on animal studies the crop engineers believed that the particular protein they were generating would not be allergenic. Still, they checked their assumption by partnering with the University of Nebraska, which had blood samples from individuals with Brazil-nut allergy. To the scientists' great disappointment, the blood reacted allergically to the new soybeans. The research was terminated, since Pioneer Hi-Bred concluded that on farms, in silos and during transport this GE soy designed for animals could accidentally get mixed into soy intended for humans and so pose a threat to the food supply.

This episode taught the biotech industry not to use any part of clearly allergenic foods for genetic engineering. Questions of profitability, public relations, ethics and liability all make Pioneer Hi-Bred's misfortune a cautionary tale for business executives. Thus when anti-GE activists raise fears that companies will hide known allergens inside foods, they promote an unrealistic view of business. No profit-seeking company would now use known allergens for crop engineering, and in fact, international guidelines forbid it. Companies take the guidelines seriously because they are used to adjudicate trade disputes.

But the care to avoid using known allergens cannot fully protect against unknown ones. An Australian study from 2005, oft cited both by pro-GE and anti-GE activists with respect to allergy surprises, bears discussion. The research seemed to show, for the first time, that genetic engineering could convert a non-allergenic protein into a protein evoking a definite immune response in lab mice, though under rather artificial conditions. Moreover, this unexpected immune response apparently caused the mice to react afterwards to other, ordinary proteins that they had not been sensitive to beforehand. The finding prompted Australia's Commonwealth Scientific and Industrial Research Organization (CSIRO) to drop a decade-long effort to develop weevil-resistant peas.[43]

On the one hand, the Australian scientists were prudent in handling their GE peas. Even though the peas did not induce a full-blown allergic response in the mice, and no data exists on whether the peas would produce any reaction in humans, the institute halted the work. They have not resumed it, despite a 2013 Austrian study in which mice did *not* have any out-of-the-ordinary immune reactions to these GE peas.[44] Thus scientific safeguards functioned properly. Scientific creativity was employed, and afterwards so also was a precautionary attitude.

Yet, on the other hand, although GE plants are more rigorously tested than conventional crops, not all GE testing is as thorough as that given to the peas. The unanticipated outcome of the pea project, whose results are still not fully understood, gives pause for thought. It is, in fact, conceivable that genetic modification could introduce into foods a new allergenic protein, and current testing guidelines are imperfect for detecting this kind of problem. The risk is low – actually much lower than introducing a new food from overseas (such as kiwi fruit) to a population, since whole foods include far more proteins in higher 'doses' than the couple or so proteins that are engineered into familiar foods. But all the same, a risk does exist.

Commentators generally take one of two perspectives on the Australian peas. They either feel that

> Researchers had worthy motivation to protect an important crop from a nasty pest. Despite this impetus, they responsibly prioritized avoiding any potential problem for the food supply.

or

> Scientists created the potential problem in the first place and are dangerously messing around with our foods.

These two viewpoints exemplify the documented gap between scientists' perceptions of genetic engineering and that of many in the broader public.

To these two cases, we might add the concern that GE crops approved to feed animals, but not yet approved for humans, could accidentally get into our foods. This did happen with Starlink corn (maize), which reached the market for animal feed in 1998. Maize for human consumption soon became contaminated with Starlink, leading to a large u.s. food recall in 2000. Starlink was thereafter taken off the market. Medical experts found no evidence that Starlink had caused harm to any of the 51 people who claimed adverse effects from it, but their testing was not 100 per cent conclusive.[45] The damage to public perceptions was very real, however. There was also considerable financial damage for Starlink's manufacturer, Aventis CropScience. Once again, the biotech industry learned a hard lesson, the one that Pioneer Hi-Bred had already foreseen with soybeans: do not make food crops into GE animals-only feed crops on any assumption that food and feed can always be kept separate. Fortunately for the soy industry and soy foods producers, this error has not been made in commercializing GE soybeans.

The differences between public and scientists' perceptions of GE foods are stark even in the u.s., where GE foods began and are more accepted than elsewhere. A 2015 survey by the Pew Research Center found that, overall, 'Science holds an esteemed place among citizens and professionals'; yet on specific topics the u.s. public often disagrees with the American Association for the Advancement of Science (AAAS). In particular,

> A majority of the general public (57 per cent) says that genetically modified (GM) foods are generally *unsafe* to eat, while 37 per cent says such foods are safe; by contrast, 88 per cent of AAAS scientists say GM foods are generally *safe* . . . This is the largest opinion difference between the public and scientists

across thirteen issues in biomedicine, agriculture, climate science, energy and space exploration. The public sector most in agreement with the scientists about GE crops was professional farmers.[46] Organic farmers, who constitute fewer than 10 per cent of u.s. cultivators, do not use GE crops,[47] but almost all other u.s. farmers do.

In Europe, many farmers view GE crops favourably but cannot grow them due to government restrictions. Although Europe imports a great deal of GE animal feed, many policy-makers and citizens reject GE crops for human food and brook no GE fields in their countries. In 2011–12, for example, 80 per cent of French survey respondents disapproved of GE crops in open fields within their borders, and

79 per cent were hostile to GE foods.[48] Interestingly, polls suggest that Western Europeans tend not to spurn genetic engineering in industrial and medical applications. But in Europe food is a different matter; Europeans are protective of their foods as bearers of heritage, health and a deeply embodied sense of self. Among ordinary citizens, the very idea of buying GE food is stigmatized.

Of course, European consumers could not easily reject GE foods in their marketplaces if they did not know which foods had been modified. But they do know, because in the EU all foods (and animal feeds) with more than 0.9 per cent GE ingredients must be labelled as containing genetically modified organisms (GMOs). The EU adopted this standard in 1997, following a well-organized effort by Greenpeace and other activists to influence public opinion.[49] The EU's action set the tone for many other countries.

Now global exporters must hire legal experts to advise them, as the laws vary from place to place and year to year. Some countries follow the 0.9 per cent standard, while others set a 5 per cent limit; some have exempted animal feed from GMO labelling; some only label particular ingredients and products (because of its prominence as a GE crop, soy as food is always subject to GE monitoring); some compel labelling of GE foods in retail stores but have no requirements for restaurant food; and so on. In numerous nations, growing GE crops is prohibited, but prepared GE foods can be imported as long as they are labelled.

Meanwhile, in other nations no labelling of GE foods is required, as authorities agree with the preponderant scientific opinion that these foods are equivalent to conventional ones in nutrition and health impacts. The policy-makers have also been influenced by food-producer lobbies. Businesses that design, grow, process or market GE foods intensely wish to avoid a repeat of their European experience.

In the no-labelling countries, the companies fear that adding a 'GMO' label will frighten consumers away. They argue that scaring consumers away from nutritive, non-dangerous foods just because they were made through complex and novel processes is unfair to businesses that have invested heavily to develop these useful products. They protest that labelling GE foods gives non-GE competitors – especially the organics industry – an unjustifiable advantage. For decades, these arguments particularly held sway in two major GE-producing nations, the U.S. and Canada.

In recent years the push for labelling gained traction even in the U.S., the GE giant. The little state of Vermont roared by requiring labels on GE foods within its borders. Previous labelling efforts in other states had failed, generally because corporations poured tens of millions of dollars into advertising campaigns claiming that GE labelling would raise the cost of food. Until Vermont said otherwise, it appeared that Americans were more afraid of higher food prices than of genetic modifications on their plates. With the Vermont law in place, for the first time one could find packaged food in America stating 'PARTIALLY PRODUCED WITH GENETIC ENGINEERING'. Some companies, wishing to avoid the cost of printing separate labels for Vermont-bound products and then carefully keeping them separate from non-Vermont items, simply added the notice to all their foods with GE ingredients.

But they did not do so calmly. Businesses responded to the Vermont law with panic, working with the U.S. Congress to craft an alternate labelling law with several goals. It would apply to all fifty states; would hopefully mollify the public; would nullify all state and local GE labelling laws; would pertain only to human food, not animal feed; and would be tolerably weak enough to please the agricultural industry. Their lobbying efforts succeeded. President Obama signed the measure into law in July 2016.

Pro-labelling activists are right to ridicule the new legislation. Large food companies now may disclose GE ingredients on their packages with either a written phrase, a symbol or an electronic 'quick response' (QR) code readable by a smartphone. Small food companies can avoid the expense of a QR code by providing a phone number or web address where consumers can seek more information. This system puts a burden on shoppers, as the QR symbol and web address are far less likely to be noticed and understood than a label in plain English, precisely because they put a layer of hassle between the consumer and the information. As the advocacy group 'Just Label It' points out, few consumers will find time to scan multiple QR symbols or make phone calls while pushing their trolleys or carts through supermarkets. And what of people who do not own smartphones or who forgot theirs at home?

Pro-labelling activists have nicknamed the law the 'DARK' Act, for '*D*enying *A*mericans the *R*ight to *K*now'. They are furious with the corporations and lobbyists, politicians and even the Organic Trade

Association (OTA), which supported the bill because it included compromise protections for their industry.

It is entirely reasonable for consumers to fume at companies obstructing the spread of knowledge. QR codes will not do and advertisements with happy farmers and idyllic green-and-golden fields in mellow sunlight are woefully paltry sources of information. But consumers have ample reason to be frustrated with the anti-GE activists as well. Those activists often glide over crucial scientific details, mix up risks and with blind confidence cite very small numbers of studies whose methods have been repeatedly criticized by the majority of independent scientists. For example, in 2016 a tab at the top of a website dealing with food risks for children was labelled 'Defining Food Allergies'. Clicking on it led to a page that did NOT discuss any medically verified allergies, but instead focused entirely on genetic engineering. The page cited the Australian pea experiment without mentioning the later research casting doubt on whether engineering of the peas had truly provoked any special immune reaction in mice. The website also mentioned three other GE food studies as if they provided strong reason for concern, even though numerous experts have roundly denounced all three as plagued by sloppy scientific methods. Subsequently, the website was updated with catchy graphics, more news stories and less on research, but a mission statement continues to trumpet the unproven claim that GE allergens are 'now found in the U.S. food supply'.

The rejection or superficial application of science is a serious issue for genetic engineering, just as it is for climate change. Appallingly, some prominent GE defenders are also ardent climate-change deniers, and some on the left who denounce climate-deniers as unscientific themselves make pronouncements about genetic engineering with little scientific rigour. Just because a scientist has published a study does not mean it was any good. Science is an investigative *process*, not a particular expert or study. Major scientific understandings are arrived at through painstaking research by scores of different labs, millions of hours of effort, stringent peer review, debate and discussion, revision and repetitive collection of data, and eventually the consensus of hundreds upon hundreds of scientists drawing on massive amounts of evidence – not half a dozen researchers referring to their own few studies.

'Science' as an abstract concept is respected, yet too often the rigours of the scientific process are ignored. This dichotomy produces ironies on both sides of the GE debate. The Frankenstein analogy for GE foods, for instance, contains a significant irony. In Mary Shelley's novel, the monster was a lonely being who became violent because his creator and social world rejected him. Humans found him repulsive and unnatural, assumed he was dangerous, despised him without investigation into his possible worth and gave him no chance to contribute positively to his community. He therefore did not experience the moderating effects of acceptance, with the expectations for behaviour that come with acceptance. He did not experience thoughtful assessment and effective regulation. Frankenstein is thus an odd metaphor for anti-GE activists who reject this technology immediately on the assumption that it is contrary to nature (which in fact it is not) and automatically dangerous. They have missed the lesson that total rejection invites aggressive push-back, with biotech companies becoming more antagonistic to regulations.

But there is irony, too, in biotechnology companies' insistence that they already endure more-than-sufficient supervision from governments. True, from 2002–12, the consensus of some 770 scientific studies was that eating GE foods currently on the market poses no real danger.[50] All the same, genetic engineering is potent. So far, so good – but will it always be so?

The companies minimize valid questions about risk. Just because a process has basic, understandable and practical steps does not mean it is risk free. Companies assure the public over and over that their work is highly regulated and astoundingly safe – but is genetic engineering regulated *enough*? Is the process quite as safe as the companies believe – or quite as dangerous as anti-GE activists contend? Reasoned debate can easily be lost in the din of mutual accusations.

History is filled with the unintended, injurious consequences of under-regulated technologies. Seeking a free hand to conduct their businesses, companies pour hefty funds into convincing politicians to leave them alone. The corporations pledge to police themselves. But each company weighs the risks of harm their business might cause against the risks of having their business fail. Their tolerance for risks to the environment or to human health can reach unacceptable levels, especially when a risk unfolds slowly and the danger is to someone other than the corporate executives and their families. If protecting their business from being out-competed means taking more chances with health and safety, they are often willing to tilt the balance in favour of entrepreneurial success. And so, across various economic sectors we find oil spills, increases in obesity, deceptive tobacco-company advertising, birth defects, microbial food poisoning, mine collapses, marine dead zones and global warming figuring among the results of corporate activity. Human history underscores the irony in corporate claims that they can regulate themselves and need few legal interventions.

A worrisome trend in corporate genetic engineering is a lack of transparency. Companies cannot be expected to publicize trade secrets, but they should present accurate information about the safety and efficacy of their work. Deceptions such as Dow's regulatory sleight-of-hand with Enlist Duo (see Chapter Seven) should not be tolerated. Nor should academics accept corporate 'research grants' in exchange for pronouncements supporting company products. At a minimum, there should be full disclosure about the agribusiness funding behind any pro-GE statements emanating from a supposedly unbiased ivory tower.

Unfortunately, the 'ivory washing' of products and scientific positions is in full swing in the U.S. and on the Internet. It has, for instance, come to light that a food microbiologist who has oft written for the 'neutral' website 'Academics Review' has received tens of thousands of research dollars from Monsanto.[51] The monetary connection has not been apparent on the website, which is highly pro-GE and revels in ridiculing anti-GE advocates.

Similarly, an email has been exposed in which a University of Florida molecular biologist thanked Monsanto for an unrestricted $25,000 grant, assuring them that he would 'write whatever you like'. He also participated in a biotech-industry website called 'GMO Answers' as a seemingly dispassionate commentator – when actually Monsanto employees almost entirely penned some of his answers. When the links between this 'independent' scientist and the company came to light, the scientist promised to cut his ties to Monsanto and donate his funding to a charity food pantry. He is a sincere believer in genetic engineering, and it does not appear that either he or the company did anything illegal.[52] But the lack of disclosure is unnerving. A public that wishes to make sense of a controversial technology is justifiably resentful of muddled motives.

Monsanto is hardly alone in this strategy. Many biotech businesses cultivate cosy relationships with professors to their own advantage. At the same time, anti-GE associations and organic-food companies have also covertly used academics in public-relations campaigns.[53] Thus a former Washington State University professor whose work was heavily funded by the organic food industry co-authored an anti-ge commentary in the prestigious *New England Journal of Medicine* without initially disclosing any corporate ties.[54] His conflict of interest was not revealed, while the cloak of university affiliation suggested objectivity. Although conceivably he and his academic opponents are able to remain impartial despite the influence of bounteous corporate money, this phase of the public-relations war is disturbing. It highlights the way food is laden not only with nutrition, pleasure and profits, but also with propaganda and hypocrisy.

In the end, the right to know should genuinely be the right to *know*, not merely to speculate, not to believe things just because a company or a politician or an activist or a little handful of scientists says it is so; neither to be blinded by the aura of an expert's opinion nor that of moral righteousness, neither to allow oneself to be manipulated by slick advertisements nor by sweeping conspiracy theories. We, the public, *can* understand genetic engineering; we should not tolerate being talked down to in the egregiously distorted ways that currently pass for GE information.

We should demand up-to-date, engagingly taught science in schools. The children there will be the scientists, activists, executives, farmers, policy-makers, jurors, voters and food preparers of our later years, so whether or not we are parents, it will matter what those students learn. We ourselves need to search out sources that explain the evolving science, risks, benefits and relevant ethical questions in clear, thoughtful language. We need to hold all stakeholders accountable to show large-scale, well-replicated proof – where is the proof of benefit to society from this technology? Where is the proof of harm?

SOY FOR THE SUFFERING

The genetic engineering debate matters not only for us, but also for the planet's most vulnerable. Once again, there are two ways of looking at the issues. Some hold that GE crops could powerfully help the poor. In 2009, during the papacy of Benedict XV – a Pope not known for avant-garde ideas – a group of Vatican scholars published a paper supporting careful GE agriculture on behalf of the impoverished.[55] Then in 2016, more than a hundred Nobel laureates, many of them medical scientists, sent an open letter to Greenpeace asking them to drop their opposition to GE crops, particularly those designed to serve the undernourished.[56]

The Vatican, the laureates, development experts, the Bill & Melinda Gates Foundation and many other charities and agronomists hope for a day when genetic engineering will be properly regulated rather than stymied. Then rice enhanced to provide vitamin A, drought- and pest-resistant soybeans and more nutritious root crops could benefit the one in ten people on earth afflicted by malnutrition. Pro-GE, pro-poor activists point out that the silent, suffering population of the undernourished is larger than the populations of the U.S. and EU combined. The miserable deserve timely solutions. The advocates further argue that although those in industrialized nations who shun biotechnology are genuine idealists, unwittingly they are also elitists. They are people whose well-fed bellies can afford to spurn a promising technology, and they believe it is justified to deny other, less fortunate people that technology as well.

In reply, GE opponents protest that conventional breeding is sufficient to fortify crops with vitamins and minerals, as well as improve drought- and pest-resistance. Such breeding is already happening; for example, with funding from the Gates Foundation, HarvestPlus has used conventional breeding to iron-fortify beans, thereby reducing anaemia in African women and children. If such advances are happening too slowly, GE opponents argue, then the time lag is remediable with better funding for plentiful non-GE research; to them, the hyped-up speed of genetic modification is *not* the right answer. Anti-GE activists find it unconscionable to introduce GE crops to vulnerable populations, deeming it unethical to spread suspect products to places where the people already have enough burdens.

Ultimately, it is up to governments and consumers in developing countries themselves to assess the pros and cons of different agricultural options. They must weigh the risks of novel techniques against the often permanent losses caused by nutritional deficiencies. They must assess the economic costs and benefits of the various approaches. In deciding whether or not to cultivate GE soy, they must also consider trade implications, a topic examined in the next chapter.

Aside from debates about genetic engineering, there is another far-reaching connection between soybeans and the poor. Ordinary soy is excellent fare for people lacking adequate protein and calories. Soy provides the best protein among widely available plant products, and it is far cheaper than animal protein. Soy is therefore often sought for distressed populations, appearing as a major ingredient in rations provided to refugees and to malnourished schoolchildren.

Institutions using soy for disaster relief and long-term feeding programmes are quite varied. The UN's World Food Programme, Doctors without Borders, USAID, the International Federation of Red Cross and Red Crescent Societies, the Christian organizations of the ACT Alliance, the Catholic Church's Caritas Internationalis, India's Akshaya Patra Foundation and many others distribute soy protein mixed with maize and often milk powder as well. Not only soy's protein, but also soy oil is offered; it is relatively easy to store and provides fat and calories.

Heartening examples of soy in relief work abound – as in 1996 when the little town of Zimmi, Sierra Leone, ran out of food. Trapped by a vicious war surrounding them, they were unable to access agricultural fields or trade for food from other areas. Venturing out of town was extremely dangerous, as both sides in the conflict were assaulting ordinary citizens. Rebels wished to bring the government to its knees by ruining the nation's agriculture-based economy, so they frequently punished cultivators attempting to tend their fields. In retaliation for farming, cultivators were subjected to on-the-spot amputations. In addition, combatants on both sides rained horrific war crimes on civilians. Rural folk suspected of helping the opposing side were beheaded, raped, disembowelled, shot, had their lips cut off or sewn together, had their eyes gouged out or ears cut off, or were rounded up into buildings that were set alight. Children were often kidnapped – little boys, forced to serve the fighters as scouts;

Instant corn-soy blend is fully pre-cooked. It can be extruded into cracker shapes, used powdered in recipes, or mixed with tepid water to make a porridge. It is common in disaster relief and development work.

older boys drugged and brainwashed into carrying out atrocities; and girls forced into sexual and domestic service for the fighters. By early 1996, 10,000 people had already died, the majority near Zimmi, and hundreds of thousands more had fled to the bigger cities. Hunger stalked the remaining local population.

In late March, the International Committee of the Red Cross (ICRC) published this understated news release:

> Zimmi . . . has been virtually cut off from the rest of the country for several years by the fighting . . . From 20 to 22 March, the ICRC for the first time supplied food aid to this town . . . Since the roads are too dangerous to use, all travel between the towns of Kenema and Zimmi takes place in a helicopter displaying the Red Cross emblem. Some 40 tonnes of oil, and corn and soya flour were brought in by air and distributed to 5,600 people.[57]

ICRC's delivery of soy protein and calories was a matter of life or death. Here, in a small place where people yearned for the safe, routine lives they had lost, soy was a nearly miraculous gift from the skies. Of course, it was neither a cure-all for their country's massive problems, nor some dangerous plant undermining their well-being. It was simply good food, deliverance from wasting away and another chance at surviving the nightmare their world had become.

Soy has been delivered countless times in the wake of sudden calamity. Poignantly, soy was a medium both of succour and reciprocity after the 2011 earthquake-tsunami-nuclear accident in Japan. At Japan's time of great need, South American farmers returned some of the support the Japanese government had bestowed on them for years.

The mutuality had begun years before with the Japan International Cooperation Agency (JICA) which, among other missions, assists Japanese emigrants and their descendants. In Latin America, JICA has helped emigrant communities (called *Nikkei*) with medical clinics, elder care, teachers for Japanese-language classes and scholarships for study in Japan. JICA has also provided loans to South American Nikkei farmers – cultivators who, it happens, especially grow soy.

The magnitude of the 2011 crisis filled the Nikkei with empathy. The quake was so forceful that it shifted the earth's axis between 10 and 25 cm (approximately 4–10 in.) and generated a tsunami with waves as high as 40 m (131 ft). The waters led to radiation leaks at three nuclear reactors. The intertwined disasters caused nearly 25,000 casualties; the collapse of nearly 130,000 buildings; an uninhabitable zone for 20 km (12½ miles) around the reactors; the destruction of 26,000 fishing boats; severe damage to ports, roads, railways and airports; and the death of as many as 8 million chickens whose feed ingredients, including soy, could not be delivered.[58]

The shocked Nikkei responded quickly. In Paraguay, they demonstrated their solidarity partly with soybeans. A cooperative of Nikkei soybean producers donated a hundred tons of soybeans and, as JICA later explained,

> The Federation of Japanese Associations in Paraguay collected donations from all over Paraguay for the cost of shipping and producing tofu, with the cooperation of Gialinks Co., Ltd, a Japanese company with years of experience in importing soybeans grown by the *Nikkei* farmers. The soybeans [were] used to produce tofu . . . distributed to the victims of the Great

East Japan Earthquake. By February 2012, this project supplied enough soybeans to make one million packets of tofu.[59]

More recently, soy was delivered in the wake of another notable natural disaster. In July 2016 in northeast India, torrential storms filled rivers to overflowing, flooding over 1,000 villages. Waters normally bringing life instead destroyed tens of thousands of hectares of crops. People who lost their homes crowded onto roads and bridges, and into relief camps. Indian governments quickly rescued many citizens from drowning, but the situation was overwhelming. Relief agencies responded too, among them the Lutheran World Service India Trust (LWSIT). LWSIT brought food for 1,500 severely affected households in sixteen villages, particularly the disabled, single-mother families and widows from minority ethnic groups. Among the rations was Nutrela, a commercial meat substitute manufactured in India from soy flour, nicknamed 'soy-chunk'. People received ten days of sustenance as they began to recobble together their lives.[60]

Soy has also mitigated the devastating nutritional effects of endless, crushing poverty. In Mozambique, a multilateral partnership delivers soy-fortified meals and nutrition education to impoverished children at their schools, free of charge. The USDA donates the food. Then the charity Planet Aid and its local partner deliver hot corn porridge blended with soy to more than 250 schools.[61] The World Initiative for Soy in Human Health (WISHH), an organization founded by U.S. soy farmers in 2000, provides nutrition training to teachers and children, with hefty funding from Mozambique's government. The value of the multi-pronged programme is manifold: it helps children grow properly and maintain healthy immune systems; the free meals attract parents to the concept of schooling; it encourages teen girls to stay in school, which reduces a teen pregnancy rate among the highest in the world;[62] and it disseminates nutritional knowledge. This school feeding programme is not alone: it is just one among many worldwide deploying soy as a source of protein.

The University of Illinois has taken a different tack. Since 1973 it has provided technical expertise for small entrepreneurs in developing countries who wish to manufacture soy foods or fortify traditional foods with soy. The university's 'International Soybean

Program' (INTSOY) receives funding from the USDA and U.S. soy advocacy groups to host seminars for food technologists, factory owners, government policy-makers and other stakeholders from overseas. Staff from INTSOY and the university's National Soybean Research Laboratory (NSRL) have also worked directly 'on the ground' in 21 countries in Africa, Asia, Latin America and the Caribbean. They have taught how to sustainably extract and extrude, ferment and flavour, curdle and cook soy.

WISHH similarly trains entrepreneurs in developing countries. The organization promotes soy food consumption everywhere and has assisted sister organizations, such as Soy Southern Africa, in expanding their influence. WISHH's cross-cultural reach even led in 2015 to collaboration with the Ghanaian Atomic Energy Commission (GAEC), which sought a donation of defatted soy flour.[63] The GAEC is a scientific institute with many departments, including ones focusing on radiation for disinfecting foods, and on crop irradiation to induce mutations for breeding. The GAEC had been asked to improve the country's *gari*, a popular cassava mash that is fermented, turned into flakes or flour and then used in recipes. Some gari brands had already been enhanced with full-fat soy flour, but the public had not readily accepted them. GAEC's food experts envisioned an alternative using defatted U.S. soy flour. Within a few months of GAEC's contacting WISHH, the latter had delivered a bag of the defatted flour of nearly 23 kg (50 lb). The now-provisioned research is ongoing.

The NSRL/INTSOY and WISHH provide longer-term solutions than handing out soy foods to desperate people. Although they are mindful that short-term gifts can be crucial, that is not their mission. Instead, they teach others – those who are needy but not desperate – how to turn soybeans into soy foods on their own, and why soy products are a good idea in the first place. But these organizations rarely take the still further step of teaching others how to *grow* soybeans. Their missions are more oriented towards encouraging people to eat soy imported from the U.S., so they aid others with the specialized aspects of soy food production, providing genuinely valuable technical and nutritional advice. They seek to help U.S. farmers do well financially while they do good morally. Because WISHH is directly accountable to U.S. soy farmers, it particularly emphasizes long-term market development for U.S. soybeans.

Charitable organizations have assumed the role of promoting soy cultivation among the world's poor. The Mennonite Central Committee spent decades teaching soy farming in Bangladesh, and the ICRC has sponsored soy production in the Democratic Republic of the Congo. N2Africa, an organization funded by the Gates Foundation, works to promote nitrogen-fixing crops such as soy in eleven countries. World Vision International has made soy more profitable for small farmers in Uganda, facilitating their post-harvest access to a Ugandan oilseed processing company.

As an aspect of development aid – to the dismay of U.S. soy farmers – the U.S. government has also promoted soy production overseas. The U.S. Soybean Innovation Lab, funded by USAID and located at the University of Illinois, is working with the Syngenta Foundation for Sustainable Agriculture on field trials to test soybean varieties in Malawi, Kenya and Zambia. USAID explains that this work is overdue, since 'Soybean farmers in Africa may either only have access to a few seed varieties with an unimpressive yield potential, or a few high-yielding varieties for which no performance data exists for their latitude and altitude.'[64]

Similarly, to boost Mozambique's chicken industry, the USDA spurred that country to develop a steady, home-grown supply of soy-based poultry feed. They provided farmers with high-quality soybean seeds and technical advice. They note their successes in

> helping farmers to become seed replicators to supply others, and helping to increase yields . . . Soy farmers expanded in number from 2,000 to 30,000. Small and medium sized entrepreneurs expanded into soybean oil production as a new agro-industry.[65]

The Mozambican poultry industry, in turn, grew in value from $25 million in 2005 to $165 million just five years later.[66]

Yet another U.S. agency, the Peace Corps, has taught soy farmers in Burkina Faso how to use imperfect beans – ones that buyers rejected and so previously were discarded – to make soy milk, yoghurt and tofu. One Peace Corps volunteer further assisted the women's soy cooperative in her village to package the soy foods, advertise them at a regional market and calculate profits. These efforts, like many in the U.S. government's history, have focused on making soybean cultivation both feasible and rewarding for the world's needy.

The governments of other countries with soy expertise – Japan, Brazil, China and South Korea – have similarly encouraged soy farming in faraway places. As explained in Chapter Six, Japan initially helped Brazil become a world soybean power, and Brazil now assists other developing countries in growing soy. Thus in 2009 when the presidents of Brazil and Venezuela met, with much fanfare they unveiled a Venezuelan soy-farming project that included Brazilian technical assistance.

In Indonesia, Japan's JICA has trained farmers in how to inspect and produce high-quality soybean seeds, and the South Korean government has assisted research to improve soy varieties suitable to the climate. In Angola, Chinese government loans have supported soy cultivation in partnership with the Angolan Ministry of Agriculture and private Chinese enterprises. The philosophy behind all these efforts can be summed up by paraphrasing a famous adage: Give a man a soy food, and you feed him for a day. Sell a man some soybeans, then teach him how to process and market them, and you give him profits that might feed him for a long while. But if you *also* teach a man to grow soy on his own, his profits might increase enough that you have fed him for a lifetime – and he might have a surplus to export to your own growing population. You might also develop trade with him in farming supplies.

These distinctions have far-reaching implications, since simply giving people food can create as many problems as it solves. Not only do frequent handouts encourage dependency in recipients, but also food from abroad can undermine local farmers. Why would consumers in Malawi, for example, pay normal prices for local farmers' crops if, thanks to reduced-cost sales or giveaways from rich nations, they can get corn-soy blend for little or no cost? The Malawian farmer, seeing that her crops cannot compete with foreign foods flooding the market, decides to grow less next year. Or perhaps she hopes to grow just as much every year, but her depressed profits now make her unable to buy fertilizer for the next season. When thousands of farmers face such a situation, the rural economy is damaged. The region's ability to feed itself in future years can be seriously compromised.

Food donations are unquestionably necessary in dire circumstances, but whenever possible aid workers should purchase that food from local suppliers. If an entire region's agriculture has failed, then food from afar may be required. But that kind of delivery should be the last resort. With this insight, in 2005 the giant U.S. charity CARE decided to phase out accepting food from the U.S. government. This 'no thanks' meant turning down $45 million yearly in soy, corn and other crops. The move was bold for development workers, yet not unprecedented; CARE was following the lead of the EU, which in 1999 also eliminated detrimental flows of their food overseas. Canada similarly 'untied' its food aid from Canadian-produced foods in 2008.

The world's biggest food donor, by far, is the U.S., which has typically provided about half the world's donated comestibles. In the 2000s, calls grew for the U.S. to reform its food aid to avoid undermining poor farmers. In theory, U.S. law already prohibits such undercutting. But laws and intentions do not always align with realities. Successive U.S. presidents have therefore sought flexibility to provide nutritional aid by purchasing crops within distressed countries, or in countries nearby. In reply, the powerful American farm lobby has repeatedly balked at sending less of their surplus abroad. Doing so would mean keeping more surplus within the U.S., which would push down crop prices – and profits – at home.

There is, then, a great irony in soy donations: by destabilizing local agriculture, the giving of this protein-rich food can at times reduce long-term dietary security in poor countries. Complexity abounds, as this particular paradox of soy and nutrition joins so many others worth spelling out.

Thus as we have seen, soy is ubiquitous in our food supplies, since even in places where people eat no soy at all, they often eat animals that eat it – yet the soy frequently goes unnoticed. Then, when soy is noticed, its natural isoflavones are wildly praised – and also thoroughly demonized. These contradictory judgements arise from dramatic pronouncements in mass media about soy and health, yet medical researchers have *not* found that soy foods have dramatic effects, except when they save lives in situations of severe protein deprivation.

The lack of dramatic health effects applies also to GE soy, which generates a further set of contradictions. First, GE soy is extremely popular among farmers – yet consumers who are aware of it tend to mistrust it. Second, although soy is among the more difficult plants to modify, genetic engineers do frequently alter it. Third, virtually all science on currently planted GE soy has found it safe to eat – but new biotechnologies offer such power that unless they are handled responsibly, unexpected dangers could arise. Fourth, GE soy could offer profits to people who farm under difficult conditions – or it could expose vulnerable populations to excess risk.

Soy's relationship to those vulnerable populations creates even more paradoxes. As we have seen, in distressed places worldwide, donated soy can save lives – or undermine agriculture – or both at the same time. Further, in developing countries, small farmers' cultivation of soy can increase their food security – but in the hands of wealthy farmers, soy can displace smallholders and their sub-sistence crops, thereby diminishing food security for the poor. And finally, growing soy is a very efficient way to produce protein for human food, yet soy is massively fed to animals instead. Some 70 per cent of all soy protein in the world is used in the *in*efficient process of providing humans with protein in pork and poultry.[67] The way we use soy today is less than optimal for feeding a hungry, growing human population.

THE INTRICACIES OF soy's genome are thus matched by humans' convoluted relationships with it. Soy is a useful food, but we some-how keep turning it into a 'frenemy'. We are so very complicated in our nutritional attitudes and behaviours. And because humans are complicated about everything, how we handle soy in our economies is also multifaceted. The sometimes labyrinthine ways that we trade soy are probed next.

NINE

BEANS AS BUSINESS: *BIG* BUSINESS

Imagine a couple, Abe and Melora Roth, in LaSalle County, Illinois. They live in the heartland of soy farming in the u.s., the nation with the world's most bountiful crop. Although the Roths tend their GE soybeans and corn with care, their 120-hectare (300-acre) farm does not give them enough income; Melora also works at a nearby farm-machinery manufacturer. Farming, second jobs and raising children are common activities in the county; social relations are mostly stable. Most of the drama resides in agricultural conditions – weather, pests and crop-price fluctuations. The supreme adventures are reserved for the soybeans.

The tiny, mature beans will make a fantastic voyage, courtesy of big business. The journey begins in October with the transfer of 8,400 bushels (nearly 230 metric tons or over 0.5 million lb) into a tractor-trailer. To move the crop, the Roths use a long pipe attached to their combine harvester. The couple then trucks the beans to the LaSalle Terminal of the Archer, Daniels, Midland Company (ADM), strategically located on the Illinois River near the intersection of two interstate highways. They make about nine trips to bring in their harvest. Once unloaded, each trailerful of beans is inspected, weighed and graded, and if the beans are too flawed, their value is reduced. ADM pays the Roths for them at the current prices for their grades.

ADM personnel place the beans in drying machines and then cool them to prevent two problems: mould, and the metabolism that could set the seeds on the way to germination. These steps require serious attention to safety, as soybean dust can ignite if exposed to sparks. Next, the Roths' beans are stored in giant aerated bins within a grain elevator and diligently kept separate from non-GE soy. Fortunately, ADM has decades of experience loading crops into storage, with strict safety procedures to protect workers from the hazards of heavy equipment and of cascading beans. Cascade accidents do happen on farms, with over two dozen 'entrapments', in which a person is too buried to escape without assistance, occurring yearly in the U.S. About half end as fatal 'engulfments': the victim is entirely covered and suffocates.[1] Handling bulk soy and other crops is not child's play.

In our scenario, international demand for soybeans is currently high, so ADM will send the Roths' beans, blended with those from other farms, down the Illinois River to the waters of the mighty, moody Mississippi. Before leaving the U.S. mainland, the beans will travel some 2,253 km (1,400 miles) to the sea. This shipment is ultimately bound for China, recipient of some 70 per cent of America's exported soy.

As soon as a covered barge is available, ADM transfers the Roths' beans into it. At around 9 m wide x 60 m long (around 30 x 200 ft), the barge holds 50,000 bushels of soybeans, weighing 1,361 metric tons (3 million lb).[2] Rivermen laboriously attach the barge with rigging to a towboat and to several other barges filled with grain or beans – up to fourteen more. Despite the word 'tow' in the boat's name, the powerful little vessel will actually push the barges, rather than pull them, through an elaborate system of dams and locks.

The towboat with its barges moves fairly fast at times and is heavy – weighing as much as 870 semi-trucks added together – so steering is challenging, and it can take up to 2.5 km (1½ miles)[3] for the assemblage to stop. The captain must avoid water skiers, recreational boaters and other cargo haulers, with constant alertness to the changing position of the navigational blind spots, which can impede vision for a significant distance in front of and to the sides of the barges. Here, too, the work is not for amateurs.

The towboat and barges, carrying soybeans and grain worth millions of dollars, reach the Mississippi River at St Louis, Missouri. The crew transfers their barges to another towboat pushing even more barges – as many as sixty![4] The new, larger assemblage travels for six days, approximately 1,600 km (1,000 miles), to a transfer point in the middle of the river just above New Orleans. Here a specialized company using high-tech equipment pulls the contents

In the port of New Orleans, a towboat pushes barges filled with soy or cereal grains for export.

of the barges out and reloads them onto a mammoth, oceangoing ship. This stevedoring can take up to three days. In addition to the crop transfer, there are also safety checks and much paperwork to be filled out.

The giant ship is designed to protect the beans from moisture and overheating. Moisture can not only lead to moulding but also promote biological activity within the beans; however inert they may seem, the beans are still living organisms. In moist conditions they can begin sprouting, undergoing cellular respiration and so releasing heat. Mountains of beans in active respiration can generate so much heat that they spontaneously self-ignite. Of course, no captain wishes to deliver scorched beans or experience a full-blown cargo fire. Bean respiration is also dangerous because it releases carbon dioxide. The cargo hold must always be well ventilated, and as a protection against fatalities a gas measurement must be made before anyone enters it.

The ship then heads downriver to the sea. Once again, risk is always present, as became starkly clear in 2016 when high water and an unusually fast current at the river's mouth caused three rock-laden barges to break away from their moorings and crash into nearby ships. One of the ships carried bulk soybeans that spilled into the river. This kind of mishap receives close scrutiny afterwards;

profits and reputations are on the line. Shippers and their customers also investigate delays, as in their industry time is definitely money: daily costs for running a bulk vessel range from $10,000 to $20,000.[5] Contracts require crop delivery within specified time frames – under penalty of reduced payments – and besides, the sooner a boat empties a load, the sooner a new paying load can be picked up.

It is time for the Roths' beans to glide through the Gulf of Mexico and the Caribbean Sea. Though by now hurricane season is winding down, a major storm is still possible, so the captain vigilantly studies weather forecasts. The ship is a 'Panamax', sized to fit through the Panama Canal and carrying between 50,000 and 60,000 tons of cargo.[6] The canal's recent expansion allows even larger ships to pass through, yet most of the world's grain and beans are still carried on Panamax vessels. Ships larger than Panamax are often too big to enter destination ports.

Our hypothetical ship now passes through the canal to the Pacific. The captain pays dearly for this privilege – about $155,000 in cargo tolls, fees for tugboats to guide the ship, ground assistants and ground wires – but using the canal is still cheaper than rounding the tip of South America.[7] Crossing the canal takes nine methodical hours.

Fortunately, the Pacific typhoon season is mostly over by now. But tempests and ocean accidents are still always possible. A dramatic case occurred in December 2004 when a storm blew a malfunctioning ship onto the shoals of an island in Alaska's Aleutian chain. Called the *Selendang Ayu* ('Beautiful Scarf' in Malay), the ship was bound from Seattle to China when its engines failed. The crew radioed for help. During the rescue mission a massive wave hit the ship and splashed into a helicopter's engines, causing it to crash. Six people perished. The *Selendang Ayu* then broke apart. The wounded ship spilled about 750 tons of fuel oil into the sea. Its cargo of more than 60,000 tons of soybeans was lost, sinking or washing up on the shores of an island with the quirky name of Unalaska. Soybeans rotted on Unalaska and in nearby waters for eighteen months, harming wildlife when their decomposition used up the oxygen in the water.[8]

We imagine no such mishap with the Roths' beans, which spend a few weeks traversing the ocean. As the crew finally leaves the endless lonely waters and begins nearing land, they watch for pirates.

Assailants are most likely at or near ports. Often land-based thieves who sneak onto docked ships, they can be armed and dangerous, and seafarers have been tied up, injured and even killed. Yet threats do also occur on the high seas; in these cases the attackers are skilled seamen.

By contrast with days of yore, pirates today rarely covet a ship's commercial cargo – raiders generally prefer to get in and out of a ship quickly. On bulk carriers, thieves target electronic and maintenance equipment, the crew's personal possessions and the consumer goods and cash in the ship's store. Sometimes the goal is ransom money in exchange for a kidnapped crew. In the case of our prototypical ship, no one would want to steal any actual soybeans – just the wealth that the beans generate.

Not having encountered any pirates on open waters, our ship peacefully enters the port of Shanghai. Shanghai is a massive, bustling place and the world's largest port for the shipping of 6- or 12-m (20- or 40-ft) containers filled with consumer goods. But our ship is not stopping here. Shanghai sits at the mouth of the Yangtze River, one of the two great waterways of China and the longest river in Asia. Our ship makes its way 275 km (170 miles) up the Yangtze to the industrial city of Nanjing, one of the world's largest inland river ports and a regional hub for rail and highway traffic. The unwieldy ship must be guided cautiously into the busy port, since its enormous weight could cause punishing damage if it smashed into anything. ADM has a factory here for crushing soybeans to produce vegetable oil and animal feed. Soon the Roths' beans will be on local Chinese dinner plates and in the bellies of the region's pigs.

But even for the pigs there is uncertainty, as soy meal needs proper storage to prevent it from spoiling, and the region around the Yangtze River is flood-prone. Anhui Province, just to the west, has experienced serious floods in 1996, 2003, 2006–8 and every year from 2011 to the present.[9] In 2016 a photo of a weeping Anhui farmer wading among his pigs' flooded stalls was picked up by Internet news providers worldwide. A rescue was soon organized for as many of his 3,000 pigs as could be saved – which saved the farmer, too, from financial ruin. Unfortunately in such situations soy meal does not fare so well; flood waters destroy it. Once again, the soy is ever at risk.

But excess rain tends to come in the summer, well after the Roths' beans became pig feed and were consumed. Soybeans for

China's summertime come from South America, rather than from the u.s. So it is the South American beans that may end up destroyed or washed away by floods. We can safely imagine that the Roth beans are finally no longer soy at all – their oil has become part of human bodies, and their protein meal has become pork flesh. On the other side of the earth from Illinois, at last the beans' journey has ended – satisfactorily, as sources of income for many different actors along the way and, finally, as nourishment.

Soybeans sometimes take a different route from the u.s. to Asia. As soybean agriculture has moved into the more northern and westerly states of Nebraska, Minnesota and the Dakotas, more beans have travelled from the Pacific Northwest. The beans are trucked from farms to rail depots, and there fed into 'hopper' train cars with special chutes for unloading cargo. Trains haul the soy to shipping terminals along Puget Sound and the river city of Portland, Oregon. Ships leaving for Asia from the Pacific Northwest spend eighteen to twenty fewer days at sea than those taking the New Orleans/Panama Canal route.[10] Shortened sea time reduces costs, often making up for the increased cost of rail transport within the u.s. compared to the barge system in the Mississippi River Basin. Other export routes for

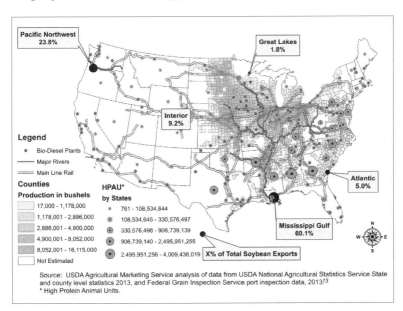

Production of soybean per u.s. state in 2013; proportions of total soybean exports travelling particular transportation routes; levels of high-protein animal feed consumption by state, and geography of u.s. biodiesel factories.

whole soybeans, much less used but still not trivial, are from Great Lakes or Eastern Seaboard ports, either to the Middle East or to the Netherlands, where soy is processed for distribution in Europe.

But only about 45 per cent of America's soy is exported at all.[11] The remaining beans are trucked and crushed within the u.s. Most are processed at factories owned by Bunge North America (a publicly traded company), ADM (also public), Cargill (private) and Ag Processing Inc. (farmer-cooperative owned). The companies clean, dehull and crush the beans into flakes. Then they use hexane to extract the oil. The oil is treated to remove the hexane and is refined, degummed, bleached, deodorized and often hydrogenated. The companies also remove residual hexane from the leftover flakes. They heat the flakes to inactivate anti-nutrients, dry and cool them and grind them into soy meal.

As in the handling of soybeans for export, without watchful management these activities are perilous. Solvent extraction releases flammable fumes; there have been explosions at soy factories. In 1981 Ralston Purina's soy oil factory in Louisville, Kentucky, accidentally emitted hexane into the city's sewer system. The chemical emitted volatile gases, and on a Friday the thirteenth, 3 km (2 miles) of sewer pipes burst in a series of explosions, ripping streets apart and leaving craters. Residents were thrown out of their beds. Fortunately, no one died. In 1984 Ralston Purina paid some $33 million to the agencies, local businesses and residents whose lives had been disrupted.[12] Within a year the company had left the soy-processing business, selling almost all of their facilities to Cargill.

Likewise, the Central Soya Company (which Bunge eventually purchased) suffered a hexane explosion in 1994 in Indianapolis; that blast in turn ignited surrounding grain dust, causing an even larger second explosion. Eleven people were injured, four critically. Six thousand gallons of soy oil spilled from the factory – some of it into storm sewers and from there into the White River. The processing facility was severely damaged and never reopened. The company ended up paying over $600,000 in fines.[13]

But the u.s. is not alone: a hexane fire broke out in a soy factory in Germany in 1977, and an explosion in Denmark in 1980 caused 27 casualties. And, too, such problems are not merely something of the past and not only related to hexane, as a 2016 incident in South Dakota showed. A welder, Randy Satter, was working atop a tank containing soybean soapstock, a by-product of soy oil refining that is further treated and sold for animal feed or biodiesel. No one had told Mr Satter that the tank emitted highly flammable gases. When sparks from his equipment ignited the tank, it exploded, killing him.

Yet danger is not truly the most dramatic aspect of soy processing and trade around the globe. In fact, storms, pirates and accidents are rare. Employees at Central Soya, for example, had worked constantly for decades with hexane and never had an explosion until that fateful night in 1994. The most startling feature of soy's presence in modern life is, instead, the simple fact of its vastness. Its enormity startles us because most activities using soybeans are so routine that people outside the industry barely perceive them. Sudden difficulties in the industry's usual smooth functioning are like the tip of an iceberg that makes us notice, 'Oh, there's ice here'; in the same way, an accident or terrible problem makes us notice the normally unobtrusive soy in our world. And, just as we can easily fail to realize the immensity of a berg hidden under visible floating ice, so too we are often ignorant of how soybeans hugely undergird our daily lives. If we are the Roths in LaSalle County, we understand soy's importance, but unless we are connected to the industry, we may know little of it.

Soy is the most grown oilseed in the world by far, and the fourth most cultivated of all crops (the first three global plants – maize, wheat and rice – are all cereals).[14] The internationalism of the soybean trade is striking; as scholar Mariano Turzi notes, soybeans can be 'harvested in Paraguay, sent by barge to Brazil for export or to Argentina for processing, and sold in Geneva to Asia after the operation has been authorized by headquarters in the United States'.[15] The sheer bulk of soy production, along with its globalism, has made soy the third most internationally traded plant on earth by weight.[16] Soy fields bestow the u.s. with its second most valuable legal harvest, after corn (both are likely behind marijuana).[17] Soy and soy products constitute the most valuable crop export for six countries: the u.s., Brazil, Argentina, Paraguay, Bolivia and Uruguay. According to the un's Food and Agriculture Organization, worldwide the value of harvested soybeans came to an impressive $123 billion in 2013.[18]

Globally farmers produce some 2 quadrillion individual soybeans each year (that's 200 times more than a trillion). If all of the

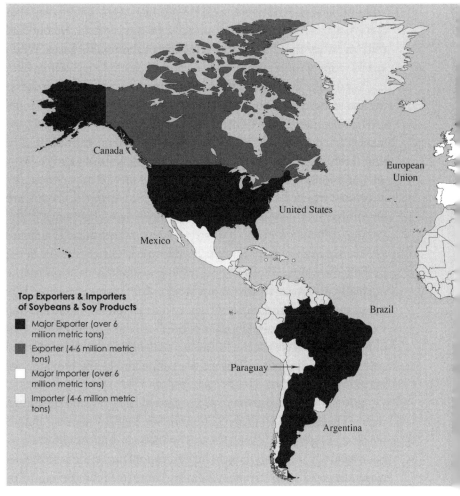

Major exporters and importers of soybeans and soy products, 2017.

soybeans harvested in 2016 were laid end to end in a belt around the equator, it would circle the earth almost 400,000 times! If we imagine uncurling the belt and launching it into space, it would quite easily reach the Sun. It would, in fact, be able to extend out to the Sun and back fifty times.[19]

But apart from some successful experiments with growing soybeans at the International Space Station, the beans do not leave our planet. They go into animal bellies, human bellies and certain industrial uses. This distribution flows from two powerful motivations, money and nutrition – each complex in its details but straightforward as incentives.

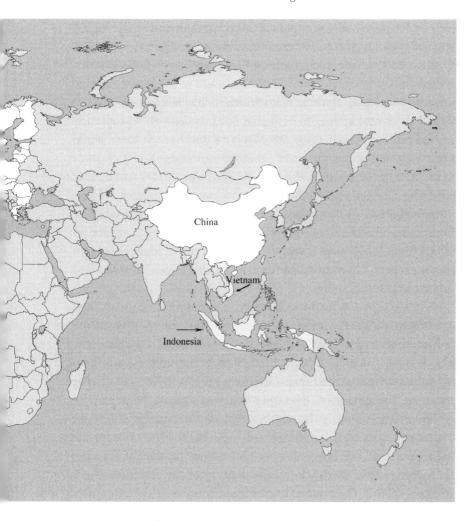

Farming is an inherently unpredictable means of making money. Human control of pests fluctuates, and rather than having the power to make the weather do our bidding, it seems that since the Industrial Revolution our lifestyles are making the weather more chaotic, not less. Farmers need protection against the ways that these problems, as well as overproduction, can affect crop prices. They need a modicum of assurance that all their hard work will actually enable them to provide for their families. Futures contracts on their harvests are one way they find that protection.

By locking in prices at an agreed-upon level, futures contracts make budgets more predictable for cultivators like the Roths, as well as for processing companies. Merchants invented the highly specific, modern form of these contracts at the Chicago Board of Trade (CBOT) in the mid-nineteenth century (soybeans were not traded until 1936, however). The merchants wished to regularize unruly agricultural markets where farmers had sometimes arrived to sell their crops, only to find that overproduction had already caused prices to crash. Crop prices were sometimes so low – while transportation prices were not – that farmers had found it cheaper to let their harvests rot on the streets than to search for and deliver to buyers. Conversely, at other times processing companies – bakeries, for example – encountered the opposite problem: scarcities of unprocessed ingredients sent prices so high that they struggled to afford them. They were forced to pass most of the higher costs on to consumers, creating discontent when the prices of bread and other staple foods soared.

The solution, a futures contract, is a detailed, standardized agreement between a seller and a buyer. What commodity will be delivered, with what level of quality, in what quantity, on what dates and at what price are all specified. This is not unlike signing an agreement of sale with a furniture store for future delivery of a living room set; the agreement lists the brand and style of the items, the colour or fabric chosen, the number of pieces in the set and the date of delivery. Because the agreement also specifies a fixed price for the living room set, the buyer does not have to worry that in between the signing of the contract and the delivery of the furniture, there will be a spike in the price of his desired furniture. If the price goes up for other people, that does not affect his contract. The seller benefits too, because she is protected from a fall in the furniture's price and can count on the amount laid out in the agreement of sale.

The most important difference between an ordinary retail furniture agreement and a commodity futures contract is that although the futures contract is based on the real projected value of a raw material such as soybeans, the parties to the agreement usually finish their dealings without exchanging any actual beans for cash with each other. Instead, the board of trade keeps track of all the buyers and sellers and, as the contract is expiring, assigns who will deliver to whom. To clarify this, let us imagine a contract that the Roths make to deliver a single bushel of their soybeans for $10 to Fictitious Feedlot on 18 July (actually futures contracts are made for thousands of bushels at a time). The Roths make this deal because they fear that the price could go down to only $9 by July; Fictitious Feedlot makes the deal because they fear the price could go up to $11. The two sides are 'hedging', as in 'hedging one's bets'. The $10 price is immediately recorded as a transaction in the accounting system at the CBOT.

If either party wishes to get out of the contract early, however, they could sell their obligations in the contract to a speculator. This could be desirable to Fictitious Feedlot, for instance, if they have a cash flow problem and need the money. Let us say then that the price of soybeans goes up to $11 before the contract expires. Now in order to buy soy, Feedlot will have to pay a price they had wished to avoid. But to offset this potential problem, they had sold their part of the futures contract for $11 to Trader Trisha. They will lose $1 buying actual soybeans from a local farmer, Nearby Ned, for $11 instead of the $10 in their original contract with the Roths, but they gained $1 by selling their side of the contract itself to Trisha for more than the value they had originally promised and had been recorded on their CBOT ledger. The $1 loss is offset by a $1 gain, so the risks have been successfully hedged.

So why would Trisha buy this contract – why would she pay to have Fictitious Feedlot's accounting ledger for this contract transferred to her? The reason lies in an opposite strategy from that of hedgers – a strategy in which luck, knowledge of the soy industry, vigilance and speed could lead Trisha to big profits, but in which she could also have big losses. Whereas Fictitious Feedlot had originally been afraid that the price might rise too high and had used the futures contract to reduce risk, Trisha embraces the risky *hope* that the price of soy will rise yet higher. If the price rises to $12 for the bushel, however briefly, Trader Trisha will quickly sell the contract to Speculator Sam for the higher price. She pledged $11 for it, and now she sells it for $12. Her ledger is credited 'plus one dollar' on this bushel, without her ever touching a soybean.

Speculator Sam is hoping the price will rise higher still, but he misjudged the market, as there is an announcement that the soybean harvest in Brazil will be larger than expected. Because of anticipated greater supply of soy, the price drops. It never bounces back up high enough for Sam to make a profit. He takes a loss, having bought the contract for $12 and in the end selling it for a bit less than $10 to

Hungry Hogs, Inc. CBOT records the sale in the ledger for Hungry Hogs, which, having pledged their payment, now owns the right to collect that bushel of soybeans. To feed their animals, the staff of Hungry Hogs does want the real soybeans, not just the speculative possibilities for a quick profit. When the contract expires, they turn to collect the bushel of beans from the board of trade, which will assign someone to deliver it to them. Possibly that assignee will be whomever the Roths sold their side of the contract to as part of their own hedging strategy, but it might be someone else altogether. If the holder of the assigned delivery contract is not a soy farmer, that individual or company will have to buy a bushel of soybeans on the cash market at the going rate in order to fulfil the promise of soybean delivery.

It can be hard for people unfamiliar with the complexities of commodity finance to wrap their minds around the abstractness of all this trading. Yet it is even more complicated and abstract than this, because it is also possible for an investor to pay for the *option*, but not the requirement, to purchase a futures contract at a specified price. That is to say, for an advance fee, the investor will be able to buy that futures contract any time before it expires, if desired.

Moreover, in the case of soybeans there is the added wrinkle that not only are contracts made for whole beans but, separately, for processed beans in the forms of soybean oil and soy protein meal. Differences in prices of whole bean contracts and processed soy contracts reflect the value that processing adds to the beans. The price difference is called the 'crush spread' because it indicates the 'spread' of value at any given time between leaving the soybeans whole rather than, instead, crushing them. The crush spread varies with changes in supply and demand for the whole beans versus the two processed products, with changes in transportation and processing costs, and with the effects of speculation on soy's three different futures markets.

Soy-processing companies study the crush spread carefully, using it to make decisions about when and how much crushing to do – that is, when and in what quantities to sell the processed products in order to optimize profits. They also use futures contracts in soy oil and meal to hedge their financial risks, while speculators once again use these contracts to court quick profits. The speculators seek instances in which prices for the futures contracts inaccurately reflect the actual financial conditions in the cultivation, processing and marketing spheres. Exploiting the discrepancies, they trade astutely for profits.

Both hedgers and speculators look carefully, too, at differences in supply and demand *between* the two processed products (oil versus meal). Which contracts to buy and which to sell, and when, depend also on these distinctions. Underlying trends for the oil and meal must be studied assiduously – for example, what is the expected upcoming production of palm oil in Malaysia as competition for soybean oil? Futures traders must also be very comfortable with the jargon of commodity exchanges and with the differences in how values are listed. At the CBOT, whole soybeans are listed in cents per bushel, soybean meal in dollars per (non-metric) ton and soybean oil in cents per pound. At the whole soybean exchange in Dalian, China – the second largest after the CBOT – the beans are listed in Chinese Yuan per metric ton. Add to all this the inherent financial risks in futures speculation – and the recent price-distorting effects of large institutional investments in futures markets – and it becomes abundantly clear that trading soy futures is not for the faint of heart.

The financial risks of futures speculation were starkly captured in the 1983 hit movie *Trading Places*. Approaching a commodities exchange centre, a seasoned broker expounds to his protégé, Billy Ray Valentine,

> Think big, think positive, never show any sign of weakness. Always go for the throat. Buy low, sell high. Fear? That's the other guy's problem. Nothing you have ever experienced will prepare you for the absolute carnage you are about to witness. Super Bowl, World Series – they don't know what pressure is. In this building, it's either kill or be killed. You make no friends in the pits and you take no prisoners. One minute you're up half a million in soybeans and the next, boom, your kids don't go to college and they've repossessed your Bentley. Are you with me?[20]

The film is so emblematic of how trading has worked that Gary Gensler, chairman of the U.S. Commodity Futures Trading Commission, cited it in testimony to Congress about the need to tighten futures rules. He repeatedly requested a new 'Eddie Murphy' rule – invoking the actor who played Billy Ray Valentine because in the movie that character profits massively from misappropriated USDA information.[21] Congress agreed that trades based on unreleased government information did indeed need to be prohibited, and in 2011 President Obama signed the new rule into law.

Financial ruin can loom for multiple actors when commodity dealers collude in insider trading, otherwise cheat the system, attempt to corner markets or get in over their heads monetarily. An egregious case involving soybean oil occurred in 1963 when Anthony De Angelis, a commodities salesman who ran the Allied Crude Vegetable Oil Refining Corporation, overplayed his devious hand. De Angelis already had a history of shipping substandard soy oil through the Food for Peace programme. Unfortunately, his actions in the early 1960s were even less ethical.

At that time the Soviet Union was experiencing agricultural shortages, and rumours circulated that they might be interested in purchasing large quantities of vegetable oil from the U.S. Hoping to make a fortune in sales and futures contracts, De Angelis bought shipments of soy and cottonseed oils and stored them in New Jersey. Next, as the *New York Herald Tribune* later explained, 'using warehouse receipts for the stuff, Allied went to banks, factors, all sorts of firms in the lending business, and borrowed to buy more oil. It had not yet paid for some of the oil it was using as collateral.'[22]

The U.S. political climate at the time was fraught; any agricultural deal with the Soviets was highly controversial. Wrangling over details pitted the U.S. Congress against the Kennedy administration, the shipping industry against the diplomats and the Americans against the Soviets. All the uncertainty caused commodity prices to slide. De Angelis's backers eventually insisted, as per contract, that he forward some $19 million more in cash to them. Instead, Allied filed for bankruptcy. Soon, according to the *Herald Tribune*, Allied's creditors started 'a frantic search through a spaghetti-like maze of pipes and tanks in Bayonne, NJ for millions of gallons of vegetable oil'. Little was ever found; it turned out that many of the arriving ships were filled mostly with water, with only a thin layer of oil floating on the top – just enough to fool inspectors. As Isadore Barmash explains in *Great Business Disasters*, this was the great soybean scandal of the mid-Sixties . . . a $150 million swindle . . . The fiasco in 1963 forced Ira Haupt & Co., a respected brokerage, out of business, caused another to merge, stuck twenty banks with bad loans, embarrassed trading companies, and brought still other concerns to the brink.[23]

When yet further losses are included, the value of this fraud expressed in 2016 purchasing power came to nearly $1.4 billion. One of the hardest hit enterprises was American Express; its stock dropped 50 per cent in the swindle's aftermath. The financial nightmare had a bright side for a young investor named Warren Buffet, however. He bought 5 per cent of American Express for a bargain price.[24] It also benefited the *Wall Street Journal* reporter who covered the story: he won a 1964 Pulitzer Prize.[25]

There have been other scandals, too. In 1989 the CBOT accused an Italian firm that at the time owned the Central Soya company, Ferruzzi, of trying to corner the summer soybean market – that is, of buying so many futures contracts *and* actual harvests that they would effectively have controlled soybean prices for everyone else. CBOT forced Ferruzzi to sell its soybean contracts. Furious at their loss of profits, the company sued CBOT and began a high-profile media campaign against CBOT officials. In 1992 the Italians and CBOT reached a settlement in which Ferruzzi paid all legal costs and a $1.65 million fine, relinquished their membership in the CBOT and admitted no wrongdoing.[26]

The year 1989 was a difficult one at CBOT, as a two-year FBI investigation also came to a head. FBI agents, extensively trained to go undercover as commodities brokers, had gathered enough evidence to indict 46 of their 'fellow' brokers and local traders at CBOT and the Chicago Mercantile Exchange. The defendants were charged with multiple crimes, including defrauding the customers they were supposed to represent. Eight soybean traders pleaded guilty and received leniency; ten were convicted in court and paid fines and restitution, or served time in prison, or both.[27] Fortunately, apparently only a few of the exchanges' 6,000 agents (in various commodities) had engaged in the worst trickery.

Despite protections developed after these scandals, problems still do pop up from time to time as cheaters find ways around rules and technologies. Thus in less than three months of 2011, high-frequency trader Michael Coscia made an illegal profit of nearly $1.4 million by manipulating the electronic commodity trading systems in Chicago and London.[28] He did so using software he had specially commissioned in order to perform a prohibited manoeuvre repeatedly. Among the commodity markets he tampered with were those of soy oil and soy meal. He was sentenced to three years in prison.

Yet such incidents are actually fairly rare. Most of the time, trades in soybeans and soy products, and in the futures contracts for them, unfold in a conventional manner. The legal safeguards usually work, although the stakes for futures speculators are always high.

Not only is there a lively trade in soy and soy contracts, so too the companies – big and small – that develop, distribute, process and export soy; that manufacture products using soy; and that provide services to soy farmers and industries are themselves frequently traded. Among myriad examples, one can trace the dizzying evolution of a company that a group of Iowa landowners, along with Henry A. Wallace, a farm journal editor, founded in 1926. Wallace would go on to become u.s. Secretary of Agriculture, then the country's 33rd Vice President and later Secretary of Commerce, but first he would shepherd his business, the Hi-Bred Corn Company, to a resounding success.

Although the enterprise would eventually become a major seller to soy farmers, it first focused on marketing a novel product, the seeds of hybrid corn (maize). Over time executives experimented with selling egg-laying chickens, broiler chickens and cattle. By 1935 the company had added the word 'Pioneer' to its name to help it stand out within an increasingly competitive market. In 1973 they purchased the Peterson Seed Company, acquiring the diverse soybean varieties that would catapult them to prominence in the world of soy.

A 'musical chairs' game of buying and selling ensued. In the 1970s company leaders purchased further agricultural firms and assets, and in 1978 they spun off their egg-laying poultry business as an independent company. In 1983 they sold to Cargill some of the same assets they had purchased in the 1970s (Cargill in turn sold them to the Delta and Pineland Company in 1994; Monsanto purchased that entire company in 2007). Then in 1991 Pioneer purchased 2 million shares in Mycogen Seeds, with whom they developed a GE partnership including work on insect-resistant soy. The wheeling and dealing kept apace, as in 1992 Pioneer paid Monsanto nearly half a million dollars for the advance right to sell Roundup Ready soybeans once they had passed their regulatory hurdles.

Pioneer sold its Mycogen shares in 1998. By this point Pioneer was the top brand for soybean seeds in North America. This dominance attracted the attention of DuPont, which purchased a 20 per cent stake in Pioneer in 1997; the two enterprises formed a joint venture. In 1999 the takeover was complete: for $7.7 billion, DuPont purchased Pioneer, making it into a wholly owned subsidiary. Then in 2006 Pioneer partnered with its Swiss rival, seed giant Syngenta, to form Greenleaf Genetics, a joint venture that provided more GE choices to soy farmers. In 2010 Pioneer left that collaboration. Next, in 2013 Pioneer acquired majority ownership of a prominent South African seed company in order to extend its influence on that continent. Meanwhile, DuPont and Monsanto sparred in bitter patent and anti-trust court battles over seed technologies – but in 2013 they put their differences aside, settling out of court. DuPont agreed to pay Monsanto a minimum of $1.75 billion in royalties for seed technology licensing, and Monsanto dropped its insistence that DuPont pay them a $1 billion earlier jury award.

The settlement did not offer Pioneer a calm moment, however; in business there is no respite. Recently rumours have circulated that DuPont might sell Pioneer. Iowa's *Des Moines Register* explained that, 'Falling corn and soybean prices, with stubbornly high prices for land, seeds and other inputs, are squeezing farm income. The downturn has sharply lowered the values of DuPont, Monsanto . . . and other agricultural companies.'[29] Farmers with lower incomes buy fewer farm products. In this economic environment, DuPont wondered whether it might want to divest itself of Pioneer.

Nobody was off the hook: in 2016 a company owned by the government of China began the regulatory petitions for purchasing Syngenta for $43 billion, and Bayer AG similarly began the process of persuading governments in North America and Europe that its purchase of Monsanto for $56 billion would not create any monopolies. As for Pioneer, as of 2016 they were still selling soybean seeds, even as their parent company, DuPont, was planning to merge with Dow Chemical. The companies thus buy and sell soybeans even as they buy and sell each other.

The fear of monopolies wielding excess control over markets is only the first of many concerns in the sphere of soy economics. Ironically, although governments may oppose mergers of the largest companies, at the same time those very companies and soy farmers alike often benefit from government assistance. Government aid is a second major source of concern and takes various forms.

Startlingly, government aid can involve *multiple* international governments working in tandem. Twelve governments finance and manage the Initiative for the Integration of the Regional Infrastructure of South America (IIRSA), whose transportation projects directly benefit that continent's soy industry as well as other businesses. In northwest Argentina, for example, the IIRSA has paid for highway construction and rehabilitation of abandoned railway lines. With this infrastructure assistance, soy barons can more profitably move their beans to export markets. Such transportation initiatives are controversial mainly for environmental reasons, since they encourage ever more soy plantings and deforestation.

The South Americans are hardly alone in propping up soy producers. The U.S. government's aid to farmers frequently sparks international anger because it distorts trade to Americans' advantage. Federal subsidies of various types to U.S. soybean farmers between 1995 and 2014 totalled $31.8 billion.[30] Although periodically the government changes the conditions and rules for assistance, farmers and the politicians they influence remain addicted to what has been called agricultural 'welfare'.[31] The largest share of this funding has been doled out to insurance businesses as hefty subsidies for farmers' coverage; the insurers also receive federal payments to offset their administrative costs. Along with the insurance companies, the complex system of subsidies and payments favours wealthy farmers with large landholdings. It has often been criticized as promoting inequality.

Yet many U.S. farmers argue that if their insurance were not subsidized, they would be unable to afford it. They are unconvinced that the futures market would be able to adequately substitute for insurance to safeguard their finances from drought, pest epidemics, floods, hail or free-falling soybean prices. Without insurance subsidies, they would simply go without enough protection, a situation they obviously wish to avoid. Farmers and their lobbyists insist that the entire nation should also avoid that problem because, they say, protecting farmers' incomes is crucial for assuring the u.s. food supply.

But these subsidies make it hard for soy producers in poor countries – in Ghana, for example – to market their own soybeans. Although the Ghanaian government has nascent financial supports for soy farmers, it cannot afford a protective largesse towards them comparable to that of the u.s. government. Consequently, Ghanaian farmers cannot grow soybeans as securely or cheaply as u.s. culti-vators can. Although Ghanaians do receive aid from international development experts, they still shoulder far more financial burden, relative to their incomes, than their American counterparts. They also face a long-term risk of competition from cheaper imported soy. This threat looms because, over time, the Ghanaian soy-processing industry will presumably improve its capacity to store and crush very large shipments of soybeans. That situation will make it pos-sible for the crushers to buy bulk shipments of beans from America at prices lower than those Ghanaian farmers can offer. Soy farm-ers in the u.s. can sell their beans so cheaply in part because their government cushions (coddles?) them in a way that African govern-ments cannot. In the soy trade, as in many other agricultural sectors, African farmers rightly feel that the economics of world commerce are stacked against them.

The economic imbalance is exacerbated when nations with sur-plus crops 'dump' them into fragile markets at low prices. Recall that the u.s. government helps America's farmers by buying up surpluses and then donating them to charities or selling them at low cost to other countries' governments. Too often this has propped up u.s. farmers' profits by sacrificing the profits of impoverished farmers overseas; wherever that wave of extra corn and soy goes, it lowers local market prices. It also provides handsome profits for the u.s. shipping companies that must, by u.s. law, be contracted with to transport those foods overseas.

Adding to this unfairness to poor farmers, the culinary expect-ations of urban consumers in a receiving country can shift; they start to prefer the flavour or consistency of imported products over their country's own traditional crops. The impact of subsidized exports of u.s. soy oil to Bangladesh illustrates the process. Beginning in the 1960s, the Bangladeshi government received large quantities of semi-processed u.s. soy oil that it could sell inexpensively to local refiners. The programme relieved the u.s. of surplus oil and so helped protect the price of soy for u.s. farmers. The programne also provided the Bangladeshi government with a revenue source, and it made cheap cooking oil available to Bangladeshi consumers, who did need more fat in their diets. Although those consumers initially rejected the oil, its price soon made it popular. Unfortunately, this chain of events deeply undermined Bangladesh's traditional mustard oil farmers. Even after the cheap shipments stopped and Bangladesh began importing soy oil from South America rather than the u.s., the impact of the u.s. programme continued as a lasting change in the flavour and price preferences of Bangladeshi consumers.

Financial supports for soy farmers also spark international legal disputes. In 2016 a consortium of Brazilian soy farmers hired a Chicago law firm to research whether a complaint against the u.s. government's farm supports could successfully be lodged with the World Trade Organization (wto). Founded in 1995, the wto is the global organization that handles the rules of trade between nations and mediates quarrels among them. Brazil and the u.s. are among its treaty-bound participants.

The Brazilian soy farmers were alarmed by how the subsidies in America's 2014 farm bill were playing out. Because the bill tied support levels to market prices, which dropped significantly following the law's passage, u.s. soy farmers were receiving much more assistance than previously anticipated.

The Brazilian farmers felt unfairly outcompeted. They took inspiration from Brazil's 2014 receipt, after a ten-year legal battle at the wto, of $300 million for Brazilian cotton farmers who had objected to u.s. cotton-farm subsidies. Brazil's soy farmers decided to explore persuading their government to file a similar complaint on their behalf.

The wto also handles tariff policies, placing strict limits on the taxes nations can levy on agricultural imports. Although trade in whole soybeans is fairly free of tariffs worldwide, countries wishing to encourage a domestic crushing industry impose tariffs on imported soy oil and meal to spur buyers to purchase locally crushed soy. While such tariffs are permitted within the wto framework, at times the major soy-producing nations are quite upset about them. They strive for new, more favourable relations with their trading partners. Thus the Trans-Pacific Partnership (TPP), negotiated by the Obama administration for seven years with eleven other countries, would have eliminated many tariffs on soy products, making U.S. soy businesses big winners.

But the TPP had far-reaching economic implications and met opposition in many quarters. Responding to his supporters' distrust of the agreement, President Trump immediately nixed U.S. participation. For their part, some of the other eleven countries also witnessed heated arguments against the treaty. Protests broke out over controversial provisions it contained, including one that would have allowed corporations to sue governments for what they considered unfair trade practices. Populations wishing to keep out GE soybeans feared lawsuits from Monsanto or Cargill if they continued to insist that GE imports be labelled as 'genetically modified'. Without U.S. participation, the TPP withered. Yet its detailed provisions could easily provide templates for future trade negotiations. Their existence continues to unnerve detractors.

The TPP is scarcely the only arena in which GE soy has generated controversy in international trade. Disputes about the handling of GE products in import markets constitute a third contentious area in the economics of soy. Right from its introduction as an internationally traded product, GE soy met resistance. As a genetics textbook explains, in 1996

> several British newspapers ran frontpage photographs of inflatable rafts belonging to the Greenpeace organization blocking the entry of a freighter into Liverpool harbor. Nearby, Greenpeace had erected a huge banner on a barge, showing the words 'Floodgate: Genetic Pollution'. The protest was against the first shipment of genetically engineered soybeans from the United States to Britain. In the next month, Greenpeace was in Hamburg harbor, Germany, using a powerful slide projector to beam the words 'Genetic experiment – don't buy it' onto the side of a similar freighter.[32]

Greenpeace also roused ordinary consumers to write to European grocery chains to protest GE imports. Meanwhile, farmers in France destroyed GE seeds, slashing open their bags, spraying them with fire extinguishers and even urinating on them to damage them as much as possible. Similarly, off and on over many years and in multiple European countries, bands of saboteurs have vandalized field trials of GE crops.

Some of the saboteurs were prosecuted and punished, but at the same time public outcry against biotechnology convinced European governments to adopt stringent labelling requirements and a 'precautionary principle' towards genetic modification. That principle holds that if there is a plausible risk that an action could do harm, then the action must be considered 'guilty until proven innocent' – that is, the burden of proof lies with those who wish to undertake the action. The principle raises to legal status the advice that one is 'better safe than sorry'.

Inspired by events in Europe, in the year 2000 Ecuadoran activists positioned two small boats outside the port of Guayaquil to block the unloading of 30,000 tons of GE soy that the U.S. Food for Peace programme had sent for animal feed. Protesters boarded the delivery ship and impeded its entry into port. Meanwhile, environmentalists and sympathetic government officials entered the port authority's office, demanding that the ship turn back. Their arguments rested on the principles of environmental caution in Ecuador's 1998 constitution. The activists won a temporary injunction stopping distribution of the soy, but before all legal requirements were completed to send the ship away, different Ecuadoran officials auctioned its contents off.[33] The frustrated activists had to wait until 2008 for a long-sought partial victory. In that year, although the government allowed the import of GE products when labelled, it took the very strong step of writing an explicit ban on the growing of GE crops right into their new constitution.

In places where GE cultivation is disallowed, not everyone is happy about it. Romania is illustrative. In 1999 Roundup Ready soy was introduced to that country's farmers and quickly adopted. RR soy became the country's most profitable crop, by 2006 occupying 137,000 hectares (nearly 340,000 acres). Romania began exporting whole soybeans and greatly reduced its imports of soy meal.

But then in 2007 Romania joined the EU, and farmers had to comply with EU rules against cultivating RR soy. The farmers switched to conventional varieties of soy. To their chagrin, they struggled with weeds, profitability dropped, and then so did the amount of soy they were willing to produce – decreasing by more than 75 per cent within two years.[34] Romania returned to high dependence on soy imports; by 2013 the value of those imports had shot up thirteen times higher than their value in 2006.[35] Although recent years have seen an upturn in Romanian cultivation of the beans, the quantity grown still comes to little more than half the harvest of 2006.[36] Membership of the EU has provided Romania with many benefits, but those have come at the expense of soy profitability and independence. Many farmers who had made a good living growing RR soy in the past deem the EU's stance injurious.

To some, the most disturbing GE trade controversy centres on the rejection of GE foods even when they come as donations for severely malnourished people. This phenomenon began in 2002 when, even as Zambians were literally starving, their government rejected a large shipment of maize (corn) that had come from the U.S. through the World Food Programme (WFP). Zambian officials were suspicious of the health effects of GE foods. They also worried that their farmers might save some of the donated maize to plant in their fields, thus introducing a GE crop into the country.[37] Zambia's agricultural exports made up 30 per cent of its gross domestic product,[38] and since European countries were a major market, the officials worried that Europe could begin refusing Zambia's exports as 'contaminated'. They feared the eventual ruin of their country's finances.

GE soybeans have similarly come under fire. In 2010, 2.2 million Zimbabweans needed emergency food due to inadequate rain and crop failure, but the government rejected any donated GE crop that was not milled first, so as to prevent it from being planted. This was not an easy requirement for aid agencies to meet. Yet, agreeing with his government's decision, soil science professor and soybean farmer Sheunesu Mpepereki of the University of Zimbabwe remarked, 'Recently, the National Soya-bean Taskforce received an inquiry from a prospective client in Europe who requested for non-GM Soya beans. So if we allow GM products and seed into the country, we lose that market.'[39] The restrictions in Europe have thus had perturbing, controversial consequences elsewhere in the world.

To GE or not to GE, that is the question. Yet amid such large tides of world trade, there have also always been small, unexpected ripples. Sometimes little ripples even lead to major changes: as we have already seen, President Nixon's short-term decision to restrict soy exports led over time to enormous shifts in trade. Many less sweeping examples also abound in which modest soy commerce is intertwined with global developments.

The more nimble entrepreneurs have found ways to flourish in changing circumstances, as for example Ralston Purina in 1976. The u.s. Congress had just established a 320-km (200-mile) fishery conservation zone surrounding its territory. The Japanese food industry reacted with concern to the restriction of Japanese fishing in Alaskan waters. A Japanese company quickly partnered with Ralston Purina. Together they developed a soy protein isolate that could partially substitute for fish in the traditional fish pastes of Japanese cuisine. The joint venture's sales went from zero to 3,600 metric tons annually in the space of two years.[40] Ralston Purina had cleverly exploited a changed global context. In a similar way, currently organic soybean farmers have found niche markets for limited but lucrative sales of non-GE soybeans around the world.

But business opportunities provide fertile ground for conflict, too. A fourth area of soy-trade dispute is that which ensues between business entities. The most internationally inflammatory of these arguments regards the contracts that agro-tech companies require of farmers who wish to grow their GE seeds. Trailblazer Monsanto developed 'Technology Stewardship Agreements' – contracts in which farmers promise to use GE seeds for only one harvest. Dow AgroSciences, Bayer Crop Science, BASF Plant Science and DuPont Pioneer now all use this system to protect their enormous financial investments in genetic research. The companies argue that if their GE seeds can be used to generate multiple harvests, the seeds' profitability will be so curtailed that the companies will have no incentive to keep creating them.

On the political left, worldwide fury over these contracts has been intense. Oft-cited philosopher and activist Vandana Shiva has been particularly vocal in rejecting both GE technology and the patenting of any seeds, whether engineered or not. Championing farmers' ancient practice of saving seeds from whatever they grow to use for the next season's plantings, Shiva decries any patenting of life forms as 'biopiracy' and considers the corporations' business model immoral. She is so adamantly anti-GE that she even denounces Golden Rice, the plant genetically enriched to provide vitamin A and therefore prevent blindness among the poorest of the poor.

Nevertheless, the technology deals between biotech companies and farmers are legally binding. Monsanto, wishing to show it is serious about the agreements, has sued nearly 150 farmers for breach of contract over the last twenty years.[41] Most of the cases have been settled out of court, but in the eleven instances that did go to trial, Monsanto has won every time, in part because the company does not sue farmers for merely small amounts of unauthorized crops in their fields. They choose their cases well.

The most infamous case began in the late 1990s when Monsanto discovered that a Canadian farmer, Percy Schmeiser, was growing its RR canola (rapeseed) even though he had no contract with the company. Monsanto sued for patent infringement. Schmeiser claimed that RR seeds had blown in from his neighbour's farm or a passing truck, causing some RR plants to grow in his vicinity. He claimed he saved seeds from those plants and intentionally sowed them the following year. Schmeiser felt it was completely within his rights to save seed.

Monsanto's case against him went all the way to the Canadian Supreme Court, which ruled in the company's favour. Schmeiser, meanwhile, became a hero to 'seed freedom' activists. In 2005 Schmeiser discovered unwanted RR canola in his fields and successfully brought Monsanto to the small claims court to pay for its removal.

A prominent ruling involving soybeans further enunciated how lasting a seed patent can be. In *Bowman* v. *Monsanto Co.*, the U.S. Supreme Court affirmed that Indiana farmer Vernon Bowman erred in purchasing RR soybeans from a local grain elevator and then planting them in his fields without a Monsanto contract. The court ruled that in the case of seeds, patent rights continue far beyond an initial sale – *if* the seeds are used to make more of themselves. In other words, Bowman had the right to buy RR soybeans from the grain elevator and then resell them without being under contract to Monsanto or paying them royalties, but he did not have the right to use the patented seeds to make more of such seeds without a contract. The decision was a resounding victory for the biotech industry.

More recently, Monsanto quarrelled (once again) with the government of Argentina about its GE soy. Having finally won the right to patent its newer soybeans in that country, Monsanto pressured

Argentine exporters to test all their soybeans before sending them out of the country. Monsanto wanted exporters to verify that farmers bringing them crops made from Monsanto-patented seeds had actually followed the rules by being under contract with the company. If a shipment tested positive for Monsanto seeds, but there was no record of the farmer's having an agreement with the company, then the exporters would report the farmer to Monsanto.

In May 2016 the Argentine government publicly reacted to this tactic, insisting that any such testing would require advance government approval. Monsanto responded by suspending all sales of its newest soybean technologies in the country. Talks ensued between the government and the corporation for several weeks until it was determined that Argentina's National Seed Institute would oversee all inspections for the current harvest, and Monsanto's latest GE soybeans would again become available to farmers. Negotiations also began on a new comprehensive seed law.

Mostly, for the farmers and companies involved, these contract disputes are about who gets to make money. A fifth area of controversy in soy economics is also about profits – and persuasion. Companies vehemently care about rules for how products may be presented to consumers, as shown with Chapter Three's anti-margarine laws and Chapter Eight's discussion of GE labelling. Arguments about what counts as 'milk' provide another example of such sensitivity, with the different sides manoeuvring to guard or expand their market shares. How soy (or nut) beverages can permissibly be advertised is contested.

Countries vary in what they call 'milk'. The EU prohibits the word 'milk' on a label unless the product comes from mammary secretions, so soy milk producers label their products 'soy drink', or in France, *tonyu* (from its Japanese name). In China, the beverage has for centuries been called 'soy broth' without reference to 'milk'. By contrast, in other Asian nations (North and South Korea, Thailand, Vietnam, Japan), the drink's name overlaps with the name for dairy milk.

In the U.S., a dairy-loving nation, the soy industry has fought to follow those latter nations' lead; associating soy with dairy milk boosts their business. When in 2000 and 2010 the dairy industry asked the FDA to prohibit the word 'milk' on containers of non-dairy beverages, soy companies protested. Soy interests also entered the fray when dairymen proposed two different class-action lawsuits against soy-milk companies for using the word 'milk' on their boxes. In each of these instances, the Soyfoods Association of North America, an industry group, battled the dairy producers.

So far, the soy industry is winning. While the FDA has occasionally warned soy-drink companies not to use the word 'milk' on their packages, it has generally focused on more pressing matters. As for the court cases, judges in 2013 and 2015 decried the dairy industry for underestimating consumer intelligence. They deemed it obvious that 'soy milk' does not contain cow secretions, in the same way that an 'ebook' obviously does not contain paper.[42]

A poignant sixth controversy in the business of soy involves the further disempowerment of already disadvantaged people. The issue is 'land grabbing', such as the brasiguayos are accused of perpetrating in Paraguay. According to the watchdog organization Land Matrix, in nearly two hundred deals between 2001 and 2016, large private investors and corporations crossed national boundaries to purchase or lease extensive tracts for soybean agriculture. Thirty-six per cent of these acquisitions took place in Africa, often in countries such as Ethiopia and Mozambique that have weak or corrupt governance – and also hungry, poor populations.[43]

The spate of appropriations for various crops and forestry has been called a 'global land rush', alarming the UN's Committee on World Food Security (CFS). In 2009 the CFS began a three-year consultation with an array of actors on five continents. Together they hammered out voluntary guidelines for land purchases, with the goal of protecting indigenous peoples, small farmers with informal rights to the land and those already unfairly evicted from their fields, for whom a restitution process was outlined.

But the proof will be in the pudding; it remains to be seen how carefully the guidelines will be followed. At least nine transnational land deals for soy cultivation of over 6,000 hectares (14,800 acres) each have been negotiated in developing countries since the guidelines' 2012 release. Notably, Australians purchased 37,000 hectares (91,400 acres) in Brazil, and a contract enabled South Africans to lease 50,000 hectares (about 123,500 acres) in the Republic of the Congo.[44] How well the rights of local residents have been and will be respected remains to be seen.

THE MANY CONTESTED arenas of soy economics constantly affect prices for the beans. Futures traders therefore keep a perpetual eye on all the controversies: on corporate mergers and anti-trust rulings; on government aid to soy farmers and international rulings on such subsidies; on the variable restrictions placed on GE products in different markets; on what contracts and courts affirm about patents; on advertising rules for soy products; and on how land-tenure regulations influence soy production levels. The traders also pay attention to transportation costs for soy, weather patterns, prices of competing crops, pest outbreaks, new soy products, consumer consumption trends and, of course, new rules in the futures trading business itself. They keep their fingers on the pulse of anything that could affect the value of Abe and Melora Roth's humble crop, including the relatively new realm of biodiesel, to which we now turn.

TEN

FAT IN THE FIRE: SOY DIESEL

Imagine if the U.S. military developed a weapon that could threaten millions around the world with hunger, accelerate global warming, incite widespread instability and revolution, provide our competitors and enemies with cheaper energy, and reduce America's economy to a permanent state of recession. What would be the sense and morality of employing such a weapon? We are already building that weapon – it is our biofuels program.

Navy Captain T. A. 'Ike' Kiefer, 'Twenty-first Century Snake Oil:
Why the United States Should Reject Biofuels as Part of a Rational
National Security Energy Strategy' (2013)[1]

Biodiesel use is good for the environment, human health, local economic growth, and the national economy. It provides meaningful fuel choice – and helps decrease threats associated with petroleum dependence . . . Over its lifecycle, biodiesel reduces greenhouse gas emissions by as much as 86 percent compared to petroleum . . . Biodiesel is non-toxic; in fact, table salt is more toxic . . . More biodiesel use means . . . less cancer risk and less risk of respiratory disease [and] . . . Biodiesel enhances the world's protein supply.

From the web pages of the National Biodiesel Board[2]

Is turning soy oil into diesel fuel a bad idea, or a good one? The answer is yes – and no – to both. Using soybeans for diesel has shifting, kaleidoscopic effects on the world. Its consequences are many, varied and sometimes unpredictably transmitted in multiple directions.

Consider the unrest in Jakarta, Indonesia, in 2008. In January, thousands of tempeh and tofu vendors took to the streets to protest the more than doubling of soybean prices the previous year. They demanded more government intervention to bring the price of soybean imports down. Their livelihoods were on the line; as the price

Street vendors in Jakarta, Indonesia, sell many types of snacks, including soybeans fermented as tempeh.

kept rising, office workers who previously purchased soy foods were turning to cheaper options.

The Indonesian government eliminated import tariffs on whole soybeans, since the country's poor rely on the beans for protein. Authorities also took steps to control soaring prices of other foods. Yet by March, the media reported on babies dying of malnutrition: the government's efforts had not been enough. Outraged, the Islamic organization Hizb ut-Tahrir staged protests in multiple Indonesian cities. Their orators exhorted hundreds in attendance to embrace 'the advantages of Islamic civilization through the establishment of the Caliphate and Sharia' law as solutions to price spikes and poverty.

The international diverting of soy to biodiesel contributed to these events. Numerous intertwined forces beyond biodiesel also played a role. They included:

- mediocre staple crop harvests in multiple countries that year;

- the high price of petroleum (which added to food transport costs);

- China's growing demand for soybeans;

- the diversion of u.s. land away from soybean production in order to grow maize (corn) for subsidized ethanol; and

- Indonesia's reduction of import tariffs in the 1990s. It became difficult for local farmers to compete with cheap imported soybeans. As maize and rice became more profitable, many Indonesian farmers shifted away from soy. This increased the country's dependence on foreign soybeans, leaving them at the mercy of rising international soybean prices in 2007–8.

But although a multiplicity of troubles were to blame for the high Indonesian food prices, some of the blame does belong to the production of soy biodiesel – and speculation in soybeans encouraged by u.s. government subsidies for biodiesel. The high soybean prices contributed, in turn, to wrenching economic distress among Indonesia's poor. By 2007–8 the ever-increasing globalization of food sourcing had created a web in which problems or policies in one part of the world reverberated intensely elsewhere.

Consider also a very different situation. Medford Township, New Jersey, has had the longest continuous school-bus biodiesel programme in the u.s. It began with a u.s. Department of Energy grant, which made experimenting with alternative fuel possible in those early days when buying even small amounts of soy biodiesel added considerable expense to fuel budgets. In Medford's pilot project, starting in late 1997, half the town's school buses used 20 per cent soy biodiesel mixed into petro-diesel, and half used 100 per cent petro-diesel. During the project's four and a half years, in the buses running on partial biodiesel the school system documented a significant reduction in the tailpipe emissions that form smog and threaten health.

Benefiting from transportation manager Joe Biluck's experience as a diesel-engine mechanic, the school system could adjust vehicles so that the soy diesel led to fewer mechanical problems than regular diesel caused. Biodiesel lubricates better and in older vehicles burns cleaner than petro-diesel. In the buses assigned to biodiesel, these differences extended the life of exhaust and fuel systems, radiator struts, hood or bonnet brackets and mounts and fibreglass work. When the district adopted biodiesel for all its school buses, the wear-and-tear savings came to between $10,000 and $12,000 per year.[3]

Finding over time that improvements in the price and quality of soy diesel made grant money and special adjustments unnecessary, the school district has continued buying soy diesel for over twenty years. Although the township in general suffers from the same pollution as other populated areas near highways, the environment in and around school buses is safer than before. Since 1997, the district calculates that using soy diesel has eliminated around 56,000 kg (123,000 lb) of smog-forming gases and about 1,088 kg (2,400 lb) of diesel particulate matter that schoolchildren and bus drivers would otherwise have been exposed to.[4]

The community has responded positively. Biluck remembers a bus driver in the early years who was unhappy with the imminent change in fuels; she worried about the biodiesel's performance. But she drove a route for children with disabilities, and after six months with biodiesel in the tank, she apologized to Joe for her earlier scepticism. She was won over when she observed a child with serious respiratory problems struggling less to breathe each time he entered, exited and rode in her bus. The odour inside her vehicle was less obnoxious, too. Some Medford residents even say their school bus exhaust smells like French fries! This is the aroma of soy biodiesel helping people, a counterpoint to the soybean stresses in Jakarta.

The smell of biodiesel is actually variable, since it is made from diverse fats – principally now from virgin rapeseed (canola) oil in Europe, virgin soybean oil in the u.s., Brazil and Argentina, and virgin palm oil in Southeast Asia. But sometimes these oils become biodiesel *after* they have been used to cook French fries, doughnuts, chicken and other fried foods. In Southern California, biodiesel sometimes smells like the Mexican foods that local eateries serve. Here and there in cities all over the world, biodiesel entrepreneurs collect leftover oil, called 'yellow grease', from restaurants and institutional kitchens and then make it into biodiesel.

Biodiesel is distinct from either the virgin or used vegetable oil that is its 'feedstock'. Using straight vegetable oil in an ordinary diesel engine subjects it to inappropriate wear and tear, as the straight oil is too viscous and can combust incompletely, causing damaging carbon build-up. By contrast, biodiesel flows and combusts more appropriately. It is the chemical creation that results from treating oils or fats with alcohol and breaking off glycerine as a saleable by-product. Although worldwide most biodiesel comes from soy or rapeseed, it can be made from other sources, too. Despite the title of Kiefer's book quoted at the opening of this chapter, biofuels are not made from snakes – but in Louisiana, biodiesel has been made from alligator fat![5]

Biodiesel is also different from 'renewable diesel', although the two can be made from the same starter feedstocks, including soy oil. Renewable diesel is concocted through a more complex chemical process and is very similar to petro-diesel; it can, in fact, be shipped through the same long-distance pipes as petroleum. Renewable diesel is expensive and currently little used.

Whether processed from virgin soy oil, yellow grease or some other oil source, the more widespread product, biodiesel, can either be blended with petroleum diesel or burned in a vehicle that can handle it unblended. Blends are labelled according to the percentage of biodiesel they contain; thus the common blend of 20 per cent biodiesel and 80 per cent petro-diesel is called 'B20'. Blended biodiesels up to B20 require few if any adjustments to diesel vehicles and so are easy to adopt from a technical standpoint. The main concern is that biodiesel has a solvent effect; it cleans deposits on tank walls and pipes that petro-diesel previously left behind. The release of deposits can clog filters unless they are regularly cleaned in the initial months after biodiesel is introduced.

Blends higher than B20 can be more complicated to introduce to an ordinary diesel engine. Higher blends are problematic for parts made of rubber and certain metals; these must be replaced with more suitable alternatives. In addition, biodiesel at too high a level (or biodiesel that was improperly made) can congeal at colder temperatures, which causes engines to stall. Hence in colder climates and seasons, retailers sell blends lower than B20.

Yet vehicles can be adapted to handle 100 per cent biodiesel quite successfully, as motorcyclist Geoffrey Baker demonstrated in 2009. Baker adapted a bike and drove on biodiesel north through the U.S. from Mexico to Canada. In California, Baker stopped by the ruins of Manzanar, a Second World War internment camp whose Japanese residents made rapid-method soy sauce for themselves and other camps – by 1943 Manzanar's workers were making about 19,000 litres (4,180 gallons) of soy sauce a month.[6] Baker's arrival there made for a poignant juxtaposition of soy in different time periods: modern fuel uses versus the downtrodden internees' longing for familiar soy sauce. Soy played an important role both for those subjugated ghosts of the past and for the engine of Baker's present.

In the southern part of his route, Baker used 100 per cent biodiesel, manufactured mostly from soy-laden yellow grease. In the more northern areas 100 per cent biodiesel was not available, so he filled his tank with soy-oil diesel blends. Neither form of biodiesel gave him any trouble. The motorcycle made the entire 2,585-km (1,606-mile) trip on just 42.5 litres (9.36 gallons) of fuel.[7] For Baker, the trip was an adventure – but it was also a proof of concept.

Biodiesel companies wish to see many more Geoffrey Bakers on the road. They look to governments for support to make their nascent industry more viable, to spur the manufacture of more biodiesel fuel and biodiesel-friendly vehicles.

Around the world, energy companies do receive financial incentives (and prods) to create biodiesel blends. Assorted tax credits, grants and subsidies are available from federal, state, provincial and local sources in countries as varied as the U.S., Brazil, Argentina, Canada, Indonesia, Switzerland, South Korea, South Africa, Ireland and Belgium, along with many others. Governments provide financial assistance primarily for three reasons: to support their farmers with an additional market for crops, to lessen dependence on imported fuels and to reduce air pollution.

Powerful agricultural lobbies push their governments to devise and maintain the subsidies. In the U.S. – the country with the largest biodiesel production – the American Soybean Association (ASA) advocates strongly for the nation's renewable fuels programme. This programme operates with both a carrot and a stick. The carrot has been a $1 tax credit for each gallon of biodiesel that a registered blending company adds to petro-diesel. This credit has frequently been due to be phased out but, thanks to industry lobbying, has just as frequently been renewed before expiring.

The stick has been a Renewable Identification Number (RIN) system whereby each gallon of guideline-compliant biofuel created in or imported into the U.S. is given a unique identifying number. Companies that refine or blend petro-diesel for retail sale have been

Japanese American internees line up for lunch at the Manzanar Relocation Center in California in 1943. Residents produced soy sauce for themselves and other internment camps.

obligated by law to obtain and 'retire' a certain number of RINs yearly. This forces them to support the biofuel industry.

Understanding how companies fulfil their legal obligation requires grasping the way RINs are handled. Each gallon's RIN is carefully recorded and transferred during any change in the gallon's ownership. However, any owner of a gallon-plus-RIN is allowed to *detach* the RIN from the gallon. Although the RIN is not an object, it can be treated as if it were one and sold separately. The owner of the gallon-plus-RIN may choose either to keep the two together, or keep one and sell the other, or sell each to a different buyer.

Petro-diesel retailers can acquire RINs either by creating biodiesel themselves, by buying biodiesel gallons along with their accompanying RINs from other companies, or by purchasing RINs once those RINs have been detached from their fuel gallons. The detached RINs are sold by companies that ended up with more than the number of RINs required of them; detached RINs are thoroughly tradable. As the U.S. Congressional Research Service explains, legally 'RINs have value as a replacement for the actual purchase of biofuels.'[8] Whereas a gallon of biodiesel has value as fuel, the RIN has value as a unit of compliance with government demands.

Biofuels' supply and demand vary over time in relation to many factors including the size of crop harvests; the price of biofuels' chief competitor, petroleum; and the demand for relevant crops for purposes other than biofuel. Supply and demand also vary across regions. All of this variability causes the value of RINS to fluctuate. The fluctuations have, in turn, encouraged development of a RIN futures market.

The value of RINS has also tempted some to generate them fraudulently. The U.S. government takes such crime seriously, investigating and prosecuting offenders. They wish to protect a system they find useful for meeting policy goals. By contrast, smaller petroleum companies unable to produce their own biodiesel wish to abolish the RIN system. They resent being forced to buy fuel from their competitors to blend with their own, or else to buy detached RINS from a market they believe is rife with scams.

While the ASA does publicly note this programme's economic benefit to soy cultivators, to non-farmers the organization also touts biodiesel's positive environmental impacts.[9] Scientists have indeed found that when burned in older engines – many of which are still on the roads – biodiesel emits less carbon monoxide and fewer toxic compounds than regular diesel. As the Medford school district noticed, biodiesel also releases considerably less particulate matter into the air – the microscopic soot that can lead to lung, vascular and heart illnesses. Blends higher than B20 emit more nitrogen oxides (NO_x) than petro-diesel, however, which can in their own way exacerbate asthma and other lung conditions. EPA scientists published reports in 2015 indicating that blends of around B20 are probably better for human health than either pure petro-diesel or pure biodiesel.[10] The EPA also applauds soy biodiesel because the carbon it releases when burned is later taken in by the next soybean crop that farmers grow to make more biodiesel: it is a carbon-in, carbon-out, carbon-in system. Overall the EPA deems biodiesel an improvement over petro-diesel in addressing climate change.[11]

Yet the impact of biodiesel on global climate change is not entirely clear. While producing and burning biodiesel releases less permanent carbon into the air than relying on fossil fuels, the farming of crops such as soy for the biodiesel feedstock may release more nitrous oxide (N_2O), an especially potent greenhouse gas. In addition, when fields are dedicated to growing crops for biodiesel instead of food, an indirect consequence can be that somewhere else in the world, forests are cut down in order to supply the world food system with the now 'missing' food. Loss of forests adds significantly to climate change and destroys wildlife. Nature Conservancy scientists make several recommendations to reduce such indirect land-use changes:

- hardy, high-yield plants should be grown for biofuels on marginal farmland that is unsuitable for food crops;

- wastes, residues and wildlife-friendly plants should be used for biofuels;

- food-crop yields and cattle pasturing systems should be continually improved, so that less land is required for them; and

- developing countries that preserve forests should receive financial compensation, since protecting forests reduces greenhouse gases and is thus as important for the quality of our atmosphere as using biofuels instead of petroleum.[12]

Soy is neither a particularly hardy nor particularly wildlife-friendly crop, and the Nature Conservancy does not recommend using virgin soy oil for biodiesel. It should be noted that producing biodiesel from virgin soy oil also uses far more fresh water than the drilling and processing of petroleum. In an era when the earth's freshwater resources are strained, this disadvantage is notable.

Meanwhile, the impact of biodiesel on energy independence has been meagre. True, biodiesel production has grown dramatically in the past two decades. The EU went from processing about 1 billion litres in 2001 to over 12 billion in 2014, mostly from rapeseed.[13] In the U.S., where biodiesel is primarily based on soy, production multiplied 146-fold from 32 million litres in 2001 to approximately 4.7 *billion* litres in 2015.[14] In South America, soy biodiesel production took off in the mid-2000s, rising to over 6 billion litres in 2015.[15] But although all this expansion is exciting to the biodiesel industry, the overall numbers pale in comparison with fossil fuel use.

Argentina uses soy biodiesel domestically and also exports it, mainly to the U.S., Peru and, off and on depending on tariffs, to the EU. Brazil and the U.S. produce it overwhelmingly for internal consumption. In all three soy-producing countries, biodiesel consumption is small compared to consumption even merely of petro-diesel, not to mention gasoline, coal, natural gas and other petroleum-based fuels. In the u.s., biodiesel in 2015 was only about 5 per cent of all diesel used; the other 95 per cent was petro-diesel.[16] Soy oil contributes far, far less to energy consumption worldwide than oil pumped out of the earth's crust.

Ultimately, although producing biodiesel can be one of multiple strategies for reducing petroleum dependence, biodiesel cannot be a major solution. Crops are simply not energy-dense enough: the amount of land needed to grow oil-rich plants for truly large quantities of biodiesel would be colossal. Kiefer calculated in 2013 that using diesel from virgin soy oil to provide 'the 28 exajoules of energy that the u.s. uses every year just for cars and trucks and airplanes would require . . . 3.2 billion acres – one billion more than all u.s. territory including Alaska.'[17] Solar, water and wind power are, in the long run, more promising.

An attractive alternative to growing crops for virgin-oil biodiesel is to recycle edible oils that have already been used. Even stern, analytical critics of virgin-oil biodiesel like Kiefer have no great quarrel with biodiesel made from yellow grease, although they warn that it is nowhere near abundant enough to replace fossil fuels.

Yellow grease requires special steps to be converted to biodiesel, but the process is not fundamentally difficult. It can be cost-effective for fuel businesses, particularly when there are tax incentives and yellow grease can be obtained for free. In the triad of big soy-producing countries, only the u.s. uses much yellow grease for biodiesel; there it grew from 6 per cent of the feedstock in 2010 to 12 per cent in 2015.[18] Much of this yellow grease has its origin as soy oil.

Yellow grease is also used, however, in animal feed; the grease makes feed less dusty and provides extra calories – and cattle love it. Chickens and pigs consume it, too. Smaller amounts are used to manufacture paint, make-up, soap, rubber and detergents. These uses for yellow grease create competition for obtaining it. Depending on the quality of the grease and its location, a grease-handling company might or might not be able to acquire it for free. The little ski resort community of Summerhaven, Arizona, for example, is lucky that a small biodiesel manufacturer is willing to come up Mount Lemmon to retrieve their used oil; those restaurants are not paid for the yellow grease. In more easily accessed locales, processing companies do pay for grease. In the past, it was the restaurants who paid for the service of having someone get yellow grease off their hands, since it is cumbersome to dispose of properly. But with the growth of biodiesel in the u.s., the market dynamics switched.

Biodiesel processors in America compete with several large rendering companies for grease. Small firms jokingly refer to their large, price-setting rivals as the 'Tallow Ban' – though they recognize that the big players are not as tyrranical as the actual Taliban! Both small and large companies also compete with grease thieves. People do steal used cooking oil, though some police departments are unaware that grease removal is a crime.

Thieves strike in the middle of the night in the alleys behind restaurants where companies have placed grease-collection tanks. When the rendering industry got savvy and started putting locks on the tanks, burglars responded by damaging the tanks to get the valuable gunk; it is worth the extra effort to be able to siphon off the rancid, dirty liquid because the heists can yield thousands of dollars in profit in a single night.

In addition to losing biodiesel feedstock, companies are burdened with considerable clean-up costs when hurried, sloppy thieves spill grease. Large grease-collection companies, such as Griffin Industries in the u.s., hire detectives to track the crooks down. Griffin has investigated bandits in many states, yet it remains unclear where all the stolen grease is going. Some of it may land in the hands of crime syndicates overseas.

Some suspect that yellow grease ends up in the tanks of rival collection companies. The bitter feud between two yellow-grease processing companies in Boulder, Colorado, shows just how much animosity can bedevil the industry. The feud began with accusations by one company that its rival had stolen yellow grease from its bins. The drama continued with an after-hours, unannounced visit of two executives from one company to the property of the other, then a trespassing lawsuit, blogs and YouTube videos with accusations that one of the companies was a 'criminal organization' misusing federal funds, a libel suit, a counter-suit claiming interference with free speech, a guilty plea, a different guilty verdict and settlement of the libel suit in favour of the defamed company. Both sides behaved badly. They also glaringly exposed the competition that exists in the used cooking oil market.

Who acquires yellow grease, and how, can thus be fraught with tension. But for city sewer authorities, the tension is worse when no one is collecting the grease at all. Too often, soy oil and other fats go down drains into sewer systems. The grease congeals there – first a little, then a new layer, then another layer, and so on until a grease 'log' develops – with embedded rubbish, hair, food and 'flushable' wipes, which are notorious hitchhikers in grease. The problem is so severe for sewage backups that some cities hire grease managers to address it.

Notably, in the early 2000s authorities in San Francisco felt frustrated by the $3.5 million they spent annually to deal with grease blockages.[19] At that time, city restaurants paid rendering companies to take their yellow grease away. Temptation always lurked: although it was illegal, restaurant managers could save money by just pouring used oils down the drain. Officials tackled this menace in 2007 by offering a free, city-run service of yellow grease collection. They filtered the grease and sold it to local biodiesel factories. The city then purchased the biodiesel to blend with petro-diesel for its transportation fleet. The programme was a success. It inspired efforts elsewhere in the state to reduce both yellow grease in municipal pipes and petro-diesel pollution in the air.

Meanwhile, California studied 'renewable diesel' for government vehicles across the state. Because renewable diesel burns much like petro-diesel, it can entirely replace regular diesel with virtually no changes to a vehicle. In addition, renewable diesel burns more cleanly than either petro-diesel or biodiesel. Since the switch improves local air quality, in 2015 San Francisco completely replaced its diesel and biodiesel in municipal vehicles with renewable diesel, and the state mandated that its public agencies immediately begin purchasing renewable diesel to help meet air-quality goals.

California's renewable diesel comes from the world's largest producer, the Finnish company Neste, and includes very little soy in the feedstock. Up to half of the feedstock is palm oil, whose harvesting in tropical countries has been the subject of a Greenpeace campaign protesting deforestation.[20] In various areas of California, problematic petro-diesel in government vehicles was thus at first partly replaced with eco-friendly, soy-laden yellow grease, and then completely exchanged for mostly foreign, eco-questionable renewable diesel. Clearly, complexities and trade-offs abound.

Cleaner air in California risks causing greenhouse gas emissions from deforestation, affecting the planet as a whole. U.S. soy farmers and soy-diesel processors are also very unhappy that biofuel imports are edging them out of a market they laboured to build.

Governments in California used an unusually large amount of yellow grease for biodiesel. Elsewhere in the U.S., virgin soy oil is the typical feedstock – one that soy cultivators ardently advocate. To those who argue that using soy oil for biodiesel poses environmental risks, the farmers counter that in order to comply with federal regulations for RINs, the soy oil in fuels must come only from fields that were *already* farmland. No wild lands can be cleared to produce fuel feedstock. Moreover, farmers assert that continuing agricultural improvements will enable them to grow ever more soy on the same amount of land; extra land has not, and will not, be needed even when biodiesel creates demand for extra soy. Finally, to those who argue that diverting soy to biodiesel production pushes food prices upwards, worsening food insecurity among the poor, the soy producers of the National Biodiesel Board (NBB) answer that

> biodiesel actually benefits the world's protein supply. Processing biodiesel from soybeans uses only the oil portion of the soybean, leaving all of the protein available to nourish livestock and humans. By creating a new market for soybean oil, we increase the availability of protein-rich meal for human and livestock consumption. The increased meal supply results in a more cost-effective food and feed source.[21]

The NBB further notes 2016 data showing a drop in U.S. food prices even as biodiesel production increased.[22] The U.S. biodiesel industry does not appear to be creating financial pressure for American grocery shoppers.

An ecological concern lies, however, with how increasing the demand for soy oil could affect world prices. Whenever the price of soy oil goes up, farmers in places like Paraguay are motivated to convert untouched lands to soy agriculture. They surmise that high prices should allow them profitably to sell an expanded harvest to Argentine processing companies. Thus, because commerce and pricing are globally interconnected, even if the soy oil in U.S.-produced biodiesel did not come from any recently wild lands, somewhere else in the world natural ecosystems may still suffer.

Humans who depend on whole soybeans for food may also suffer. True, more soy protein meal may become available to international markets, but not everyone wants to use only one part of the beans. For the poor in several Asian societies, it is the beans with their oil intact – an inexpensive source not only of protein, but of calories and lipids – that are needed. For vulnerable Asian families, it matters that the U.S. Congressional Research Service has predicted that using soy for biofuels is expected to reduce U.S. whole soybean exports 14 per cent by 2022.[23] Fewer exports can mean higher world soybean prices – unless some other country fills in the export gap.

Of course, an international shift in suppliers could prompt its own troubling questions: did the new purveyors of soybeans convert virgin lands to soy agriculture? Did big soy landowners displace small farmers lacking documents to prove their land ownership? It is easy for North American soy biodiesel producers to see these issues as far away and irrelevant. But in a world that is commercially ever smaller, they are, in fact, germane for everyone.

In a globalized world, disadvantaged people can be especially hurt. Indonesian poet and political commentator Goenawan Mohamad captured this reality in a poignant 2008 column about a street vendor named Slamet.[24] Mohamad's words are worth attending to, bearing in mind that in the previous year, growing corn (maize) in America for ethanol had been more profitable than growing soy. Then suddenly the value of soybeans had shot up. Mohamad's column decried how Slamet was affected:

> Slamet's story is a negative indicator of our civilization . . . This man was a diligent trader, though poor. Since 1993 he had peddled fried cassava, tofu, tempeh and bananas . . . In the first years, his wife Nuriah says, there was hope: he could make a profit of up to 20,000 Rupiahs [about $1.50 U.S.] per day.
> But then, recently, the price of soybeans rose quickly from 3,400 Rupiahs to 8,000 Rupiahs per kilo . . . What could he do? He could not make enough profit to buy his family's groceries. His debts were mounting. He and his family lived in a home that was only 7 meters by 7 meters. But his fate wasn't determined there. It was determined far away: by bureaucrats

in Indonesia's Department of Agriculture and Commerce, by turbulent world markets, by fields and barns in the United States, by the weather and harvest in Brazil, by the structure of agribusiness in Argentina.

What power did Slamet have on the sidelines of this giant network? How much power could he have, when American farmers find it more profitable to grow maize for biofuel than to grow soybeans, and so the world's supply of soybeans shrinks? . . . When China and India, two very populated countries with rapidly growing economies, keep pushing up the demand for soy?

The soaring of soybean prices was inevitable. And so Slamet fell.

What could he do? He lived in a country with bureaucrats who fail to act in time . . . Slamet is an indicator of negligence.

His ruin is also a symptom of agricultural mistakes. In 1974, Indonesia grew enough soybeans for its own needs, but . . . it shifted crops and began importing soy . . . The policy-makers have been chaotic, or dumb, or confused. It seems that Slamet's story is also about soy donkeys . . . and Slamet's story is not just about tempeh and power and absurdity. It is also about a nation where a person can be desperately in debt . . . while not far from where he hanged himself there are people who spend hundreds of millions of Rupiahs for a single night's event. Slamet's story is the story of murder by indifference. Among his last words was a portent to his child Oji, in third grade, whose school fees Slamet could no longer afford. Slamet whispered that he would die soon. His death was inaudible.

But it was also a cry.

So also Mohamad's words are a cry. They ask us to examine our actions carefully. They ask us to consider the reverberations our soybeans, and agriculture, and biofuels have around the world.

Hope perhaps lies in a different kind of ordinary person – ones who are not so vulnerable as Slamet, and are able to make a little difference in their local regions. Every year Pima County, Arizona, hosts a household grease drive. The tradition started in 2005 as a way for families to drop off the used oils and fats they had after

Thanksgiving. Billed as 'Green Friday', the event helped protect Tucson's sewers while also providing feedstock to a local biodiesel company, Grecycle. Over twelve years, the drives have collected around 13,600 kg (30,000 lb) of grease.[25] This is a straightforward way in which citizens have contributed to a cleaner environment.

Grecycle collects yellow grease from 150–200 restaurants and institutional kitchens in a 640-km (400-mile) radius. The company makes about 3.8 million litres (836,000 gallons) of biodiesel yearly.[26] They sell their product mostly to a local truck stop that mixes it with petro-diesel. School districts and government fleets in the area remember the bad old days when poorly made biodiesel clogged their equipment and are sceptical of Grecycle's wares. The truckers understand it, though, and the truck stop appreciates that in their market, the price of Grecycle's biodiesel is lower than that of petro-diesel.

Grecyle's CEO, Michael Kazz, cares about the environment and is pleased to help improve air quality. Kazz also notes that from start to finish his fuel stays within a single region – the yellow grease comes from his own corner of the American West, and the biodiesel he makes is purchased locally. This kind of geographically 'closed-loop' recycling is more environmentally sustainable than the shipping of feedstocks, biodiesel or renewable diesel long distances – sometimes across oceans – before they are used.

But the satisfaction of making a difference cannot sustain a business. In order for his company to survive, Kazz needs the federal government to keep supporting biofuels. The tax credit he receives helps keep the price of his biodiesel low enough to entice a middleman to purchase it. The same is true for processors who use virgin soy oil to make biodiesel – they too still need the government, especially when competition from foreign biofuel suppliers or petroleum depresses their profits.

But what if? What if more governments, citizens, companies and foundations invested more effort in local grease biodiesel systems, and in the vehicles, like Geoffrey Baker's motorcycle, that could run on biodiesel without any petro-diesel blended in? What if investments helped make biodiesel production consistently cheaper and less dependent on government assistance in the long run? Although many towns have recycling programmes for residential grease, the fact remains that around the world large quantities of grease are simply wasted. The untapped grease certainly could not replace petroleum – human consumption of that commodity is far too high – but that extra grease could make another dent in humanity's fossil fuel consumption.

Using sustainably grown soy oil for cooking, collecting the left-over oil (and other fats) in household tanks, periodically taking our tanks to a recycling station or rolling them out to a curb for oil pick-up, and then having an entrepreneur turn that yellow grease into eco-friendly fuel – these would be the reasonable behaviours of an enlightened population that had been given the appropriate equipment and infrastructure. It would not be so logistically or technically difficult for us to pattern our relationship to soy oil in these ways; what is mostly lacking is will.

Biodiesel derived from virgin soy oil, too, could benefit us by reducing local pollution. But with the virgin oil we should proceed cautiously. Careful monitoring and regulations must be in place on a global scale to prevent deforestation for soy agriculture. Policies and programmes must also exist to reduce spikes in the price of whole soybeans and their effects on the poor. When land is diverted from cultivating soy to, instead, corn for ethanol, and at the same time some of the soybeans that *are* grown are diverted from exports to production of biodiesel, malnutrition can result in developing countries. Places like Indonesia should be assisted in returning to a higher level of soy self-sufficiency, and ceilings should be placed on speculators' ability to send the price of whole soybeans skyward.

THE RUSSO-JAPANESE WAR that opened this book was metaphorically 'fuelled', in part, by conflict over soybeans. Now we have vehicles that can be literally fuelled by soy. Many questions about this fuelling remain. Ultimately, the most important question about soy in biodiesel is about us: what will motivate us to optimal responsibility?

AFTERWORD

They come in the semi-darkness, or sometimes in blinding light. Travelling by truck and jet and small plane, they arrive at a high-security bunker in a remote and deeply inhospitable landscape. Invited, they enter through doors and double doors with locks and more locks as they penetrate a frozen mountain. Only those sending them are truly certain of their identities. Escorted through a long steel tunnel and recorded on camera at every step, they journey down to an ice-encrusted 'cathedral' room. They pause, facing a wall scooped out to deflect shock waves should the bunker ever endure an explosion. Carrying extraordinary treasures, they enter a vault room with shelves upon shelves of precious cargo in carefully marked boxes.

They remain in that vault room, hidden away from the blizzards, polar bears and robbers of the outside world. Sensors and monitors constantly gauge conditions inside – temperature, oxygen, methane and radon levels – to keep them healthy. Here they wait, ready for their next mission, whenever they may be needed. Here they are supremely safe: any attempt to capture or harm them would require cunning beyond that even of Professor Moriarty.

They are the seeds. They are the seeds of humanity's most important food crops, and they arrive at the Svalbard Global Seed Vault in Norway as 'backups' for the seed samples of facilities elsewhere. In case the genetic diversity tended in the world's usual seed banks were to be compromised – by fire or flood, combat or epidemics, budget cuts or incompetence – the seeds with copies in the vault could be reproduced.

Inaugurated in 2008 with international funding, the vault is a frigid tunnel-fortress lying far inside the Arctic Circle in the Svalbard archipelago. It already stores some 1 million unique seed samples. They include approximately 27,000 different varieties of soybean and 1,200 varieties of soy's wild cousins.[1] Each sample preserves DNA that could be used to breed for higher yields, or better resistance to a variety of pests, or improved adaptation to specific soil, atmospheric, latitude, elevation and climatic conditions. The soy samples have come primarily from collections in the U.S., South Korea and Nigeria; seed banks in Germany, Sweden, Canada, Kenya and Colombia have sent soy seeds too. The samples each contain up to 500 individual seeds, adding up to some 6.5 million soybeans resting in a carefully calibrated deep freeze.[2]

But not everyone trusts the idea of an international vault. Although strict agreements stipulate that only the institution depositing a sample can access it – just as with a safety deposit box in a

The Svalbard Global Seed Vault in far-northern Norway keeps approximately 27,000 different varieties of soybeans in a deep freeze. The vault serves as a back-up supply in case calamities befall seed banks in other parts of the world.

monetary bank – some countries worry that their genetic resources will be stolen at Svalbard, and then even perhaps patented by a rival country or corporation. Some have hence sent hardly any seeds – notably China and India. Yet past expeditions to collect soy, such as those recounted in Chapter Three, have rendered the origins of the soybeans at Svalbard far-flung. The ancestors of Svalbard's soybeans were first collected in countries as varied as China, North Korea, Japan, Taiwan, Indonesia, Vietnam, India, Nepal, Russia, Kyrgyzstan, Georgia, Poland, Hungary, France, Turkey, Burundi, Rwanda, Tanzania, Cameroon, Chile, Argentina, Brazil, Australia and many others.[3]

By Norwegian law, none of the seeds in the vault may carry engineered genes. All of the beans there do carry genes evolved during soy's wandering past, during humanity's many efforts to adapt it to multiple environments and purposes. And just as we have shaped the genetics of soy through selective breeding, the seeds at Svalbard in turn carry genes that will allow soy to shape our world, as the plant has been doing for thousands of years.

How far soy has come from its humble origins in northeast Asia! It has been ground and boiled, fermented, toasted, rolled into flakes, extruded, pressed and chemically treated. It has been turned into tofu and soy milk and tempeh and miso and soy sauce; and also into plastic and paint and fuel and fire-extinguishing foam. It has been fed to animals to make meat, and it has served as a substitute for meat. It has nourished millions and yet been caught up in the violence of war. Watching soybeans travel through history has been a way to watch humanity: our neediness, our creativity, our violence, our intelligence, our greed, our generosity, our recklessness, our fears and our hopes.

The quest for food has been the single most decisive shaper of human history because of its far-reaching effects on human social organization and health, and on the physical environment. First the agricultural revolution, and then many shifts in farming have had extraordinarily profound effects on our lives, though they garner less attention in the news than car bombings and celebrity weddings. We ignore agricultural shifts at our peril. Soy, as a primary world crop, is implicated in numerous controversial, world-changing processes – deforestation, extinctions, trade negotiations, genetic engineering, renewable energy, global warming and the global rise in meat production (with further impacts on animal welfare, human nutrition and air and water quality). Soy is massively important to the way our world functions. In these pages we have therefore sought to understand it.

But *how* should we understand soy? With multiple perspectives: from the viewpoint of the creatures with which we share the planet, which could see soy as the proliferating weed (and the humans who plant it as overabundant, destructive mammalian 'weeds'). From the viewpoint of the hen living in an extremely cramped cage. From the viewpoint of the Egyptian city boy whose family can feed him chicken and eggs only because soy poultry feed is cheap. From the viewpoints, too, of:

- the impoverished Bangladeshi girl whose health could greatly benefit from the protein in soybean-enhanced foods; and

- the impoverished Paraguayan worker labouring in soy plantations, who is barely paid enough to feed his or her family; and

- the Argentine economist who sees taxes from soy agriculture bolstering the federal budget; and

- the Brazilian scientist who finds hope for feeding humanity in genetic engineering; and

- the European agricultural corporation profiting from the international soy trade; and

- the North American conglomerate protesting against GE food labelling as a scare tactic lacking scientific validity; and

- the food-labelling activist who argues that consumers have an unequivocal right to know how their foods were produced; and

- the bewildered consumer wondering whom to believe, and why; and

- the biodiesel regulators striving to resolve conflicting data and motivations; and

- the Japanese office worker who nibbles on edamame at a bar after work; and

- the Chinese man laughing his way through a meal of stinky tofu.

IN THESE PAGES we have visited such actors; we could explore the perspectives of myriad more. Grasping the role of soybeans in our world by understanding stakeholders' motivations, struggles and genius has taken us to many realms of human experience. Ultimately, soybeans serve as a lens for new perspectives on our very selves.

REFERENCES

INTRODUCTION: HIDDEN GOLD

1 Tadayoshi Sakurai, *Human Bullets: A Soldier's Story of Port Arthur*, trans. Masujiro Honda (Boston, MA, 1907).
2 Joseph Hammond, 'Siege of Port Arthur: Verdun in Manchuria', http://thediplomat.com, 4 November 2014.
3 John W. Steinberg et al., eds, *The Russo-Japanese War in Global Perspective: World War Zero* (Leiden, 2005).
4 K. Asakawa, *The Russo-Japanese Conflict: Its Causes and Issues* (New York, 1904); David Wolff, 'Bean There: Toward a Soy-based History of Northeast Asia', *South Atlantic Quarterly*, XCIX/1 (Winter 2000), pp. 241–52.
5 Gary L. Cromwell, 'Soybean Meal: An Exceptional Protein Source', www.soymeal.org, accessed 1 July 2017, p. 4.
6 USDA Economic Research Service, 'Table 47: World Vegetable Oils Supply and Distribution, 2012/13–2016/17', www.ers.usda.gov, 29 March 2017; weight to volume conversions from www.thecalculatorsite.com, accessed 7 December 2016.
7 Cromwell, 'Soybean Meal', p. 4.
8 Sophia Murphy, David Burch and Jennifer Clapp, 'Cereal Secrets: The World's Largest Grain Traders and Global Agriculture', Oxfam Research Reports (August 2012), p. 16.
9 FAO *Statistical Yearbook, 2013* (Rome, 2013), p. 18, chart 66; Peter Best, 'World Feed Panorama: A Year of Resilience for the Feed Industry', www.wattagnet.com, 4 March 2013.
10 E. L. Miller, 'Protein Nutrition Requirements of Farmed Livestock and Dietary Supply', www.fao.org, accessed 2 July 2017, p. 10.
11 Owen Fletcher and Andrew Johnson Jr, 'Bull Market for Chicken Feed', *Wall Street Journal*, section C, p. 1, 25 April 2012.
12 Earth Policy Institute, 'Rising Meat Consumption Takes Big Bite out of Grain Harvest', www.earth-policy.org, 22 November 2011.
13 Christopher Doering, 'Smithfield Urges Farmers to End Use of Gestation Crates', www.usatoday.com, 7 January 2014.
14 National Oceanic and Atmospheric Administration, 'Average "Dead Zone" for Gulf of Mexico Predicted', www.noaa.gov, 9 June 2016.
15 Chesapeake Bay Foundation, 'Bad Water and the Decline of Blue Crabs in the Chesapeake Bay', www.cbf.org, December 2008.

16 See www.trademap.org, accessed 24 October 2016.

17 See Trade section, 'Crops and Livestock Products', in FAOSTAT, www.fao.org, accessed 7 December 2016.

18 Lucia Kassai and Raymond Colitt, 'Brazil Soy Boom Bottlenecked as China Left Waiting', www.bloomberg.com, 26 March 2013; Gustavo Bonato and Caroline Stauffer, 'In Brazil, a New Road to the Amazon Offers Grain Export Relief', www.reuters.com, 16 October 2013.

19 ISAAA, 'Global Status of Commercialized Biotech/GM Crops: 2016', ISAAA Brief, no. 52 (Ithaca, NY, 2016), p. 1.

20 Charles E. Hanrahan, 'Agricultural Biotechnology: The U.S.–EU Dispute', Congressional Research Service Reports 69, http://digitalcommons.unl.edu (2010), p. iii.

21 ISAAA, 'Global Status', p. 4.

22 Ibid., p. 10.

23 USDA, 'World Agricultural Production', WAP 05–17, www.fas.usda.gov, May 2017, Table 11. For whole soybeans, see USDA, 'Table 21: United States Soybeans and Products Supply and Distribution Local Marketing Years' and 'Table 22: Brazil Soybeans and Products Supply and Distribution Local Marketing Years', https://apps.fas.usda.gov, accessed 5 June 2017.

24 USDA, 'Top 25 Export Commodities, with Level of Processing, by Calendar Year, Current Dollars', www.ers.usda.gov, accessed 2 July 2017.

25 Smitsa, 'Lecithin – One Really Powerful Tool For Emulsification', https://foodwrite.co.uk, 29 January 2014.

26 USDA, 'Table 22'; Randall D. Schnepf, Erik Dohlman and Christine Bolling, 'Agriculture in Brazil and Argentina: Developments and Prospects for Major Field Crops', Report WRS-01-3, www.ers.usda.gov, 28 December 2001.

27 Schnepf et al., 'Agriculture in Brazil and Argentina', p. 25.

28 FAO, 'World Hunger Again on the Rise, Driven by Conflict and Climate Change, New UN Report Says', www.fao.org, 15 September 2017.

1 ASIAN ROOTS

1 Juzhong Zhang and Qilong Cui, 'The Jiahu Site in the Huai River Area', in A Companion to Chinese Archaeology, ed. Anne P. Underhill (Hoboken, NJ, 2013), pp. 194–212.

2 Gyoung-Ah Lee et al., 'Archaeological Soybean (Glycine max) in East Asia: Does Size Matter?', PLOS ONE, VI/11, http://journals.plos.org, 4 November 2011.

3 Ibid.

4 See Katarzyna J. Cwiertka and Akiko Moriya, 'Fermented Soyfoods in South Korea', in The World of Soy, ed. Christine M. Du Bois, Chee-Beng Tan and Sidney Mintz (Champaign, IL, 2008), pp. 165–6.

5 Donald L. Philippi, trans., Kojiki (Princeton, NJ, 1969), pp. 404–5.

6 H. T. Huang, Fermentations and Food Science, vol. VI, pt 5 of Biology and Technology of Science/Civilisation in China (Cambridge, 2000), p. 337.

7 H. T. Huang, 'Early Uses of Soybean in Chinese History', in The World of Soy, ed. Du Bois, Tan and Mintz, pp. 46–7.

8 Theodore Hymowitz and K. Kaizuma, 'Dissemination of Soybeans (Glycine max): Seed Protein Electrophoresis Profiles among Japanese Cultivars', Economic Botany, XXXIII (1979), p. 317.

9 Erino Ozeki, 'Fermented Soybean Products and Japanese Standard Taste', in *The World of Soy*, ed. Du Bois, Tan and Mintz, p. 150.

10 Huang, 'Early Uses', p. 52.

11 William Shurtleff and Akiko Aoyagi, 'History of Tofu – Page 1', www.soyinfocenter.com, 2004.

12 William Shurtleff, H. T. Huang and Akiko Aoyagi, *History of Soybeans and Soyfoods in China and Taiwan, and in Chinese Cookbooks, Restaurants, and Chinese Work with Soyfoods outside China* (1024 BCE to 2014) (Lafayette, CA, 2014), pp. 64–5.

13 Chee-Beng Tan, 'Tofu and Related Products in Chinese Foodways', in *The World of Soy*, ed. Du Bois, Tan and Mintz, p. 101.

14 Shurtleff and Aoyagi, 'History of Tofu – Page 1', p. 1.

15 Can Van Nguyen, trans., 'Tofu in Vietnamese Life', in *The World of Soy*, ed. Du Bois, Tan and Mintz, p. 185.

16 William Shurtleff and Akiko Aoyagi, *The Book of Tofu*, rev. edn (New York, 1979), p. 3; Zeina Makky, '12 Facts and Figures about the Beloved French Croissant', http://archive.jsonline.com, 10 July 2014.

17 William Shurtleff and Akiko Aoyagi, *Early History of Soybeans and Soyfoods Worldwide* (1024 BCE to 1899) (Lafayette, CA, 2014), pp. 110–11.

18 Myra Sidharta, 'Soyfoods in Indonesia', in *The World of Soy*, ed. Du Bois, Tan and Mintz, pp. 197–8.

19 William Shurtleff and Akiko Aoyagi, *History of Soybeans and Soyfoods in Southeast Asia* (13th Century to 2010) (Lafayette, CA, 2010), pp. 51–3.

20 William Shurtleff and Akiko Aoyagi, *History of Tempeh and Tempeh Products* (1815–2011) (Lafayette, CA, 2011), p. 785; Soewito Santoso, trans., *The Centhini Story: The Javanese Journey of Life* (Singapore, 2006), pp. 355–6, 372–3.

21 Linda Lombardi, 'Kawaii Japanese Food Characters', www.tofugu.com, 10 April 2014; David A. Henry, 'The Tale of the War between the Shôjin and the Animals (*Shôjin Gyorui Monogatari*)', abstract at http://aas2.asian-studies.org, accessed 3 July 2017.

22 Sidney W. Mintz, 'Fermented Beans and Western Taste', in *The World of Soy*, ed. Du Bois, Tan and Mintz, p. 56.

23 Hiroshi Tachi, 'Characteristics of Japanese Soy Sauce', www.kikkoman.co.jp, accessed 3 July 2017.

24 William Shurtleff and Akiko Aoyagi, *History of Soy Sauce* (160 CE to 2012) (Lafayette, CA, 2012), p. 446.

25 William Shurtleff and Akiko Aoyagi, *History of Soybeans and Soyfoods in Japan, and in Japanese Cookbooks and Restaurants outside Japan* (701 CE to 2014) (Lafayette, CA, 2014), p. 8.

26 William Shurtleff and Akiko Aoyagi, *History of Soybeans and Soyfoods in Central Asia* (1876–2008) (Lafayette, CA, 2008), p. 7.

27 Ibid.

2 EUROPE EXPLORES AND EXPERIMENTS

1 Francesco Carletti, *My Voyage around the World*, trans. Herbert Weinstock (London, 1964 [early 1600s]).

2 Carletti, *My Voyage*, p. 110.

3 Engelbert Kaempfer, *The History of Japan*, vol. I, bk 1 (London, 1727), pp. 121–2.

4 William Shurtleff and Akiko Aoyagi, *History of Soy Sauce* (160 CE to 2012) (Lafayette, CA, 2012), p. 1135.

5 Shurtleff and Aoyagi, *History of Soy Sauce*, pp. 59–60.

6 George Gordon Byron, 'Beppo: A Venetian Story', www.poemhunter.com, accessed 3 July 2017.

7 William Shurtleff and Akiko Aoyagi, *Friedrich Haberlandt: History of His Work with Soybeans and Soyfoods (1876–2008)* (Lafayette, CA, 2008), p. 70.

8 Paul M. Champion, *Industrie ancienne et moderne de l'empire chinois* (Paris, 1869).

9 William Shurtleff and Akiko Aoyagi, 'History of Soybeans and Soyfoods in Europe (incl. Eastern Europe and the USSR, 1597–mid-1980s) Part 2', www.soyinfocenter.com, 2007.

10 William Shurtleff and Akiko Aoyagi, 'The Society for Acclimatization, France – Page 2', www.soyinfocenter.com, 2004.

11 William Shurtleff and Akiko Aoyagi, 'History of Soy in Europe (incl. Eastern Europe and the USSR, 1597–mid-1980s) Part 1', www.soyinfocenter.com, 2007.

12 Shurtleff and Aoyagi, *Friedrich Haberlandt*, p. 30.

13 Nicolas-Auguste Paillieux, *Le Soya: sa composition chimique, des variétés, sa culture et ses usages* (Paris, 1881).

14 Yuying Li and L. Grandvoinnet, *Le Soja: sa culture, ses usages alimentaires, thérapeutiques, agricoles et industriels* (Paris, 1912).

15 William Shurtleff and Akiko Aoyagi, 'History of Soybeans and Soyfoods in Europe Part 3', www.soyinfocenter.com, 2007.

16 William Shurtleff and Akiko Aoyagi, 'The Society for Acclimatization, France – Page 3', www.soyinfocenter.com, 2004.

17 See the discussion at 'World War I Casualties', www.wikipedia.com, accessed 3 July 2017.

18 A. Bloch, 'Quelques Mots sur la fabrication et la composition du teou-fou (fromage de haricots chinois fourni par le *Soja Hispida*)', *Bulletin des Sciences pharmacologiques*, XIII (Paris, March 1906), pp. 138–43.

19 William Shurtleff and Akiko Aoyagi, *History of Soybeans and Soyfoods in Africa (1857–2009)* (Lafayette, CA, 2009), p. 398.

20 John F. Schmitz et al., 'Biobased Products from Soybeans', in *Soybeans: Chemistry, Production, Processing, and Utilization*, ed. Lawrence A. Johnson, Pamela J. White and Richard Galloway (Urbana, IL, 2015), p. 541.

21 Emanuel Senft, 'Ueber Einige in Japan Verwendete Vegetabilische Nahrungsmittel, mit Besonderer Beruecksichtigung der Japanischen Militaerkonserven', *Pharmazeutische Praxis* (1906–7), V/12, pp. 481–91; VI/3, pp. 81–9; VI/4, pp. 122–4, 131–2; VI/6, pp. 211–12, 219.

22 J. Rusch, 1924, 'Letter to G. Repp in Portland, Oregon', in *Die Welt-Post* (Omaha, NE, 18 September 1924), www.volgagerman.net, see under 'Villages', 'Huck', 'Letters from Hell'.

23 Artemy A. Horvath, 'The Soy Bean as Human Food', *Industrial and Engineering Chemistry, News Edition*, IX/9 (10 May 1931), p. 136.

24 F. S. Kale, *Soya Bean: Its Value in Dietetics, Cultivation and Uses* (Baroda State, India, 1936); William Shurtleff and Akiko Aoyagi, 'History of Soybeans and Soyfoods in Europe (incl. Eastern Europe and the USSR, 1597–mid-1980s) Part 7', www.soyinfocenter.com, 2007.

25 Ingrid Henriksen, 'An Economic History of Denmark', http://eh.net, 6 October 2006; Shurtleff and Aoyagi, 'History of Soy in Europe . . . Part 1', 2007.

26 Carl Freytag, *Deutschlands 'Drang nach Südosten'* (Vienna, 1945), p. 195.

27 'Unilever Buys Some Sara Lee Businesses for Almost $2B', *USA Today*, 25 September 2009, http://usatoday30.usatoday.com, accessed 3 July 2017.

28 Round Table on Responsible Soy, 'Unilever', www.responsiblesoy.org, accessed 3 July 2017.

29 'Una rivoluzione alimentare, la manna che ritorna', *Illustrazione del Popolo* (Turin, 11 December 1921), p. 2.

30 Gerhard Schacher, 'The Importance of Rumania', http://archive.spectator. co.uk, 18 November 1938.

31 William Shurtleff and Akiko Aoyagi, 'Biography of Laszlo (Ladislaus) Berczeller (1890–1955) and History of His Work with Edelsoja Whole Soy Flour', www.soyinfocenter, 2016; William Shurtleff and Akiko Aoyagi, 'History of Soy Flour, Grits, Flakes, and Cereal-soy Blends Part 2', www.soyinfocenter.com, 2004.

32 William Shurtleff and Akiko Aoyagi, 'Dr Artemy Alexis Horvath: Work with Soyfoods', www.soyinfocenter.com, 2004.

33 Christine M. Du Bois, 'Social Context and Diet: Changing Soy Production and Consumption in the United States', in *The World of Soy*, ed. Christine M. Du Bois, Chee-Beng Tan and Sidney Mintz (Urbana, IL, 2008), p. 214.

3 THE YOUNG COUNTRY AND THE ANCIENT BEAN

1 Theodore Hymowitz and J. R. Harlan, 'Introduction of Soybean to North America by Samuel Bowen in 1765', *Economic Botany*, XXXIX/4 (1983), pp. 371–9.

2 Virginia Farm Bureau Federation, 'Soybeans Are Now Virginia's Most Valuable Crop', http://southeastfarmpress.com, 23 November 2010.

3 'Property', www.monticello.org, accessed 3 July 2017.

4 'Population of Chinese in the United States, 1860–1940', http://teachingresources.atlas.illinois.edu, accessed 3 July 2017, p. 2.

5 Walter Charles Blasedale, 'A Description of Some Chinese Vegetable Food Materials and Their Nutritive and Economic Value', USDA *Office of Experimental Stations, Bulletin* LXVIII.

6 Ronald E. Yates, *The Kikkoman Chronicles: A Global Company with a Japanese Soul* (New York, 1998), p. 24; William Shurtleff and Akiko Aoyagi, *How Japanese and Japanese-Americans Brought Soyfoods to the United States and the Hawaiian Islands: A History (1851–2011)* (Lafayette, CA, 2011), p. 5.

7 'Woman Off to China as Government Agent to Study Soy Bean', *New York Times Magazine*, section 6, p. 9, column 1 (10 June 1917).

8 Theodore Hymowitz, 'Dorsett-Morse Soybean Collection Trip to East Asia: 50 Year Retrospective', *Economic Botany*, XXXVIII/4 (October–December 1984), p. 378.

9 Ibid., p. 379.

10 Ibid., p. 382.

11 Ibid.

12 USDA horticulturalist Knowles A. Ryerson, quoted ibid., pp. 382–3.

13 Mark A. Mikel et al., 'Genetic Diversity and Agronomic Improvement of
    North American Soybean Germplasm', *Crop Science*, L/4 (August 2009),
    pp. 1219–29; Richard L. Bernard et al., 'Origins and Pedigrees of Public
    Soybean Varieties in the United States and Canada', USDA *Technical Bulletin*,
    no. 1746 (October 1988).
14 Hymowitz, 'Dorsett-Morse', p. 380.
15 'Kellogg Company Fact Sheet', http://newsroom.kelloggcompany.com,
    accessed 4 July 2017.
16 William Shurtleff and Akiko Aoyagi, 'Worthington Foods (1939–): Work
    with Soyfoods', www.soyinfocenter.com, 2004; William Shurtleff and
    Akiko Aoyagi, 'Dr John Harvey Kellogg and Battle Creek Foods: Work
    with Soy', www.soyinfocenter.com, 2004.
17 Dan J. Forrestal, *The Kernel and the Bean: The 75-year Story of the Staley
    Company* (New York, 1982), pp. 64–5; paraphrased in William Shurtleff and
    Akiko Aoyagi, 'A. E. Staley Manufacturing Company (1922–1980s): Work
    with Soy', www.soyinfocenter.com, 2004.
18 Rebecca Rupp, 'The Butter Wars: When Margarine Was Pink', http://the-
    plate.nationalgeographic.com, 13 August 2014.
19 William Shurtleff and Akiko Aoyagi, 'Dr Harry W. Miller: Work with Soy',
    www.soyinfocenter.com, 2004.
20 Ibid.
21 Herbert Brill, 'Approach to Milk Protein Allergy in Infants', *Canadian
    Family Physician*, LIV/9 (September 2008), pp. 1258–64.
22 Shurtleff and Aoyagi, 'Dr Harry W. Miller'.
23 Ibid.
24 John C. Gardner and Thomas L. Payne, 'A Soybean Biotechnology
    Outlook', *AgBioForum*, VI/1–2, www.agbioforum.org, 2003.
25 Center for Food Safety and Save Our Seeds, *Seed Giants Vs. U.S. Farmers*,
    www.centerforfoodsafety.org, 2013.
26 Edward S. Jenkins et al., ed., 'Percy L. Julian', in *American Black Scientists
    and Inventors* (Washington, DC, 1975); Gaius Chamberlain, 'Percy Julian',
    http://blackinventor.com, 23 March 2012.
27 Greg Grandin, *Fordlandia: The Rise and Fall of Henry Ford's Forgotten Jungle
    City* (New York, 2010).
28 Robert Hoff, 'Brazil: Developments in Brazil's Northern Ports Move
    forward with Favorable Long-term Implications for Brazilian Agricultural
    Competitiveness', GAIN Report No. BR0815, http://gain.fas.usda.gov,
    20 July 2012; Gerson Freitas Jr, 'Megainvestimento Abre Nova Rota
    Para Soja', http://amazonia.org.br, 24 January 2013.
29 'Henry Ford and the Soybean', *Journal of the American Oil Chemists' Society*,
    LIV/3 (March 1977), p. 207A.
30 William Shurtleff and Akiko Aoyagi, *Henry Ford and His Researchers:
    History of Their Work with Soybeans, Soyfoods and Chemurgy (1928–2011)*
    (Lafayette, CA, 2011), p. 8.
31 Shurtleff and Aoyagi, *Henry Ford*, p. 86.
32 David L. Lewis, 'Henry Ford's Plastic Car', *Michigan History* (Winter 1972),
    pp. 319–30.
33 Shurtleff and Aoyagi, *Henry Ford*, pp. 309, 360.

4 SOY PATRIOTIC

1 Bob Wurth, *1942: Australia's Greatest Peril* (Sydney, 2008); William Shurtleff and Akiko Aoyagi, *History of Soybeans and Soyfoods in Japan, and in Japanese Cookbooks and Restaurants outside Japan (701 CE to 2014)* (Lafayette, CA, 2014), p. 1806.

2 Shurtleff and Aoyagi, ibid., pp. 1174–5.

3 'Food for Fighters', www.learnnc.org, 1943.

4 Edwin G. Strand, 'Soybeans in American Farming', USDA *Technical Bulletin* 966 (Washington, DC, November 1948), p. 13.

5 Am Matagrin, *Le Soja et les industries du soja: produits alimentaires, huile de soja, lécithine végétale, caséine végétale* (Paris, 1939), part II.

6 William Norton Medlicott, *The Economic Blockade*, vol. I (New York and London, 1952), pp. 669–70.

7 Von Andreas Schmidt, 'Gomorrha auf den Elbinseln', www.abendblatt.de, 1 February 2013; Warren H. Goss, *The German Oilseed Industry* (Washington, DC, 1947), pp. 34–40.

8 C. N. Trueman, 'The Bombing of Hamburg in 1943', www. historylearningsite.co.uk, 16 August 2016.

9 K. Asakawa, *The Russo-Japanese Conflict: Its Causes and Issues* (London, 1904), p. 9.

10 Lizzie Collingham, *The Taste of War: World War II and the Battle for Food* (New York, 2012), p. 60.

11 Ibid., p. 62.

12 Ibid., p. 305.

13 'Operation Starvation', https://ghb67.wordpress.com, 12 January 2014.

14 Collingham, *The Taste of War*, p. 310.

15 B. F. Johnston, *Japanese Food Management in World War II* (Stanford, CA, 1953), pp. 12, 109, 114.

16 William Shurtleff and Akiko Aoyagi, 'History of Tofu – Page 5', www.soyinfocenter.com, 2004.

17 'Rare Foodstuffs Received Here from Internees', *Minidoka Irrigator*, II/49 (Minidoka Internment Center, Hunt, Idaho, 29 January 1944), p. 1.

18 'Pieter Roelofsen', https://nl.wikipedia.org, accessed 4 July 2017; 'Pieter Anton Roelofsen's Scientific Contributions', www.researchgate.net, accessed 4 July 2017; 'Geregistreerde Pieter Anton Roelofsen, Geboren op 20 juli 1908', www.openarch.nl, accessed 4 July 2017.

19 Pieter Anton Roelofsen, 'Tempeh-bereiding in Krijgsgevangenschap', *Vakblad voor Biologen*, XXVI/10 (October 1946), pp. 114–16.

20 A. G. Van Veen, 'De Voeding in de Japansche Interneerings-kampen in Nederlandsch Indie', *Voeding*, VII/5 (15 December 1946), pp. 173–86; A. G. Van Veen and G. Schaefer, 'The Influence of the Tempeh Fungus on the Soya Bean', *Documenta Neerlandica et Indonesica de Morbis Tropicis*, II/3 (September 1950), pp. 270–81.

21 Gerold Stahel, 'Foods from Fermented Soybeans . . . As Prepared in the Netherlands Indies', *Journal of the New York Botanical Garden*, XLVII/564 (December 1946), pp. 285–7.

22 Anna Reid, 'Siege of Leningrad: Deadliest City Blockade in Human History', www.thehistoryreader.com, 6 September 2011.

23 Richard Bidlack, 'Survival Strategies in Leningrad during the First Year of the Soviet-German War', in *The People's War: Responses to World War II in the Soviet Union*, ed. Robert W. Thurston and Bernd Bonwetsch (Champaign, IL, 2000), p. 93.

24 Darra Goldstein, 'Women under Siege: Leningrad 1941–1942', http://darragoldstein.com, December 2012, pp. 2–3.

25 Richard Bidlack and Nikita Lomagin, *The Leningrad Blockade, 1941–1944: A New Documentary History from the Soviet Archives* (New Haven, CT, 2012), p. 309.

26 F. H. Gruen, 'Britain's Foreign Trade Problem and Its Effect on British Food Imports', *Review of Marketing and Agricultural Economics*, xv/8 (1947), p. 282.

27 Shuang Wen, 'Ubiquitous-yet-invisible: Soybean's Journey from Manchuria to Egypt in the First Half of the Twentieth Century', in Shuang Wen, *Imperial Mediation: Chinese-Arab Connections at the Turn of the Twentieth Century* (forthcoming).

28 Bill Ganzel, 'Changing Crops – Soybeans', www.livinghistoryfarm.org, accessed 5 July 2017.

29 USDA, 'Crop Production Historical Track Records' (Washington, DC, April 2015), p. 163.

30 'All for One: One for All: The Story of Lend-lease', www.ibiblio.org, June 1943.

31 Donald S. Payne, 'Soybeans in Lend-lease', *Soybean Digest* (September 1942).

32 'British Wartime Food', www.cooksinfo.com, accessed 5 July 2017; Collingham, *The Taste of War*, p. 394.

33 'Rations', http://pwencycl.kgbudge.com, accessed 5 July 2017.

34 'Farm Relief, 1929–1941', www.encyclopedia.com, 2002.

35 William Shurtleff and Akiko Aoyagi, 'History of World Soybean Production and Trade – Part 1', www.soyinfocenter.com, 2004.

36 Richard L. Bernard et al., 'Origins and Pedigrees of Public Soybean Varieties in the United States and Canada', USDA *Technical Bulletin*, no. 1746 (Washington, DC, October 1988).

37 Strand, 'Soybeans', pp. 13–14.

38 'Bulk of Our Soya Beans Going Abroad While Home Supply Increases 12 Times', *New York Times* (9 August 1943), p. 95.

39 Clive M. McCay, 'Sprouted Soy Beans: Some Informal Notes' (Ithaca, NY, April 1943).

40 'Governor is Host at Soy Bean Lunch: Party for 67 at Albany Is to Demonstrate Value of Meat Substitutes', *New York Times* (15 June 1943), p. 24.

41 'Food Crisis Grave, Dewey Aide Warns: People Do Not Realize How Desperate Situation Is, Mrs R. W. Straus Declares', *New York Times* (17 June 1943), p. 18.

42 William Shurtleff and Akiko Aoyagi, 'History of Soy Flour, Grits, Flakes, and Cereal-soy Blends – Part 4', www.soyinfocenter.com, 2004.

43 'Send Million Soy Leaflets', *Soybean Digest* (November 1945), p. 7.

44 Jane Holt, 'News of Food: Soy Beans, the Source of Oil, Flour, Milk and Cereals, Winning "Terrific" Popularity', *New York Times* (27 January 1943), p. 16.

45 'Vermont Ready to Launch Soy Bean Culture Tests: Fifty One-acre Plots', *Christian Science Monitor* (31 December 1935), p. 5.

46 'Always Something New: A Cavalcade of Scientific Discovery', USDA ARS [Agricultural Research Service] Miscellaneous Publication no. 1507 (Washington, DC, 1993), p. 86.

47 H. V. Parekh, *Solvent Extraction of Vegetable Oils* (Bombay, 1958), p. 24.

48 Collingham, *The Taste of War*, p. 470.

49 Alan S. Milward, *The Reconstruction of Western Europe, 1945–51* (Berkeley, CA, 1984), p. 46.

50 William Shurtleff and Akiko Aoyagi, 'The Meals for Millions Foundation and Multi-purpose Food: Work with Soyfoods', www.soyinfocenter.com, 2011.

51 William Shurtleff and Akiko Aoyagi, 'History of Soy Sauce, Shoyu, and Tamari – Page 6', www.soyinfocenter.com, 2004.

52 William Shurtleff and Akiko Aoyagi, 'History of Tofu – Page 3', www.soyinfocenter.com, 2004.

53 Michael Turton, 'Paper on Parade: Should the U.S. Grab Taiwan?', http://michaelturton.blogspot.com, 14 September 2008.

5 FATTENING WITH FEED

1 Anna-Leena Lohiniva et al., 'Poultry Rearing and Slaughtering Practices in Rural Egypt: An Exploration of Risk Factors for H5N1 Virus Human Transmission', www.influenzajournal.com, 12 November 2012, p. 1251.

2 'A Review of Migratory Bird Flyways and Priorities for Management', CMS *Technical Series*, XXVII (Bonn, 2014).

3 Irene Lorenzo, 'Ending Illegal Killing and Trapping of 5.7 Million Birds in Egypt', www.birdlife.org, 10 March 2016; Adam Welz, 'Jonathan Franzen, "Egypt Is the Worst Place to Be a Migratory Bird"', www.theguardian.com, 19 July 2013.

4 Christian Grund et al., 'H5N1 in Egypt: Situation, OIE Twinning, and Escape Mutants', www.cdc.gov, accessed 5 July 2017, p. 13.

5 'Avian Influenza A (H5N1) in Egypt Update', www.emro.who.int, 21 March 2015.

6 Grund et al., 'H5N1', p. 13.

7 'Nearly a Third of Children Malnourished – Report', www.irinnews.org, 5 November 2009.

8 'Global and Regional Food Consumption Patterns and Trends', in *Diet, Nutrition and the Prevention of Chronic Diseases: Report of the Joint WHO/FAO Expert Consultation*, WHO Technical Report Series, no. 916 (Rome, 2003), p. 7.

9 Samuel Nurko et al., 'Successful Use of a Chicken-based Diet for the Treatment of Severely Malnourished Children with Persistent Diarrhea: A Prospective, Randomized Study', *Journal of Pediatrics*, CXXXI (3 September 1977), pp. 405–12.

10 'World Protein Meal Consumption 2016/17', www.soymeal.org, accessed 6 July 2017.

11 Farid A. Hosny, 'The Structure and Importance of the Commercial and Village Based Poultry Systems in Egypt', www.fao.org, 24 November 2006, pp. 24, 32.

12 Fawzi A. Taha, 'Derived Feed Demand for Egypt's Poultry and Egg Sector to 2010 – Policies and Implications', http://ageconsearch.umn.edu, 18 February 2004, p. 12.

13 For a history of soy cultivation in Egypt and its links to British colonialism, see Shuang Wen, 'Ubiquitous-yet-invisible: Soybean's Journey from Manchuria to Egypt in the First Half of the Twentieth Century', in Shuang Wen, *Imperial Mediation: Chinese-Arab Connections at the Turn of the Twentieth Century* (forthcoming). See also Shuang Wen, 'Mediated Imaginations: Chinese-Arab Connections in the Late Nineteenth and Early Twentieth Centuries', PhD dissertation, Georgetown University (2015).

14 UN Department of Public Information, 'The Millennium Development Goals Report 2015 Fact Sheet', Document DPI/2594/3 E, www.un.org, 6 July 2015.

15 Andreina Lucchesi, 'Peru: Chicken-blood Cookbook Stamps Out Anaemia', www.wfp.org, 13 July 2010.

16 Jeremy Warner, 'How Much Methane?', http://basiceating.blogspot.com, 29 September 2008; Vaclav Smil, 'Eating Meat: Evolution, Patterns, and Consequences', *Population and Development Review*, XXVIII/4 (December 2002), pp. 614–15.

17 Gary L. Cromwell, 'Soybean Meal – An Exceptional Protein Source', Review Paper, www.soymeal.org, accessed 10 July 2017, p. 2; Sara Willis, 'The Use of Soybean Meal and Full Fat Soybean Meal by the Animal Feed Industry', www.australianoilseeds.com, accessed 10 July 2017, p. 6; Peter Best, 'World Feed Panorama: A Year of Resilience for the Feed Industry', www.wattagnet.com, 4 March 2013.

18 Christine M. Du Bois, 'Social Context and Diet: Changing Soy Production and Consumption in the United States', in *The World of Soy*, ed. Christine M. Du Bois, Chee-Beng Tan and Sidney Mintz (Champaign, IL, 2008), p. 217.

19 William Shurtleff and Akiko Aoyagi, 'American Soybean Association: History of Work with Soy', www.soyinfocenter.com, 2004.

20 Ibid.

21 James O. Howard, *Partners in Developing Farm Markets Overseas: A History of the Cooperative Program between U.S. Agricultural Commodity Organizations and the Foreign Agricultural Service* (Washington, DC, 1989), pp. 12–13.

22 Ibid., p. 13.

23 'Iowa Remembers 50th Anniversary of Japan Hog Lift', www.iowafarmertoday.com, 8 April 2010; Howard, *Partners in Developing*, pp. 8–10.

24 Howard, ibid., p. 10.

25 Ibid., p. 11.

26 Timothy K. Smith, 'Changing Tastes: By the End of This Year, Poultry Will Surpass Beef in the U.S. Diet', *Wall Street Journal*, 17 September 1987, p. 1.

27 Tara Parker-Pope, 'Chicken-nugget Boom Leads to Worries about Kids' Health', www.wsj.com, 18 March 2003.

28 For livestock statistics, http://faostat3.fao.org, accessed 6 July 2017; for soy, see 'Oil Crops Yearbook', 'Supply and Use: Soybeans, Soybean Meal, and Soybean Oil, U.S., Major Foreign Exporters, Importers, and World, 2013/14–2016/17', Table 45, www.ers.usda.gov, 29 March 2017.

29 Natalie Angier, 'Pigs Prove to Be Smart, If Not Vain', www.nytimes.com, 10 November 2009.

30 Humane Society of the United States, 'An hsus Report: Welfare Issues with Gestation Crates for Pregnant Sows', www.humanesociety.org, February 2013.

31 Sophia Murphy, David Burch and Jennifer Clapp, 'Cereal Secrets: The World's Largest Grain Traders and Global Agriculture', Oxfam Research Reports (August 2012), p. 10.

32 usda, 'Livestock and Poultry: World Markets and Trade', https://apps.fas.usda.gov, 11 April 2017.

33 fao, *Global Livestock Production Systems* (Rome, 2011), pp. 60, 73; Constanza Valdes, Charlie Hallahan and David Harvey, 'Brazil's Broiler Industry: Increasing Efficiency and Trade', *International Food and Agribusiness Management Review*, xviii Special Issue A, 2015; Roy Sun, 'China's Top Poultry Producers Continue Long-term Growth Plans Despite Difficulties', www.wattagnet.com, 26 May 2013.

34 The Pew Charitable Trusts, *The Business of Broilers: Hidden Costs of Putting a Chicken on Every Grill*, www.pewtrusts.org, 20 December 2013, p. 21.

35 Frontline, 'Inside the Slaughterhouse', www.pbs.org, accessed 6 July 2017.

36 Johns Hopkins Center for a Livable Future, 'Industrial Food Animal Production in America: Examining the Impact of the Pew Commission's Priority Recommendations' (autumn 2013), p. 2.

37 European Food Safety Authority et al., 'eu Summary Report on Antimicrobial Resistance in Zoonotic and Indicator Bacteria from Humans, Animals and Food in 2013', *EFSA Journal*, xiii/2 (2015), p. 5.

38 Alejandro Pérez, 'Salmonella Enteritidis: Surveillance Data and Policy Implications', www.marlerblog.com, accessed 6 July 2017, p. 32.

39 'Highly Pathogenic Avian Influenza: The Impact on the u.s. Poultry Sector and Protecting u.s. Poultry Flocks', www.ag.senate.gov, 7 July 2015. At audio point 1:05:21, Dr Clifford talks about the difficulty of disposing of so many birds.

40 'How Much Water Is Needed to Produce Food and How Much Do We Waste?', www.theguardian.com, 10 January 2013.

41 Du Bois, 'Social Context', p. 218.

42 'Farming: Soil Erosion and Degradation', wwf.panda.org, accessed 7 July 2017.

43 Ibid.

44 Mark Bittman, 'Rethinking the Meat-guzzler', www.nytimes.com, 27 January 2008.

45 '5 Factory Farm Spills in 3 Weeks', http://iowacci.org, accessed 6 July 2017.

46 'Understanding Iowa's Impaired Waters', and 'Iowa's 2014 Draft Integrated Report: Category 5: Impaired and tmdl Needed', www.iowadnr.gov, accessed 15 May 2015.

47 Michael A. Mallin, 'Impacts of Industrial Animal Production on Rivers and Estuaries', *American Scientist*, lxxxviii (January–February 2000), pp. 26–37.

6 SOY SWOOPS SOUTH

1 Ueslei Marcelino, 'Village of Joy', http://blogs.reuters.com, 15 May 2012.

2 'Anchovy – Peruvian Fishing Industry', https://cmast.ncsu.edu, accessed 7 July 2017.

3   Ivan Sergio Freire de Sousa and Rita de Cássia Milagres Teixeira Vieira, 'Soybeans and Soyfoods in Brazil, with Notes on Argentina: Sketch of an Expanding World Commodity', in *The World of Soy*, ed. Christine M. Du Bois, Chee-Beng Tan and Sidney Mintz (Urbana, IL, 2008), p. 235; Nicolas Rubio, 'Brazil: Oilseeds and Products Update', www.fas.usda.gov, 27 January 2016.

4   A. Allan Schmid and David Soroko, 'Interest Groups, Selective Incentives, Cleverness, History and Emotion: The Case of the American Soybean Association', *Journal of Economic Behavior and Organization*, XXXII (1997), pp. 278–81.

5   William Shurtleff and Akiko Aoyagi, *History of Soybeans and Soyfoods in South America (1882–2009)* (Lafayette, CA, 2009), p. 525.

6   Geraldo B. Martha Jr et al., 'Embrapa: Its Origins and Changes', in *The Regional Impact of National Policies*, ed. Werner Baer (Cheltenham, 2012), p. 217.

7   'Olacyr de Moraes, o "Rei da Soja", Morre aos 84 Anos em São Paulo', http://economia.estadao.com.br, 16 June 2015.

8   Pat Joseph, 'Soy in the Amazon', www.vqronline.org, autumn 2007.

9   Vanessa Dezem and Ivo Ribeiro, 'Itaoeste negocia parceria em tálio', www.newslog.com.br, 1 March 2012.

10   Vera Ondei, 'O Império da Família Maggi', www.dinheirorural.com.br, 1 July 2012.

11   Kenneth Rapoza, 'Brazil Senator Maggi Joins Forbes Billionaire List', www.forbes.com, 10 April 2014.

12   Ricardo Geromel, 'Meet Blairo Maggi: From Soybean King to Politician to One of the World's Most Powerful People to Tree Hugger', www.forbes.com, 8 November 2013.

13   World Wildlife Fund, 'Oil Palm and Soy: The Expanding Threat to Forests', wwf.panda.org, July 2003, p. 3.

14   Larry Rohter, 'Relentless Foe of the Amazon Jungle: Soybeans', www.nytimes.com, 17 September 2003.

15   Brian Kelly and Mark London, 'Home on the Tropical Range: How Ranching and Farming Are Changing the Amazon Debate', *U.S. News and World Report*, 1 May 2004.

16   Brian Kelly and Mark London, 'Bright Spots in the Rain Forest', *New York Times* (22 April 2004).

17   Joseph, 'Soy in the Amazon'.

18   Nicole Perlroth, 'Tree Hugger', www.forbes.com, 4 December 2009.

19   'The World's Most Powerful People', www.forbes.com, 11 November 2009.

20   South Dakota Soybean Association, 'A Visit to the Largest Soybean Farm in the World', www.sdsoybean.org, 19 March 2013.

21   Catarine Piccioni, 'Eraí Maggi e Mais Quatro se Livram de Acusação de Trabalho Escravo', www.olhardireto.com.br, 1 October 2013.

22   Global Witness, *Deadly Environment: The Dramatic Rise in Killings of Environmental and Land Defenders* (London, 2014), p. 4.

23   Daniel Nepstad et al., 'Slowing Amazon Deforestation through Public Policy and Interventions in Beef and Soy Supply Chains', *Science*, CCCXLIV/6188 (6 June 2014), pp. 118–23.

24   Rhett Butler, 'Calculating Deforestation Figures for the Amazon', http://rainforests.mongabay.com, 26 January 2017.

25 Geraldo B. Martha, Jr, 'Brazilian Agriculture: Development and Future Prospects', http://lemann.illinois.edu, 7–8 November 2013, pp. 17, 24.

26 Butler, 'Calculating'.

27 Martha, 'Brazilian Agriculture', p. 14.

28 Geromel, 'Meet Blairo Maggi'.

29 Marcondes Maciel, 'Grãos Estrada Afora', www.diariodecuiaba.com.br, 15 August 2010.

30 Oscar Delgado, 'The Soya Route in North West Argentina', www.researchgate.net, p. 22, accessed 18 November 2017.

31 'Tartagal: Dicen Que el Desastre Podría Repetirse', www.derf.com.ar, 28 April 2006.

32 Diego A Bernardini Zambrini, 'Neglected Lessons from the 2009 Dengue Epidemic in Argentina', *Revista de Saúde Pública*, xlv/2 (2011), p. 1.

33 Marcelo Sili and Luciana Soumoulou, *The Issue of Land in Argentina* (Rome, 2011), p. 6.

34 Fabiana Frayssinet, 'The Dilemma of Soy in Argentina', www.ipsnews.net, 12 March 2015.

35 isaaa, 'Global Status of Commercialized Biotech/gm Crops: 2016', Brief 52 (2016), p. 20.

36 De Sousa and Vieira, 'Soybeans and Soyfoods', p. 245.

37 Randall D. Schnepf, Erik Dohlman and Christine Bolling, *Agriculture in Brazil and Argentina: Developments and Prospects for Major Field Crops*, usda Report wrs-01-3 (Washington, dc, 2001), p. 33.

38 Hugh Bronstein, 'Argentina Tracks Soy Hoarding by Registering "Silo-bag" Sales', www.cnbc.com, 2 March 2015.

39 Pablo Rosendo Gonzalez, 'In Argentine Tax Battle, Bags of Soybeans Get the Knife', www.bloomberg.com, 25 February 2015.

40 Ibid.

41 Maria Cristina Carlino, '50 Silobolsas Rotos en Córdoba: Alarmante Reiteración de Agresiones contra Productores', www.sudesteagropecuario. com.ar, 31 May 2015.

42 Mariano Turzi, 'The Soybean Republic', *Yale Journal of International Affairs* (Spring–Summer 2011), p. 66.

43 Ibid.

44 'Guyra Reta Reserve', www.worldlandtrust.org, accessed 7 July 2017.

45 'Gran Chaco Region: 89,833 Acres of Forest Destroyed in January 2015', www.worldlandtrust.org, 23 March 2015.

46 'gdp Growth (Annual %)', http://data.worldbank.org, 'Browse by Indicator', accessed 7 July 2017.

47 fian International, 'Land & Sovereignty in the Americas: Land Conflicts and the Criminalization of Peasant Movements in Paraguay: The Case of Marina Kue and the "Curuguaty Massacre"', Food First Issue Brief no. 6 (Oakland, ca, 2014), pp. 3, 5.

48 un Human Rights Committee, 'Concluding Observations on the Third Periodic Report of Paraguay, Adopted by the Committee at its 107th Session (11–28 March 2013)' (New York and Geneva, 29 April 2013), p. 6.

49 Gaspar E. Nolte, 'Bolivian Soy Update', https://gain.fas.usda.gov, 30 April 2015, p. 2.

50 Mauricio Font, *The State and the Private Sector in Latin America: The Shift to Partnership* (Basingstoke, 2015), p. 94.
51 GRAIN, 'The United Republic of Soybeans: Take Two', www.grain.org, 2 July 2013; Javiera Rulli et al., *United Soya Republics: The Truth about Soya Production in South America*, www.lasojamata.net, 2007.

7 MOULDING OUR WORLD

1 'The Grasslands of the U.S.', www2.mcdaniel.edu, accessed 7 July 2017.
2 Wageningen University and Research Centre, 'Agriculture Is the Direct Driver for Worldwide Deforestation', www.sciencedaily.com, 25 September 2012.
3 Ministério dos Transportes, Portos e Aviação Civil, 'Plano Mestre Complexo Portuáriio De Santarém Versão Preliminar' (Brasilia, January 2017), p. 81; 'Informações Operacionais, Estatísticas, Movimentação de Mercadoria, Porto de Santarém Operação Aquaviária', www.cdp.com.br, 2015.
4 Maria del Carmen Vera-Diaz, Robert K. Kaufmann and Daniel C. Nepstad, 'The Environmental Impacts of Soybean Expansion and Infrastructure Development in Brazil's Amazon Basin', Global Development and Environment Institute working paper 09-05 (Medford, MA, 2009), p. 15.
5 Philip M. Fearnside, 'Deforestation in Amazonia', in 'Encyclopedia of Earth', http://editors.eol.org, 30 March 2007.
6 Vera-Diaz, Kaufmann and Nepstad, 'The Environmental Impacts', p. 15.
7 Ibid.
8 Marcelo F. Oliveira et al., 'Establishing a Soybean Germplasm Core Collection', *Field Crops Research*, CXIX (2010), p. 277.
9 R. G. Palmer and T. Hymowitz, 'Breeding of Grains – Soybean: Germplasm, Breeding, and Genetics', in *Encyclopedia of Food Grains*, ed. Colin W. Wrigley et al., 2nd edn (Cambridge, MA, 2015), vol. IV, p. 335, Table 2.
10 'Background on Value Web Component: Genetics', https://ag.purdue.edu, accessed 8 July 2017.
11 'Global Status of Commercialized Biotech/GM Crops: 2016', ISAAA *Briefs*, 52 (Ithaca, NY, 2016), pp. 97–8.
12 'International: Adoption of Biotech Enhanced Seedstock', http://soystats.com, accessed 8 July 2017.
13 'Research Finds Salt Tolerance Gene in Soybean', www.adelaide.edu.au, 8 January 2015.
14 Rongxia Guan et al., 'Salinity Tolerance in Soybean Is Modulated by Natural Variation in GmSALT3', *Plant Journal*, LXXX (2014), pp. 937–50.
15 Christine M. Du Bois and Ivan Sergio Freire de Sousa, 'Genetically Engineered Soy', in *The World of Soy*, ed. Christine M. Du Bois, Chee-Beng Tan and Sidney Mintz (Urbana, IL, 2008), p. 81.
16 'Jumping Genes', https://www.nps.gov, 31 March 2012.
17 Charles Hagedorn, 'Scientific Basis of Risks Associated with Transgenic Crops', http://vtnews.vt.edu, February 2000.
18 Clayton Myers and Elizabeth Hill, 'Benefits of Neonicotinoid Seed Treatments to Soybean Production', www.epa.gov, 15 October 2014, pp. 1–2.

19 Robert J. Kremer, Nathan E. Means and Sujung Kim, 'Glyphosate Affects Soybean Root Exudation and Rhizosphere Microorganisms', *International Journal of Analytical Environmental Chemistry*, LXXXV/15 (2005); R. J. Kremer and N. E. Means, 'Glyphosate and Glyphosate-resistant Crop Interactions with Rhizosphere Microorganisms', *European Journal of Agronomy*, XXXI/3 (2009), pp. 153–61.

20 Carey Gillam, 'EPA Will Require Weed-resistance Restrictions on Glyphosate Herbicide', www.reuters.com, 31 March 2015.

21 A. M. Henderson et al., 'Glyphosate General Fact Sheet', http://npic.orst.edu, 2010.

22 Gillam, 'EPA Will Require'; 'USGS NAWQA: The Pesticide National Synthesis Project/Maps', https://water.usgs.gov, accessed 8 July 2017.

23 Charles M. Benbrook, 'Trends in Glyphosate Herbicide Use in the United States and Globally', *Environmental Sciences Europe*, XXVIII/3 (2 February 2016), p. 6.

24 Chris Arsenault, 'Only 60 Years of Farming Left If Soil Degradation Continues', www.scientificamerican.com, 5 December 2014.

25 'Organic Farms Not Necessarily Better for Environment', www.ox.ac.uk, 4 September 2012; H. L. Tuomisto et al., 'Does Organic Farming Reduce Environmental Impacts? A Meta-analysis of European Research', *Journal of Environmental Management*, CXII (15 December 2012), pp. 309–20.

26 'Thirsty Food: Fueling Agriculture to Fuel Humans', http://environment.nationalgeographic.com, accessed 8 July 2017.

27 'Earth's Freshwater', www.nationalgeographic.org, accessed 8 July 2017.

28 Mark W. Rosegrant, Ximing Cai and Sarah A. Cline, *Global Water Outlook to 2025: Averting an Impending Crisis* (Washington, DC, and Colombo, Sri Lanka, 2002), pp. 10–11.

29 R. Bruce Hull et al., 'Collaborative Leadership for Sustainable Development in Global Supply Chains: Partnering across Sectors to Reduce Amazon Deforestation', www.thesolutionsjournal.com, IV/5 (24 January 2015).

30 Arjen Y. Hoekstra and Mesfin M. Mekonnen, 'The Water Footprint of Humanity', *PNAS*, CIX/9 (2011), pp. 3233–4.

31 M. M. Mekonnen and A. Y. Hoekstra, *The Green, Blue and Grey Water Footprint of Farm Animals and Animal Products*, UNESCO-IHE Research Report Series no. 48 (Delft, 2010), p. 7.

32 'Thirsty Food'.

33 Arantxa Gereña, *The Soy Mirage – The Limits of Corporate Social Responsibility: The Case of the Company Desarrollo Agrícola del Paraguay* (Oxford, 2013), p. 23.

8 POISON OR PANACEA?

1 'Everything Should Be Made as Simple as Possible, But Not Simpler', http://quoteinvestigator.com, 13 May 2011.

2 L. A. Johnson et al., 'Inactivation of Trypsin Inhibitors in Aqueous Soybean Extracts by Direct Steam Infusion', *Cereal Chemistry*, LVII/6 (1980), p. 76.

3 www.independent.co.uk, 5 December 2012; www.theguardian.com, 31 March 2015; www.livescience.com, 28 August 2012; http://bignaturaltesticles.com, accessed 8 July 2017; http://news.bbc.co.uk, 23 July 2008; www.newscientist.com, 16 October 2007.

4 E. Carlsen et al., 'Evidence for Decreasing Quality of Semen during Past 50 Years', *BMJ*, cccv/6854 (1992), pp. 609–13. For subsequent doubts of the 1992 study, see R. J. Sherins and G. Delbès, 'Is There a Decline in Sperm Counts in Men?', *Handbook of Andrology*, 2nd edn (Lawrence, ks, 2010), chap. 26, pp. 1–4; Marcello Cocuzza and Sandro C. Esteves, 'Shedding Light on the Controversy Surrounding the Temporal Decline in Human Sperm Counts: A Systematic Review', *Scientific World Journal*, article id 365691 (2014), pp. 1–9.

5 M. Rolland et al., 'Decline in Semen Concentration and Morphology in a Sample of 26,609 Men Close to General Population between 1989 and 2005 in France', *Human Reproduction*, xxviii/2 (February 2013), pp. 462–70; Hagai Levine et al., 'Temporal Trends in Sperm Count: A Systematic Review and Meta-regression Analysis', Human Reproduction Update, https://academic.oup.com, (2017), pp. 1–14.

6 Cocuzza and Esteves, 'Shedding Light', p. 4; J. Elia et al., 'Comparative Study of Seminal Parameters between Samples Collected in 1992 and Samples Collected in 2010', *Archives of Italian Urology and Andrology*, lxxxiv (2012), pp. 26–31.

7 Lianjun Pan et al., 'Exposure of Juvenile Rats to the Phytoestrogen Daidzein Impairs Erectile Function in a Dose-related Manner in Adulthood', *Journal of Andrology*, xxix/1 (February 2008), pp. 55–62; Christopher Robin Cederroth et al., 'Soy, Phytoestrogens and Their Impact on Reproductive Health', *Molecular and Cellular Endocrinology*, ccclv (2012), p. 197. For the Harvard study see Jorge E. Chavarro et al., 'Soy Food and Isoflavone Intake in Relation to Semen Quality Parameters among Men from an Infertility Clinic', *Human Reproduction*, xxiii/11 (23 July 2008), pp. 2584–90.

8 Roxanne Khamsi, 'Eating Soya Could Slash Men's Sperm Count', www.newscientist.com, 16 October 2007.

9 'Excess Weight May Affect Sperm Production, Reduce Fertility in Men', www.hsph.harvard.edu, accessed 8 July 2017; Nathalie Sermond et al., 'Obesity and Increased Risk for Oligozoospermia and Azoospermia', *Archives of Internal Medicine*, clxxii/5 (12 March 2012), pp. 440–41.

10 'Food Labeling: Health Claims; Soy Protein and Coronary Heart Disease; Final Rule', *Federal Register*, lxiv/206 (26 October, 1999), pp. 57699–733.

11 J. W. Erdman Jr, 'Soy Protein and Cardiovascular Disease: A Statement for Healthcare Professionals from the Nutrition Committee of the aha', *Circulation*, cii/20 (2000), pp. 2555–9.

12 F. M. Sacks et al., 'Soy Protein, Isoflavones, and Cardiovascular Health: An American Heart Association Science Advisory for Professionals from the Nutrition Committee', *Circulation*, cxiii/7 (11 February 2006), pp. 1034–44.

13 'Types of Breast Cancer', www.webmd.com, accessed 8 July 2017.

14 'Breast Cancer Age-adjusted Death Rate', www.worldlifeexpectancy.com, accessed 8 July 2017.

15 C. D. Allred et al., 'Dietary Genistein Results in Larger mnu-induced, Estrogen-dependent Mammary Tumors following Ovariectomy of Sprague-Dawley Rats', *Carcinogenesis*, xxv (2004), pp. 211–18.

16 Samira Ziaei and Reginald Halaby, 'Dietary Isoflavones and Breast Cancer Risk', *Medicines*, iv/2 (7 April 2017), p. 2; Sang-Ah Lee et al., 'Adolescent and

Adult Soy Food Intake and Breast Cancer Risk: Results from the Shanghai Women's Health Study', *American Journal of Clinical Nutrition*, LXXXIX (2009), pp. 1920–26.

17 Xiao Ou Shu et al., 'Soy Food Intake and Breast Cancer Survival', JAMA, CCCII/22 (2009), pp. 2437–43.

18 Steve L. Taylor, 'Estimating Prevalence of Soy Protein Allergy', www.soyconnection.com, accessed 8 July 2017.

19 *Kings of Pastry* follows the travails, triumphs and crashing defeats of top French pastry chefs as they compete for the prestigious Meilleur Ouvrier de France award. Their elaborate confections are assembled in front of judges over three days. Chemical interactions among the ingredients, the physics of extremely delicate sugar sculptures, and time limits all present intense challenges. The film has appeared at numerous international film festivals.

20 Philip Larkin and George G. Harrigan, 'Opportunities and Surprises in Crops Modified by Transgenic Technology: Metabolic Engineering of Benzylisoquinoline Alkaloid, Gossypol and Lysine Biosynthetic Pathways', *Metabolomics*, III (2007), p. 372.

21 Ibid., p. 380.

22 Joe Palca, 'The Human Edge: Finding Our Inner Fish', www.npr.org, 5 July 2010.

23 Aashiq H. Kachroo et al., 'Systematic Humanization of Yeast Genes Reveals Conserved Functions and Genetic Modularity', *Science*, CCCXLVIII/6237 (22 May 2015), pp. 921–5.

24 'Genome Sequencing Uncovers Unusual Genetic History of the Soybean', http://news.uncc.edu, 20 January 2010.

25 'DNA: Comparing Humans and Chimps', www.amnh.org, accessed 9 July 2017.

26 Oksana Lukjancenko et al., 'Comparison of 61 Sequenced *Escherichia coli* Genomes', *Microbial Ecology*, LX (2010), pp. 708–20.

27 UN World Health Organization, *Antimicrobial Resistance: Global Report on Surveillance* (Geneva, 2014).

28 See discussion in Philippe Gay, 'The Biosafety of Antibiotic Resistance Markers in Plant Transformation and the Dissemination of Genes through Horizontal Gene Flow', in *Safety of Genetically Engineered Crops*, VIB Report (Zwijnaarde, March 2001), p. 153.

29 J. C. Jennings et al, 'Determining Whether Transgenic and Endogenous Plant DNA and Transgenic Protein Are Detectable in Muscle from Swine Fed Roundup Ready Soybean Meal', *Journal of Animal Science*, LXXXI/6 (2003a), pp. 1447–55; J. C. Jennings et al., 'Attempts to Detect Transgenic and Endogenous Plant DNA and Transgenic Protein in Muscle from Broilers Fed YieldGard Corn Borer Corn', *Poultry Science*, LXXXII (2003b), pp. 371–80; T. W. Alexander et al., 'Use of Quantitative Real-time and Conventional PCR to Assess the Stability of the CP4 EPSPS Transgene from Roundup Ready Canola in the Intestinal, Ruminal, and Fecal Contents of Sheep', *Journal of Biotechnology*, CXII/3 (9 September 2004), pp. 255–66.

30 T. Netherwood et al., 'Assessing the Survival of Transgenic Plant DNA in the Human Gastrointestinal Tract', *Nature Biotechnology*, XXII/2 (2004), pp. 204–9.

31 Suzie Key et al., 'Genetically Modified Plants and Human Health', *Journal of the Royal Society of Medicine*, CI (2008), p. 291.

32 Mae-Wan Ho et al., 'CaMV 35S Promoter Fragmentation Hotspot Confirmed, and It Is Active in Animals', *Microbial Ecology in Health and Disease*, XII (2000), p. 189.

33 'No Safety Implications of GM Viral Gene Says Professor', www.farminguk. com, 25 January 2013.

34 F. Cellini et al., 'Unintended Effects and Their Detection in Genetically Modified Crops', *Food and Chemical Toxicology*, XLII (2004), p. 1099.

35 Xiuchun Zhang et al., 'Compositional Equivalency of RNAi-Mediated Virus-resistant Transgenic Soybean and Its Nontransgenic Counterpart', *Journal of Agricultural and Food Chemistry*, LXII (2014), pp. 4475–9.

36 Alessandro Nicolia et al., 'An Overview of the Last 10 Years of Genetically Engineered Crop Safety Research', *Critical Reviews of Biotechnology*, Early Online (2013), pp. 1–12.

37 'IARC Monograph on Glyphosate', www.iarc.fr, 12 April 2016; Danny Hakim, 'Key Element of Monsanto Weed Killer Not a Carcinogen, European Agency Says', www.nytimes.com, 15 March 2017; 'Glyphosate Not Classified as a Carcinogen by ECHA', https://echa.europa.eu, 15 March 2017.

38 'Joint FAO/WHO Meeting on Pesticide Residues/Geneva, 9–13 May 2016 Summary Report' (Geneva and Rome, 16 May 2016).

39 Eliot M. Herman et al., 'Genetic Modification Removes an Immunodominant Allergen from Soybean', *Plant Physiology*, CXXXII (May 2003), pp. 36–43.

40 Raymond Sanchez, 'Low-allergen, Non-GMO Soybean Could Have High Impact', https://uanews.arizona.edu, 1 May 2015.

41 Yonghua He et al., 'Transgenic Soybean Production of Bioactive Human Epidermal Growth Factor (EGF)', *PLOS ONE*, XI/6 (2016); Eric Swelund, 'Modified Formula Aims to Prevent Death in Premature Infants', https://uanews.arizona.edu, 9 May 2013.

42 Laura C. Hudson et al., 'Advancements in Transgenic Soy: From Field to Bedside', in *A Comprehensive Survey of International Soybean Research: Genetics, Physiology, Agronomy and Nitrogen Relationships*, ed. James E. Board, chap. 21 (Rijeka, 2012), p. 466.

43 See Christine M. Du Bois and Ivan Sergio Freire de Sousa, 'Genetically Engineered Soy', in *The World of Soy*, ed. Christine M. Du Bois, Chee-Beng Tan and Sidney Mintz (Champaign, IL, 2008), pp. 79–80.

44 Rui-Yun Lee et al., 'Genetically Modified a-Amylase Inhibitor Peas Are Not Specifically Allergenic in Mice', *PLOS ONE*, VIII/1 (2013).

45 U.S. Centers for Disease Control and Prevention, 'Investigation of Human Health Effects Associated with Potential Exposure to Genetically Modified Corn' (Atlanta, GA, 11 June 2001), pp. 5–6, 10.

46 Cary Funk, 'Public and Scientists' Views on Science and Society', www.pewresearch.org, 29 January 2015.

47 '2012 Census Drilldown: Organic and Local Food', http://sustainableagriculture.net, 16 May 2014.

48 U.S. Library of Congress, 'Restrictions on Genetically Modified Organisms: France', www.loc.gov, June 2014.

49 Jan M. Lucht, 'Public Acceptance of Plant Biotechnology and GM Crops', *Viruses*, VII (2015), pp. 4254–81.

50 Nicolia et al., 'An Overview'.

51 Carey Gillam, 'The True Inside Story of How a College Professor Sells Out to Monsanto', www.alternet.org, 30 January 2016.

52 Ibid.

53 The present author has interviewed and been treated to dinner both by representatives of Monsanto during a two-day trip, and by the CEO of White Wave, the large organic soy milk producer. She has received no other industry gifts, grants, endorsements or favours whatsoever.

54 Eric Lipton, 'Food Industry Enlisted Academics in G.M.O. Lobbying War, Emails Show', www.nytimes.com, 5 September 2015; Philip J. Landrigan and Charles Benbrook, 'GMOs, Herbicides, and Public Health', www.nejm. org, 20 August 2015; see critique at 'Charles Benbrook: Former Washington State Adjunct Consultant for Organic Industry', www.geneticliteracyproject. org, accessed 9 July 2017.

55 Andy Coghlan, 'Vatican Scientists Urge Support for Engineered Crops', www.newscientist.com, 30 November 2010.

56 'Laureates Letter Supporting Precision Agriculture (GMOs)', http://supportprecisionagriculture.org, 29 June 2016.

57 'Sierra Leone: A Humanitarian Wedge', www.icrc.org, 27 March 1996.

58 '2011 Tōhoku Earthquake and Tsunami', and 'Aftermath of the 2011 Tōhoku Earthquake and Tsunami', www.wikipedia.org, accessed 9 July 2017; Becky Oskin, 'Japan Earthquake and Tsunami 2011: Facts and Information', www.livescience.com, 13 September 2017. 'Japanese Earthquake Aftermath Claimed 4.37 Million Chickens', http://www.poultryworld.net, 1 March 2012. Despite its headline, this article indicates that 8 million may be the more accurate number.

59 'Support for Japanese Emigrants and Their Descendants', in JICA *Annual Report 2012*, www.jica.go.jp, p. 135.

60 'Rapid Response Fund Payment Request No. 4/2016', http://reliefweb.int, 28 July 2016.

61 'USDA Brings Food to Schools in Mozambique', www.planetaid.org, 31 May 2013.

62 'Keeping Girls in School in Mozambique', www.planetaid.org, 20 October 2014.

63 'ASA/WISHH Donates Soy Flour to Ghana Atomic Energy Commission', www.wishh.org, 25 April 2016.

64 Dana Sanchez, 'Selling Soybean Seeds in Africa: Public-private Partnership Seeks Funds to Expand Variety Tests', http://afkinsider.com, 19 February 2016, pp. 1–2.

65 'U.S. International Food Assistance Report Fiscal Year 2013', https://decsearch.usaid.gov, accessed 10 July 2017, p. 25.

66 Ibid.

67 Gary L. Cromwell, 'Soybean Meal – An Exceptional Protein Source', Review Paper, www.soymeal.org, accessed 10 July 2017, p. 2; Sara Willis, 'The Use of Soybean Meal and Full Fat Soybean Meal by the Animal Feed Industry', www.australianoilseeds.com, accessed 10 July 2017, p. 6; Peter

Best, 'World Feed Panorama: A Year of Resilience for the Feed Industry', www.wattagnet.com, 4 March 2013.

9 BEANS AS BUSINESS: *BIG* BUSINESS

1 Darrin Pack, 'Purdue Reports Grain Entrapments Up Nationwide in 2014', www.purdue.edu, 29 April 2015; Chris Bennett, 'A Steady March of Grain Bin Deaths', www.agweb.com, 3 February 2016.
2 Informa Economics, *Farm to Market: A Soybean's Journey from Field to Consumer* (Memphis, TN, August 2016), p. 276; 'Conversion Table', https://ussec.org, 6 October 2015.
3 U.S. Army Corps of Engineers, 'Locks & the River: A Boater's Guide to Safe Travel on the Upper Mississippi River & the Illinois Waterway' (Rock Island, IL, 1998), pp. 5, 12.
4 Ibid., p. 5.
5 'Chapter Four: Transporting U.S. Soybeans to Export Markets', in *Buyers' Guide*, www.ussec.org, Resources/Soy Market, p. 4-2.
6 Ibid., p. 4-1; Informa Economics, *Farm to Market*, p. 337.
7 'How Much Does it Cost to Go through the Panama Canal?', www.cheapestdestinationsblog.com, 19 July 2013.
8 'Recipes for Disaster: Cleaning Up after Food Spills', www.noaa.gov, 26 November 2013.
9 'Heavy Rain and Floods in China', www.factsanddetails.com, accessed 10 July 2017; see also http://floodlist.com.
10 'Chapter Four: Transporting', p. 4-3.
11 Mark Ash and Shelbi Knisley, 'Oil Crops Outlook October 2016', Report OCS-16J, www.usda.gov, 14 October 2016, p. 1.
12 'Around the Nation: Company Pays Millions in 1981 Sewer Explosion', *New York Times*, 9 December 1984.
13 'Central Soya Agrees to Pay Settlement in 1994 Oil Spill', Associated Press State & Local Wire, 16 August 2001.
14 FAO, *Food Outlook: Biannual Report on Global Food Markets* (Rome, October 2016), p. 42; Nikos Alexandratos and Jelle Bruinsma, *World Agriculture towards 2030/2050*, 2012 Revision, FAO/ESA Working Paper no. 12-03 (Rome, June 2012), Table 4.12, p. 121.
15 Mariano Turzi, 'The Soybean Republic', *Yale Journal of International Affairs* (Spring–Summer 2011), p. 63.
16 See www.trademap.org, accessed 24 October 2016.
17 USDA, *Crop Values 2015 Summary* (Washington, DC, February 2016), p. 9.
18 See http://faostat.fao.org, accessed 29 October 2016.
19 See USDA, 'World Agricultural Production', Circular Series WAP 9-16, September 2016, Table 11, p. 23; Keith Whigham, 'What Is the Best Soybean Seeding Rate?', www.ipm.iastate.edu, 27 April 1998; H. Kibar and T. Öztürk, 'Physical and Mechanical Properties of Soybean', *International Agrophysics*, XXII (2008), p. 239; 'Earth', https://en.wikipedia.org, accessed 10 July 2017.
20 See 'Trading Places 1983', Quotes, www.imdb.com, accessed 10 July 2017.
21 'Insider Trading in Commodities and the Eddie Murphy Rule', newsletter at http://ccrow.com, February 2011.

22 'The Great Soybean Scandal', *New York Herald Tribune*, 8 December 1963; 'Cornering Markets Past, from Silver to Salad Oil', *New York Times*, 13 July 1989, p. D6; Isadore Barmash, ed., *Great Business Disasters: Swindlers, Bunglers, and Frauds in American Industry* (Chicago, IL, 1972), pp. 81–6.

23 Barmash, *Great Business Disasters*, p. 81.

24 Mary Buffet, 'A Fire Sale at Tesla', www.huffingtonpost.com, 15 October 2013.

25 'The Great Salad Oil Swindle', www.wikipedia.org, accessed 10 July 2017.

26 William B. Crawford Jr, 'Ferruzzi Leaves CBOT over '89 Soybean Fray', http://articles.chicagotribune.com, 11 January 1992.

27 Jack Lesar, 'Judge Orders Jail, Forfeitures for Soybean Traders', UPI Archives, www.upi.com, 24 May 1991.

28 'High-frequency Trader Convicted of Disrupting Commodity Futures Market in First Federal Prosecution of "Spoofing"', www.fbi.gov, 3 November 2015.

29 Donnelle Eller and Christopher Doering, 'CEO: DuPont Exploring AG Mergers; Pioneer Fate Uncertain', www.desmoinesregister.com, 28 October 2015.

30 'Soybean Subsidies in the United States Totaled $31.8 Billion from 1995–2014', https://farm.ewg.org, accessed 10 July 2017.

31 Brian M. Reidl, 'How Farm Subsidies Became America's Largest Corporate Welfare Program', www.heritage.org, 25 February 2002; 'Farm Subsidies: A Welfare Program for Agribusiness', http://theweek.com, 10 August 2013; David J. Lynch and Alan Bjerga, 'Taxpayers Turn U.S. Farmers into Fat Cats with Subsidies', www.bloomberg.com, 9 September 2013.

32 A.J.F. Griffiths, J. H. Miller, D. T. Suzuki et al., *An Introduction to Genetic Analysis*, 7th edn (New York, 2000), at www.ncbi.nlm.nih.gov, accessed 10 July 2017.

33 Inter Press Service News Agency, 'Environment-Ecuador: Activists Block Ship Carrying Transgenic Soy', www.ipsnews.net, 13 January 2000; 'Soya Transgenica en el Ecuador', www.accionecologica.org, 31 December 2000.

34 Jan M. Lucht, 'Public Acceptance of Plant Biotechnology and GM Crops', *Viruses*, VII (2015), p. 4256.

35 See http://faostat.fao.org, accessed 19 November 2016.

36 Ibid.

37 Jennifer Clapp, 'The Political Economy of Food Aid in an Era of Agricultural Biotechnology', *Global Governance*, XI/4 (October–December 2005), pp. 467–85.

38 Alexandra C. Lewin, Case Study #4-4, 'Zambia and Genetically Modified Food Aid', in *Food Policy for Developing Countries: Case Studies*, ed. Per Pinstrup-Andersen and Fuzhi Cheng, at https://cip.cornell.edu, p. 3, accessed 18 November 2017.

39 Thulani Mpofu, 'Starving Zimbabwe Rejects GM Maize', www.zimdaily.com, 7 June 2010.

40 Kent Holt of the former Solae Company, personal communication with the author, 22 March 2010.

41 Gil Gullickson, 'Time's Up for Trait Patents', www.agriculture.com, 14 February 2013.

42 Greg Ryan, 'No Cows Needed for "Soymilk" Label, Judge Says', www.law360.com, Case *Ang et al.* v. *WhiteWave Foods Co. et al.*, 10 December 2013.

43 See data sets at www.landmatrix.org, accessed 21 November 2016.

44 Ibid., deal numbers 747 and 1167.

10 FAT IN THE FIRE: SOY DIESEL

1 T. A. Kiefer, 'Twenty-first Century Snake Oil: Why the United States Should Reject Biofuels as Part of a Rational National Security Energy Strategy', WICI Occasional Paper no. 4 (Waterloo, Ont., January 2013).

2 'More Benefits', www.americasadvancedbiofuel.com, accessed 5 December 2016; www.biodiesel.org, 'Biodiesel Fact Sheets', accessed 5 December 2016.

3 Joe Biluck, personal communication with the author, 17 December 2016.

4 Medford Township Public Schools, 'Biodiesel – A Renewable Fuel for Medium and Heavy Duty Vehicles', presentation to the School Transportation News 2015 National Conference and Expo Reno, Nevada (Medford, NJ, 2015), p. 10.

5 Henry Fountain, 'We Could See You in the Gas Tank Later, Alligator', *New York Times* (22 April 2014), p. F5.

6 'Manufacturing and Industrial', *Manzanar Free Press*, III/23 (Manzanar Internment Camp, CA, 20 March 1943), p. 7.

7 Geoffrey Baker, personal communication with the author, 13 December 2016.

8 Randy Schnepf and Brent D. Yacobucci, 'Renewable Fuel Standard (RFS): Overview and Issues' (Washington, DC, 14 March 2013), p. 14.

9 'ASA Praises New Senate; Renewable Fuels Legislation Bill Promotes American-made Energy from Environmentally Friendly Biodiesel', soygrowers.com, 8 June 2001; 'ASA Presents Biodiesel Benefits to U.S. Senate and House', soygrowers.com, 25 July 2001; 'California Reaffirms Environmental Benefits of Biodiesel', soygrowers.com, 1 October 2015.

10 *Inhalation Toxicology*, XXVII/11: Special issue on EPA research into health effects of biodiesel (September 2015).

11 Schnepf and Yacobucci, 'Renewable Fuel Standard', p. 7; EPA, 'Biodiesel', Fact Sheet EPA-420-F-10-009, www.epa.gov, February 2010.

12 Joseph E. Fargione, Richard J. Plevin and Jason D. Hill, 'The Ecological Impact of Biofuels', *Annual Review of Ecology, Evolution, and Systematics*, XLI (2010), pp. 351–77; The Nature Conservancy/LMC International, 'An Opportunity for Brazil: Minimizing the Environmental Costs of Biofuels Expansion', www.nature.org, accessed 11 July 2017; Cara Byington, 'Energy Sprawl Is the Largest Driver of Land Use Change in the U.S.', www.nature.org, 8 September 2016.

13 'EU-28 Biofuels Annual', GAIN report no. NL5028, www.usda.gov, 15 July 2015, p. 21; EU *Energy in Figures Statistical Pocketbook 2016*, http://ec.europa.eu, 1 July 2016, pp. 22, 113; www.thecalculatorsite.com, accessed 12 December 2016.

14 Table 4, 'Biodiesel Supply and Disappearance', www.usda.gov, 5 December 2016.

15 'Major Biodiesel Producing Countries 2015', www.statista.com, accessed 10 December 2016.

16 National Biodiesel Board, 'U.S. Biodiesel Consumption Hits Nearly 2.1 Billion Gallons in 2015', *Biodiesel Magazine* (25 January 2016); 'U.S. No. 2 Diesel Sales/Deliveries to On-highway Consumers', www.eia.gov, accessed 11 December 2016.

17 Kiefer, *Twenty-first Century Snake Oil*, p. 41.

18 Agricultural Marketing Resource Center, 'An Overview of the Biodiesel Market: Production, Imports, Feedstocks and Profitability', March 2016 Renewable Energy Report, www.agmrc.org, 9 March 2016, p. 4.

19 Rona Cohen, 'From Food to Fuel: Used Vegetable Oil among the Ingredients for Biodiesel', www.csg.org, August 2007, p. 25.

20 'Neste Renewable Diesel', www.wikipedia.org, accessed 11 July 2017; 'Greenpeace Catches Palm Oil Giant Wilmar in Forest Scandal', www.greenpeace.org, accessed 11 July 2017.

21 National Biodiesel Board, 'Biodiesel Myths Busted', http://biodiesel.org, accessed 11 July 2017.

22 National Biodiesel Board, 'Food Prices Merrier as Biodiesel Production Grows', press release, www.biodiesel.org, 22 December 2016.

23 Schnepf and Yacobucci, 'Renewable Fuel Standard', p. 16.

24 'Slamet', https://caping.wordpress.com, 21 January 2008. Trans. and adapted by Christine M. Du Bois with the permission of Goenawan Mohamad.

25 Elizabeth Walton, '12th Annual Grease Recycling Event', www.tucsonnewsnow.com, 2 January 2017.

26 Personal communications between Grecycle owner Michael Kazz and the author, December 2016/January 2017. See also www.grecycle.com.

AFTERWORD

1 Search of the Seed Portal under 'Species' using 'Species contains Glycine' at www.nordgen.org, 19 January 2017.

2 Search of the Seed Portal at www.nordgen.org, 19 January 2017.

3 Ibid.

SELECT BIBLIOGRAPHY

PRINT SOURCES

Baer, Werner, ed., *The Regional Impact of National Policies: The Case of Brazil* (Cheltenham, 2012)

Berlan, Jean-Pierre, Jean-Pierre Bertrand and Laurence Lebas, 'The Growth of the American "Soybean Complex"', *European Review of Agricultural Economics*, IV/4 (1999 [1976]), pp. 395–416

Brando, Paulo M., Michael T. Coe and Ruth DeFries, eds, 'Theme Issue: Ecology, Economy and Management of an Agroindustrial Frontier Landscape in the Southeast Amazon', *Philosophical Transactions of the Royal Society*, CCCLXVIII/1619 (2013)

Bryan, Ford R., *Beyond the Model T: The Other Ventures of Henry Ford* (Detroit, MI, 1990)

Collingham, Lizzie, *The Taste of War: World War II and the Battle for Food* (New York, 2012)

Du Bois, Christine M., Chee-Beng Tan and Sidney Mintz, eds, *The World of Soy* (Champaign, IL, 2008)

Filomeno, Felipe Amin, *Monsanto and Intellectual Property in South America* (New York, 2014)

Fowler, Cary, *Seeds on Ice: Svalbard and the Global Seed Vault* (Westport, CT, 2016)

Friedmann, Harriet, 'The International Relations of Food: The Unfolding Crisis of National Regulation', in *Food: Multidisciplinary Perspectives*, ed. Barbara Harriss-White and Sir Raymond Hoffenberg (Oxford, 1994), pp. 174–204

——, 'What on Earth Is the Modern World System?', *Journal of World-systems Research*, VI/2 (Summer/Fall 2000), pp. 480–515

Gibbs, H. K. et al., 'Brazil's Soy Moratorium', *Science*, CCCXLVII/6220 (23 January 2015), pp. 377–8

Griffiths, Anthony F. J., et al., *An Introduction to Genetic Analysis* (New York, 2015)

Heinrich Böll Foundation and Friends of the Earth Europe, *Meat Atlas: Facts and Figures about the Animals We Eat* (Brussels, 2014)

Hetherington, Kregg, *Guerrilla Auditors: The Politics of Transparency in Neoliberal Paraguay* (Durham, NC, 2011)

Howard, April, 'The Battle for Sustainable Agriculture in Paraguay', in *Agriculture and Food in Crisis*, ed. Fred Magdoff and Brian Tokar (New York, 2010), pp. 173–88

Huang, H. T., *Fermentations and Food Science*, vol. VI, part 5 of *Biology and Technology*, series *Science and Civilisation in China* (Cambridge, 2000)

Hudson, Laura C., Kevin C. Lambirth, Kenneth L. Bost and Kenneth J. Piller, 'Advancements in Transgenic Soy: From Field to Bedside, a Comprehensive Survey of International Soybean Research', in *Genetics, Physiology, Agronomy and Nitrogen Relationships*, ed. James Board (Rijeka, 2013)

Hull, R. Bruce, David Robertson, Courtney Kimmel and Barbara McCutchan, 'Collaborative Leadership for Sustainable Development in Global Supply Chains: Partnering across Sectors to Reduce Amazon Deforestation', *Solutions*, IV/5 (24 January 2015), pp. 51–9

Hymowitz, Theodore, 'Dorsett-Morse Soybean Collection Trip to East Asia: 50 Year Retrospective', *Economic Botany*, XXXVIII/4 (October–December 1984), pp. 378–88

——, 'Introduction of the Soybean to Illinois', *Economic Botany*, XLI/1 (1987), pp. 28–32

——, 'On the Domestication of the Soybean', *Economic Botany*, XXIV (1970), pp. 408–21

——, 'Soybeans: The Success Story', in *Soybeans: The Success Story, Advances in New Crops*, ed. Jules Janick and James Simon (Portland, OR, 1990), pp. 159–63

Hymowitz, Theodore, and J. R. Harlan, 'Introduction of Soybean to North America by Samuel Bowen in 1765', *Economic Botany*, XXXIX/4 (1983), pp. 371–9

Jenkins, Edward S., ed., 'Percy L. Julian', in Edward S. Jenkins et al., *American Black Scientists and Inventors* (Washington, DC, 1975)

Johnston, B. F., *Japanese Food Management in World War II* (Stanford, CA, 1953)

Lapegna, Pablo, *Soybeans and Power: Genetically Modified Crops, Environmental Politics, and Social Movements in Argentina* (Oxford, 2016)

Liu, KeShun, ed., *Soybeans: Chemistry, Technology, and Utilization* (New York, 1997)

Meyer, Daniel E., and Christel Cederberg, *Pesticide Use and Glyphosate-Resistant Weeds: A Case Study of Brazilian Soybean Production*, SIK Rapport No. 809 (Borås, 2010)

Morgan, Dan, *Merchants of Grain* (New York, 1979)

Nestle, Marion, *Food Politics* (Berkeley, CA, 2002)

Pimentel, David, and Marcia Pimentel, 'Sustainability of Meat-based and Plant-based Diets and the Environment', *American Journal of Clinical Nutrition*, LXXVIII/3 (September 2003), pp. 660s–3s

Prodöhl, Ines, 'From Dinner to Dynamite: Fats and Oils in Wartime America', *Global Food History*, II/1 (7 March 2016), pp. 31–50

——, 'Versatile and Cheap: A Global History of Soy in the First Half of the Twentieth Century', *Journal of Global History*, VIII (2013), pp. 461–82

Schlosser, Eric, *Fast Food Nation* (New York, 2001)

Shurtleff, William, and Akiko Aoyagi, *The Book of Tofu*, revd edn (New York, 1979)

Skees, Jerry, 'Agricultural Risk Management or Income Enhancement?', *Regulation*, XXII/1 (1999), pp. 35–43

Tuomisto, H. L., et al., 'Does Organic Farming Reduce Environmental Impacts? A Meta-analysis of European Research', *Journal of Environmental Management*, CXII (15 December 2012), pp. 309–20

Turzi, Mariano, *The Political Economy of Agricultural Booms: Managing Soybean Production in Argentina, Brazil, and Paraguay* (Cham, 2017)

——, 'The Soybean Republic', *Yale Journal of International Affairs* (Spring–Summer 2011), pp. 59–68

Wansink, Brian, 'Changing Eating Habits on the Home Front: Lost Lessons from World War II Research', *Journal of Public Policy and Marketing*, XXI/1 (Spring 2002), pp. 90–99

Warnken, Philip F., *The Development and Growth of the Soybean Industry in Brazil* (Ames, IA, 1999)

Wolff, David, 'Bean There: Toward a Soy-based History of Northeast Asia', *South Atlantic Quarterly*, XCIX/1 (Winter 2000), pp. 241–52

WEBSITES

American Soybean Association, http://soystats.com

Brazilian Agricultural Research Corporation (EMBRAPA), www.embrapa.br/en/international

Food and Agriculture Organization of the United Nations, www.fao.org, including their statistical database at http://faostat.fao.org

Food First, www.foodfirst.org

Greenpeace, www.greenpeace.org

International Service for the Acquisition of Agri-Biotech Applications, www.isaaa.org

ITC Trade Map, www.trademap.org

Land Matrix, www.landmatrix.org

La Soja Mata, http://lasojamata.iskra.net

National Biodiesel Board, www.nbb.org

National Sustainable Agriculture Coalition, http://sustainableagriculture.net

The Nature Conservancy, www.nature.org

Oxfam International, www.oxfam.org

Round Table on Responsible Soy, www.responsiblesoy.org

Soybean Innovation Lab, http://soybeaninnovationlab.illinois.edu

Soybean Meal Info Center, www.soymeal.org

SoyInfo Center, www.soyinfocenter.com

Statista, The Statistics Portal, www.statista.com

United Soybean Board, http://unitedsoybean.org

U.S. Department of Agriculture, www.usda.gov

U.S. Energy Information Administration, www.eia.gov

U.S. Environmental Protection Agency, www.epa.gov

U.S. Library of Congress, 'Restrictions on Genetically Modified Organisms' by country, www.loc.gov

U.S. Soybean Export Council, https://ussec.org

World Food Programme of the United Nations, www1.wfp.org

World Initiative for Soy in Human Health, www.wishh.org

World Wildlife Fund for Nature, http://wwf.panda.org

ACKNOWLEDGEMENTS

The story of humans' domesticating, analysing and devising an incredible number of uses for soybeans is one of constant learning from each other. We are all in this together, and I too have learned about soy from many others – from scholars, entrepreneurs, journalists, librarians, curators, archivists, statisticians, consumers, activists and government analysts. I appreciate their work and the free flow of ideas and information.

Some individuals deserve special thanks: George B. Du Bois, Jr, Kenneth Baron, Laurence U. Buxbaum and Rebecca Buxbaum for useful comments on portions of the manuscript; Emilie Sureau and Timm Sureau for help with German sources; Joe Biluck, Michael Kazz, Geoffrey Baker, Dallas Burkholder, Todd 'Ike' Kiefer, Dan Costa, Kathleen Georgette Jackson and Peter Behrle for information about biodiesel; Todd Bedford and Randall Nelson for information about the USDA's Soybean Germplasm Collection; Qiu Lijuan for information about China's germplasm; Wen Shuang for stimulating discussion about soy and empire; Bruce Bruemmer for setting me straight about Cargill during the Second World War; Kenneth Holt for information about Ralston Purina; Myra Siddharta for teaching me about Indonesian soy; William Shurtleff for bibliographical assistance and his amazing web pages at the SoyInfo Center; Theodore Hymowitz for advice and information through the years and for just being so smart; Helen Kennedy and Nicole Blechynden for information about Japanese internment; and Goenawan Mohamad for allowing me to adapt and print his moving column about soy prices in Indonesia.

Special thanks also belong to Pablo Flores, Ross Bender, Faith Julian, Catherine Nolan, Nathan G. Jordan, José Casado, Jody Shuart, Karla Renschler, Alex Knight and Taylor Zartman for help with images; Ulf Engström with a Swedish reference; David Blasco, Neelima Somashekar and Jan Grenci for useful leads; and Heather Streets-Salter for help with a permission.

I also wholeheartedly thank a fantastic crew of supporters: Marielle Buxbaum for the idea about how to begin the Afterword, and for adding Salchows to soybeans; Joan March, George March and Jackie Mintz for clippings about soy; Caryl Carpenter for news reports about soy and for facilitating my meeting Michael Pollan, whom I admire; Kirsten and Bill Blair, Valerie Swan, Laura Bird, Danièle Du Bois, Katarzyna J. Cwiertka, Chee-Beng Tan, Corinne Whitaker and the late Baha Malik for special encouragement in my soy studies; Karen Farinella and Rosa Romo for being my main 'laptop watchers'; and Kathy Rossiter and

Laurence Buxbaum for keeping my life organized when there was nothing left but soybeans rattling around my brain.

Last but certainly not least, I am very grateful to my editors Ben Hayes and Amy Salter, for their patient guidance; Maria Kilcoyne and Rebecca Ratnayake at Reaktion Books for their diligence; and again, Laurence Buxbaum, for library books, computer assistance, help in interpreting scientific papers and unstinting support.

The opinions and any mistakes in this book are, however, mine alone.

PHOTO ACKNOWLEDGEMENTS

The author and publishers wish to express their thanks to the below sources of illustrative material and/or permission to reproduce it:

Agência Brasil, Empresa Brasil de Comunicação: p. 134; Ansel Adams/Library of Congress, Washington, DC: p. 251; Scott Bauer/USDA Agricultural Research Service: p. 195; © Ross R. Bender: p. 170; Christine M. Du Bois: pp. 6, 184 (all); Christine M. Du Bois/created with Map Chart: pp. 24, 155, 224–5; courtesy Confederación de Asociaciones Rurales de Buenos Aires y La Pampa, Argentina: p. 143; photo courtesy of Ms Faith Julian and DePauw University Archives and Special Collections/artwork © United States Postal Service. All rights reserved: p. 65; © Pablo D. Flores: p. 140; Peggy Greb/USDA Agricultural Research Service: p. 208; Carol M. Highsmith Archive, Library of Congress, DC: p. 97; iStock via Getty images: alffoto: p. 117; ALLEKO: p. 31; bvmisa: p. 107; chengyuzheng: p. 45; DS70: p. 15; Fotokostic: p. 139; franz12: p. 106; GI15702993: p. 72; Gim42: p. 96; KreangchaiRungfamai: p. 246; MarcQuebec: p. 180; Phototreat: pp. 120, 127; post424: p. 44; RelaxedPace: p. 263; viennetta: p. 71; Yamtono_Sardi: p. 32; Library of Congress, Washington, DC: pp. 9, 27, 82, 154; Metropolitan Museum of Art: p. 37; Records of the Office of Government Reports, 1932–1947, U.S. National Archives: p. 83; United States Department of Agriculture: pp. 13, 19, 21, 28, 218, 221; courtesy U.S. National Archives and Records Administration: pp. 64, 67; courtesy U.S. National Archives at Atlanta, Georgia: p. 59.

INDEX